D0800722

Sustainable by Design

To Helen

Sustainable by Design
Explorations in Theory and Practice

Stuart Walker

London • Sterling, VA

TS
170.5
.W45
2006

840

9-13-07

First published by Earthscan in the UK and USA in 2006

Copyright © Stuart Walker, 2006

All rights reserved

ISBN 13:   9-781-84407-305-4   paperback
ISBN 10:   1-84407-353-X   paperback
ISBN 13:   9-781-84407-354-2   hardback
ISBN 10:   1-84407-354-8   hardback

Typesetting by Safehouse Creative
Printed and bound by Gutenberg Press Ltd, Malta
Cover design by Giles Smith

For a full list of publications please contact:

Earthscan
8–12 Camden High Street
London, NW1 0JH, UK
Tel: +44 (0)20 7387 8558
Fax: +44 (0)20 7387 8998
Email: earthinfo@earthscan.co.uk
Web: **www.earthscan.co.uk**

22883 Quicksilver Drive, Sterling, VA 20166-2012, USA

Earthscan is an imprint of James and James (Science Publishers) Ltd and
publishes in association with the International Institute for Environment
and Development

A catalogue record for this book is available from the British Library

Library of Congress Cataloging-in-Publication Data

Walker, Stuart, 1955–
    Sustainable by design : explorations in theory and practice / Stuart
Walker.
        p. cm.
    Includes bibliographical references.
    ISBN 13: 9-781-84407-305-4 (pbk.)
    ISBN 10: 1-84407-353-X (pbk.)
    ISBN 13: 9-781-84407-354-2 (hardback)
    ISBN 10: 1-84407-354-8 (hardback)
  1. Green products. 2. New Products. I. Title.
    TS170.5.W45 2006
    658.5′75–dc22

                                                            2006003749

Printed on elemental chlorine-free paper

CONTENTS

VI

FIGURES
AND TABLES

Figures

Tables

ACKNOWLEDGEMENTS

I am grateful to Tamsine Green at Earthscan who has advised and encouraged me as this book was prepared for publication. I am also thankful to my colleagues at the University of Calgary and around the world who have provided feedback and commentary on earlier versions of many of these chapters, which appeared as papers at conferences or in journals; especially Jack Ingram at the University of Central England, Jacques Giard at Arizona State University, Richard Buchanan at Carnegie-Mellon University, and those anonymous readers who peer-reviewed these pages in their various stages of development. I am especially thankful to my wife, Helen, who so diligently and expertly proofed and edited the manuscript, and who, along with my sons Joseph and Benjamin, has had to put up with me during the months that this book took shape.

ACRONYMS AND ABBREVIATIONS

ABS   acrylonitrile butadiene styrene
CAD   computer-aided design
OPEC   Organization of Petroleum Exporting Countries
PDA   personal digital assistant
UNEP   United Nations Environment Programme

1
INTRODUCTION

The central theme of this book is design, and more especially, the design of sustainable, functional objects. I explore this from a variety of angles to throw light on its different facets. It is my intention that the discussion will allow the reader to contemplate sustainable design from hitherto little-considered perspectives and in doing so appreciate its significant implications as well as its potential contribution to the creation of a more meaningful material culture.

To advance the subject of design one has to engage in the activity of designing. This is a critical creative stage in which the designer seeks to apply general, abstract ideas in the process of developing specific, defined artefacts. This transformative step distinguishes design from many other types of inquiry. Theoretical ideas inform the design of an artefact and, in turn, contemplation of the artefact can advance the development of ideas. It is an integrated and iterative process of development. Hence, the activity of designing is an essential ingredient in many of the discussions that follow, and I include numerous examples of propositional design work in which I have attempted to articulate and develop the ideas through the language of design itself.

These various thoughts, arguments and artefacts sometimes overlap and, in the process, they are reinforced. Occasionally they may even conflict, but these points of difference, too, can be useful and instructive. I hope the discussions and examples will provide the reader with an informative and stimulating set of ideas from which to consider sustainable design, even if this is by disagreeing with some of the views presented here; dissonance is often an effective catalyst for action and change.

I have structured the book so that the discussion progresses from broad, general issues to increasingly detailed design considerations. In Chapter 2, I look at the current state of design and argue for a radical rethinking of material culture and our understandings of good design. In Chapter 3, I trace the history of sustainable development and make the case for seeing it as a contemporary myth that helps us come to terms with, among other things, our current environmental crisis. In Chapter 4, I use the analogy of a journey to explore the design process and to present an approach that may be more fitting for a sustainable future. In subsequent chapters, I consider historically enduring artefacts as a way of learning about object significance; meaningful objects and what we mean by meaningful; and the relationship between the spiritual and the material. I also use propositional designs as a way of illustrating the application of sustainable thinking, and reflect on this design activity to develop ideas about tacit knowledge and its fundamental role in the creative process. I propose an aesthetic typology for contemporary products as a way of informing our ideas of product design, and examine our conceptions of time and its relevance to sustainable design. In the final chapters, I consider the notion that many contemporary products represent a stagnation in creativity – an endgame – and offer an alternative approach, grounded in ideas of environmental and social responsibility, which can serve to stimulate creative design development. I also discuss the transient nature of objects and suggest that one way forward may be to more consciously acknowledge this ephemerality, and design accordingly. In the closing discussion I offer an in-depth consideration of one particular object as a way of understanding its intellectual and aesthetic meanings in relation to sustainable practices. In these various explorations, I have tried to emphasize the creative and positive contribution of design, rather than focusing on the oft-cited environmental ills of contemporary production and consumption. Of course, in any discussion of sustainable design, we have to acknowledge the damaging consequences of our current activities, but the designer must go beyond this, not simply by designing environmentally friendly products, but by challenging our understandings of 'functional objects', by reframing our conceptions of products, and by reassessing our notions of product aesthetics. In recognizing the unsustainable nature of many current practices, we have the opportunity to build a more constructive and more profound approach that is, inherently, more sustainable.

Earlier versions of many of these discussions have been presented at academic conferences or published in scholarly journals; all have been edited and reworked for this book. In bringing them together for the first time, I believe they form a body of work that offers, in a way not possible within the confines of individual essays, a progression of ideas and an original conception and exploration of sustainable product design.

Sustainable design is a vast subject that we have barely begun to tackle and so it would be unwise to attempt a definitive solution to what is, in reality, an embryonic, dynamic and volatile area of human endeavour. By way of analogy, if we were to ask someone to describe their experience of long-distance flying we might receive one of several answers, such as: 'It's all rather boring – you sit down, eat, watch a film and fall asleep,' or 'Take-off and landing are the most stressful because there are dozens of instrument checks and constant instructions from the tower,' or 'It's exhausting, I'm on my feet for at least half the flight serving drinks, food and duty-free goods,' or again 'It's fun – you're given colouring books and toys and the stewards are nice.' Answers to the same question can be diverse and contradictory, but despite these differences and inconsistencies, they are all reasonable – they simply depend on the point of view of the respondent. We can also see that the contradictions are not just differences of opinion; each reply accurately reflects real differences in experience. Similarly, our understanding of sustainable design will vary depending on our perspective – because new aspects of this complex subject are revealed each time we change our angle of view. It is for this reason that I have included a variety of entry points into the subject, starting with a broad view of the current discipline of product design and ending with a detailed analysis of one design example.

3

There are many ways that sustainable design can be considered, and the issues included here are varied and wide-ranging, but I do not claim that this book is in any way comprehensive. The reader will not find within its pages detailed accounts of product life cycle assessment,[1] the Natural Step,[2] Factor 10[3] or other programmes that offer manufacturing or systems analyses and processes for moving towards sustainability; these subjects are covered more expertly than I could hope to do by other authors. My focus is creative design and it is from this standpoint that I begin my discussion.

I should also include a word on methodology. I am reluctant to call this work 'research' because the term conjures notions of scientific experiment or systematic, objective investigation and analysis. To adopt such an approach in design would be a mistake. Creative design studies do not always follow linear pathways, often they do not even follow logical pathways, and they are neither abstract nor objective. Therefore, they do not fall easily or solely within conventional understandings of systematic, scholarly research. The results of design are not verifiable by independent investigators adopting the same criteria and following the same methodology. Indeed, for a given problem, if different designers were all to arrive at the same result we would be sorely disappointed. In design we seek and expect variety not consistency.

The path I have adopted here is probably closer to a phenomenological understanding than to scientific or scholastic research, by which I mean that the ideas and propositional designs are not *only* based on rational argument and the logical development of an area of interest. They are *also* the result of informed, personal consideration, introspection and reflection; lived experiences; direct awareness through the design process; and intuitive decision making.

I am very aware that my approach to sustainable design has been informed by my own personal history. I was brought up in one of the most savagely industrialized valleys of South Wales where the hills were treeless, smothered with slag heaps and pierced by mine workings, and where the river ran orange from industrial effluent. The air was thick with the filth, smell and noise of the Bessemer converter and blast furnace, and social inequities, poverty, deprivation and ignorance were starkly apparent. A career as an engineer, working in the oil industry in The Netherlands, the Middle East and the UK, revealed to me overwhelming evidence of further environmental destruction on a

4

massive scale, unconscionably short-sighted rates of non-renewable resource depletion, and, in some areas, an arrogant trampling of ancient, inherently meaningful and, by any measure, sustainable ways of life. A personal interest in creative studies led me to a career shift, an education in art and design, and eventually to industrial design and exposure to further industrial processes with their own problems associated with resource depletion and waste production, and their own social ramifications.

All these experiences, which are strongly related to a number of interconnected industrial processes, together with some 15 years of postgraduate teaching, have informed the ideas and arguments I present here; in this, I owe a great debt to my students and colleagues, from whom I continue to learn.

The result is an approach to design studies that is, largely, normative, contingent and, because of the particular focus on sustainable design, implicitly polemical. In this way, I have endeavoured to acknowledge both the objective and subjective aspects of our nature, because design is a topic that lies at the junction of these two ways of thinking about, and interacting with, the world. It sits at the meeting place of science and art – but it is neither science nor art, it is simply and fascinatingly design.

5

In the following discussions, I frequently use the terms sustainable development and sustainability; most people tend to use these terms interchangeably. However, some authors have made a distinction between the two, arguing that sustainable development suggests an emphasis on development and economic growth, whereas sustainability gives priority to the environment.[4] While there may be merit in this view, I see both terms as being useful to describe our current attempts to come to terms with the economic, environmental and social concerns that we are facing in contemporary society. In the fields of product design and production, these three priorities are inextricably interwoven and inseparable and it does not seem to me very helpful to draw potentially divisive distinctions. I therefore tend to use the term sustainable development to describe a broad process of development where economic, environmental and social concerns are considered simultaneously, and I use the term sustainability to refer to ways of living in which these concerns are responsibly embraced and permeate our various endeavours. This way of using these terms is,

I think, reasonable, even if it is not as nuanced as some would like. As will become evident, finer distinctions may be somewhat moot because actually achieving a form of development that is sustainable or achieving sustainability may well be impossible. Nevertheless, both terms serve to focus our activities on doing things differently and working in ways that are socially, environmentally and economically responsible, and so both terms can be equally useful. The notion of the sustainable in design is not about fine distinctions in terminology, it is not about developing single-issue arguments, and it is not simply about reasoned argument. Rather, it is about fully engaging in the world in a way that is empathetic, intuitive and aesthetic. If we are to immerse ourselves in the creative design process and become aware, through this immersion, of the beauty and fragility of the world, then the fruits of our endeavours will reflect this. It is not so much a matter of rational proof but a matter of faith and hope; faith that goodness can prevail and hope for a better future for all.

The following chapters trace one particular path through the often-confusing territory of sustainable product design. En route, there are a series of encounters with design and at each of these I play with a set of ideas – by pursuing arguments and, in some cases, by engaging in the design process. Each encounter is like a game in which the play continues until a point is reached where it seems appropriate to stop; and I have endeavoured to ground all these encounters on a firm foundation congruent with sustainable goals. Together, these suggest a direction that leads away from inconsequential novelty, the utilitarian, and the design of enduring objects that are readily discarded, and towards an emphasis on the symbolic, the development of a meaningful material culture, and the design of ephemeral objects of lasting value. It is my hope that this direction will bring us a little closer to a more sustainable vision for design.

2
RETHINKING MATERIAL CULTURE
the cage of aesthetic convention

If we are to deal effectively with the many contemporary issues of environmental degradation and social disparity, we are going to have to rethink our notions of material culture, especially in the economically developed countries. Potentially, designers can make significant contributions to this endeavour by developing solutions that challenge precedents and demonstrate alternative possibilities – but to do this we will need to transform design education and design practice and develop new understandings of product aesthetics and our notions of 'good' design.

Whether we like to admit it or not, within the discipline of industrial or product design, there is a major emphasis on product appearance, in both professional practice and design education, and it is this preoccupation that, in many ways, renders product aesthetics hollow and superficial. The dominance of fashion-oriented, essentially trivial aesthetic definitions suggests a barrenness of thinking, a relinquishment of creativity, and a replacement of originality with bland, market-led, 'safe' solutions. This prevents industrial design from evolving into an authentic, substantive discipline capable of effectively tackling the important issues of our time: the pressing contemporary concerns that are not being appropriately dealt with in product design and manufacturing are the ethical and environmental ramifications of our actions. It is imperative that designers tackle these aspects of their discipline, as well as important questions of meaning, identity and culture associated with material goods.

Some years ago, I think it was at an engineering lecture, I heard it said that the majority of the world's diamond production was for industrial applications – for cutting tools, drill bits and grinders. These low-grade diamonds, which have no special aesthetic qualities, are crushed into grits of various sizes. Apparently, because of the high demand, and the relative rarity of gem quality diamonds, many of the processing systems have been geared towards the production of industrial diamonds. In these systems, the ore is crushed to the size of coarse sand and the dense diamond grit is separated out. With such a system there is no possibility of finding another Hope Diamond or Great Star of Africa – they are simply eliminated by the process.

Obviously, we need industrial diamonds, but we also need the Hope and the Great Star of Africa. Industrial diamonds are valued for *instrumental* reasons; they are a means to some other end. They are valued for their utility, they are used, they wear out and they are replaced. By contrast, the Great Star of Africa is valued for how it shines, how the light plays through its facets to inspire sheer awe – but it is totally useless in terms of function. The Great Star of Africa is not about function. It's about poetry and beauty and wonder; it is an end in and of itself. It has intrinsic value, it never wears out and it is irreplaceable.

In both education and practice, product design can be likened to industrial diamond processing. It tends to emphasize the production of competent, practical design solutions that conform to current norms and work within established notions of aesthetics, manufacturing, economics and utility. Accordingly, our mass-produced products are generally useful, ergonomic, convenient, economical and have a pleasant appearance.

However, there is also a need to generate solutions that defy current norms; that challenge convention; that re-conceive what design, production and products might be and, importantly, there is a need

8

to create solutions that inspire. To do this we must ensure that such solutions are not automatically rejected or eliminated by the processes we have put in place, in both design education and design practice. For original thinking to flourish in design, we must value and nurture the unfamiliar, the atypical and even the perplexing, in addition to technical competency and design proficiency. Inevitably, creative insights and ideas that are of lasting value will be rare and hard-won, but they are urgently needed in today's world of design and production.

Over the past century, there have been many inspiring examples of design that *have* challenged prevailing stereotypes and stimulated and influenced subsequent designers. Historically, the work of van Doesburg, Gerrit Reitveld and the De Stijl group in The Netherlands from 1917,[1] and of the Bauhaus designers in Germany, such as Marcel Breuer and Gunta Stölzl, in the period 1919–1933,[2] had an enormous effect on 20th century design, and their legacy is still influential. More recently, the work of the Memphis group in Italy during the 1980s had profound effects on design education and practice.[3] In their time, these groups were highly innovative and groundbreaking; they were also of their time. The issues and agendas to which they were responding are not our issues and agendas. Today, we are facing new challenges associated with the globalization of industrial capitalism, the environment, national and transnational socio-economic disparities, and rapidly evolving scientific and technological developments. While incremental changes that address these issues are important and necessary, it is also essential to encourage ideas that break with convention, that test preconceptions and, potentially, reframe our notions of product design and post-industrial material culture. The Droog designers, again from The Netherlands, are dealing with some of these questions in innovative ways that lie somewhere between art and product design, between clarity and ambiguity, between seriousness and wry wit. It is quite appropriate that many of the Droog designs defy existing classifications because part of the process of rethinking the current place and role of industrial design is to reconsider its boundaries and scope.[4]

When the aesthetic definition of a product is regarded as a primary objective, in and of itself, we must consider from whence our aesthetic decisions are derived. Personal experience, memory, notions of taste and conventions of beauty are all sources. However, it is these very conventions that have influenced, configured and, to an extent,

9

determined personal experience, memory and taste. Here then is the paradox of aesthetic definition. It is informed by convention – our conventional notions of beauty and taste. But it is this very influence of convention that results in the endless regurgitation of variations on a theme and imprisons product design in its own cage of introversion. The resulting derivations and repetitions disregard and deny the necessity of innovation that lies at the heart of aesthetic expression. While many contemporary products may have the attributes of being economical, convenient and pleasing to the eye, they also tend to be monotonously mundane, inherently destructive of the environment, representative of grossly inequitable employment practices, culturally damaging in their blanket distribution and ethically questionable in terms of their marketing. These observations have an honourable precedent. Over 25 years ago the design critic Stephen Bayley spoke of the 'plateau of mutual pastiche' that determined the appearance of so many consumer products.[5]

Instead of viewing aesthetics as a direct aim, it can also be considered as an outcome of an approach to product design that has different objectives. Industrial design can then focus on the meanings of material culture and thus develop and evolve. Ironically, in doing so, aesthetic definition will also evolve, unconstrained by the customs and precedents of product definition. In other words, aesthetics will begin to be more profoundly related to the whole of what a product *is*. Consequently, the aesthetic definition of a product, when derived from a different source, will, without doubt, challenge current norms. It will find its own place as an outcome rather than an all-consuming aim. In doing so, product design can respond creatively to the critical issues of our times in ways that are thoughtful and inspiring.

The rejection both of convention and of aesthetics as a direct aim is not, however, a rejection of history and experience; in fact quite the opposite. Personal and cultural experience can be embraced as providing important insights and nourishment for product definition. Such nourishment is urgently required if we are to effectively address current questions in ways that overcome fads and fashions and which are rooted in meaningful and enduring human and cultural values. This must start in our design schools and in how we educate our young designers.

10

Avant-garde artists such as Marcel Duchamp and Richard Long, the composer John Cage, and the contemporary architect and designer Frank Gehry demonstrate that true creativity can be challenging and difficult to absorb. It is often commercially unsuccessful and sometimes, at least initially, even ridiculed and dismissed. For example, Duchamp submitted the piece known as *Fountain* to an exhibition in New York in 1917 that was jury-free and open to all works of art. This white-porcelain urinal, which Duchamp had purchased from a supplier and signed R. Mutt, was, nevertheless, rejected from the exhibition. Despite this, it has become an icon of the 20th century and has caused people to reassess their ideas about art.[6,7] Cage's musical composition 4'33" of 1952, 'for any instrument or groups of instruments'[8] has been equally controversial and confusing and still prompts comment and ridicule. This piece has three movements, each of which is marked '*tacet*', indicating that the performer is to be silent throughout.

As Duchamp provoked questions about visual art, Cage caused us to reassess our preconceptions about music. Both demonstrated that new forms were possible that addressed important aspects of being human. Similarly, the works of sculptor Richard Long[9] and architect Frank Gehry[10] are challenging and, perhaps, sometimes bewildering. But such contributions allow us to see anew; they disrupt our comfort and test our attitudes. There is a need for such work in product design, before the excesses of our current preoccupations bury us alive in waste, pollution and sheer banality.

Ever since the early years of the 20th century, when mass-produced consumer goods started to become widely available, products have been promoted as 'new' and 'leading edge' based on two major features – aesthetics and technology. The first encompasses the latest in fashions, styling and colours and is the primary focus of the industrial designer. The second includes such things as functional attributes and gadgetry and is informed more by aspects of engineering. Neither has given us a lasting and meaningful material culture. Rather, they have contributed to the unsustainable, inherently damaging characteristics of our current design and production approaches.

We need to encourage and value an avant-garde in the field of design because time passes, the world changes and new issues come to the fore and need to be addressed. This is especially true if, over time, our ways of doing things are revealed to have damaging consequences.

Fashion and much technological innovation is often superficial, trivial and invariably wasteful. It is time to establish new criteria for product design, for progress in design and for our notions of good design. An avant-garde based in meaningful and pressing contemporary issues could provide the impetus for new, urgently needed thinking and innovative directions in product design; an impetus that would rouse the discipline from its current stasis.

For new ideas to be meaningful, innovative and well-grounded, designers must be educated in issues that go beyond the traditional boundaries of design. Philosophy, historical and contemporary issues, current affairs and discussions that stimulate critical thinking can all be brought to bear on how we reconfigure our notions of products, product design and the creation and meanings of material culture in today's world.

An example here might serve to expose our presumptions and prejudices. Our traditional, socially embedded understandings of business, growth and capitalism are, in fact, relatively recent. Industrial capitalism grew from the British cotton industry during the Industrial Revolution and is, therefore, only a few hundred years old.[11] The distinguishing feature of this system, which now seems so normal and unchallengeable, is that the surpluses of production began to be used to expand productive capacity itself. This gave us the notion of continual industrial growth, and the corollary of continually expanding consumption, disposable products, resource depletion, pollution and waste. We are living with the consequences of this today and are seemingly unable to free ourselves from its destructive grip. Before the rise of capitalism, however, the surpluses of production were used for other purposes. They were invested in economically unproductive endeavours, which, viewed from our current frame of reference, seems both incredible and ludicrous. The great European cathedrals are one legacy of this which, incidentally, still fulfil a valuable purpose today.[12]

I use this example not to suggest that we should somehow try to return to a pre-capitalist, medieval time, but simply to illustrate that existing norms do change, that alternatives are possible – and urgently needed, given the current rates of ecological devastation and the gross social imbalances associated with our present modus operandi. Critical thinking and the challenging of precedents and standards must begin to prefigure the design process and become more commonplace

12

and more substantive than is generally the case today. Designers will still have the important task of translating these ideas into form, but ultimately, it is the strength of the *ideas* that is crucial for the evolution of a lasting, meaningful and, hopefully, more benign material culture.

3
SUSTAINABLE DEVELOPMENT IN CONTEXT

the evolution of a contemporary myth

To understand why, in the early years of the 21st century, sustainable development has become generally and positively recognized by governments, business and society as a whole, we need to take a look at its emergence as an idea. In this chapter, I provide a brief overview of some of the key historical events that ultimately led to our current notions of 'sustainable development' and 'sustainability',[1] and consider what might be seen as a subset of these concepts, namely 'sustainable product design'. I also suggest that sustainable development can be understood as an important, but nevertheless limited, mythic story that attempts to give meaning to some of our principal modern-day uncertainties.

The publication of *Our Common Future* in 1987 by the World Commission on Environment and Development, often referred to as the Brundtland Report, popularized the term sustainable development, which it described as a type of development that would enable us to meet our present needs in ways that would not jeopardize the potential of future generations to meet their needs.[2] Since then there have

arisen hundreds of 'principles of sustainable development', designed
to suit all kinds of industries, interests and views.[3] However, in general
terms, sustainable development addresses three interrelated areas:
environmental stewardship, social equity and justice, and
economic issues.

In many respects, it can be argued that the statement of these three
concerns is simply our modern, secularized way of repeating age-old
wisdom teachings that have been expressed down the centuries in the
form of mythology and sacred literature. Myths have always existed and
will always exist because it is through the metaphorical language of myth
that a culture articulates its deepest concerns. Sustainable development
can be seen as our own myth, emerging from a culture of science,
technology and reason.

We live in an age in which it is often regarded as inappropriate to
include religious considerations in the discussion of contemporary
issues. In North America there is a somewhat uncomfortable and
certainly contentious division between Church and state, and in Europe
politicians tend to avoid reference to religious beliefs, and when such
references are made they are often surrounded by controversy.[4] Religious
concerns are almost never addressed in the business or commercial
world, academics rarely include discussion of the religious issues that
might be raised by a particular topic of debate and, increasingly,
religious symbols are being viewed as unacceptable in many public
school systems in western democracies.[5] However, while the demise of
religious considerations in public discourse is clearly evident, many of
the concerns remain that were traditionally addressed by religion.

In the 1970s, scholar George Steiner suggested that the demise of an
encompassing Christian teaching had deprived western society of critical
understandings of social justice, history, the mind/body relationship, and
of knowledge and moral behaviour.[6] In this same period we began to
see the emergence of (what eventually became known as) 'sustainable
development' as a socially acceptable, contemporary means of
framing our enduring ethical dilemmas and moral choices, as well
as our ideas of social justice and environmental stewardship. Indeed,
historian Philip Jenkins wonders if environmentalism might not be the
ideological force of our time, and he refers to the political scientist
Hedley Bull's suggestion that such a movement could be a kind of
worldwide, non-religious, political organization, equivalent to that seen

in western Christendom during the Middle Ages.[7] However, this seems rather overstated because secularism and its ideologies are simply not universally accepted, being restricted mainly to western, especially European, societies. In addition, and notwithstanding its admirable intentions, we must also acknowledge that the basis of sustainable development is less rounded, less developed, and has a far more instrumental bias and utilitarian agenda than the heritage of wisdom teachings that are present in the world's great philosophies, religions and mythologies. In the latter, we find the emphasis on the inner or spiritual development of the individual and of the community – from which one's behaviour and actions in the world can be guided. Without this inner source it could be argued that our 'worldly' endeavours tend to become superficial and, potentially, misguided.

Like many previous myths and religious traditions,[8] sustainable development aspires to an indefinable, unattainable goal – a goal which, nevertheless, many consider worth aiming for, but which forever eludes actual arrival. Furthermore, the sustainable 'myth' tells us that if the message goes unheeded and we fail to alter our behaviours we will be the cause of our own destruction. The message is both ethical and environmental. It promotes greater social equity and improvement in the living conditions for those in need, especially in developing countries, and it encourages conservation of the natural environment and reductions in energy use, consumption and human greed. For example, environmentalists Gordon and Suzuki offer advice for saving energy in the home and suggest how larger-scale energy savings can be made. They also state as a 'simple truth' that the present generation is the last one that can save the Earth.[9] Obviously, this statement is an assumption and a warning, but it is not a proven fact and it is anything but a 'simple truth'. Rather, it should be seen as a well-intentioned message to spur us into changing course. There are many other examples of writers who illustrate possibilities for moderating our impacts on the planet,[10] and others who warn of the imminent dangers to our future because of our destructive lifestyles.[11] In this context, sustainable development is seen as a way out of our predicament; a way forward that will enable us to live in closer harmony with the natural environment and achieve greater social equity and justice in our activities. This view of sustainable development, as something that encompasses all the essential elements required to achieve our goals is, as I will demonstrate, characteristic of a mythic story.

Another related aspect of sustainable development is its implicit sense of loss: a loss of a perfect state, a loss of innocence and a loss of harmony with nature and community; but we are urged by its advocates that, through right effort and right judgement, we can regain this lost idyll. These ideas are anything but new; in fact, they are a constant theme throughout human history. Our yearnings are always for a paradise that has been lost through our own making – through foolishness, corruption or greed;[12] such stories appear time and time again in the world's mythologies and religious texts. In the Greek Myths, we are told that Pandora's curiosity led her to open the box that released suffering and disease into an ideal world[13] and, in the Bible, Adam and Eve's disobedience results in their expulsion from the Garden of Eden,[14] to which we are forever trying to return. Similarly, today we point to our own recklessness and indulgence in destroying habitats, air quality, water quality and the ozone layer and are now striving to regain a vanished ideal through something we have termed sustainable development.

The possibility that sustainable development may not actually be achievable in any practical sense does not, however, make it any less important. We have always created and will continue to create myths that allow us to understand our world and our place in it. The point of the stories in the Greek Myths, the Bible or the Bhagavad Gita is not so much about achieving an end state as about taking on the task of learning how to live in the world. Sustainable development can be seen as our contemporary, secularized version of the same idea. Caring for and respecting the natural environment, together with ideas of socio-economic security and social justice are notions that have been with us for a very long time. However, their importance and mutual interdependence have only been reconfigured into an acceptable language for contemporary, developed, secularized societies relatively recently.

Economics and commerce go back to time immemorial, but in Christian cultures, profit and business have often been viewed with ambivalence. (I mention Christian cultures in particular because Christianity is the religion that has most strongly influenced the development of western industrialized societies.) There are numerous passages in the New Testament that cast riches and wealth in a poor light,[15] and, whether taken literally or in terms of metaphor and symbol, these stories have undoubtedly contributed to western society's love–hate relationship with the economic aspiration. Ironically, it was the accumulation of vast wealth within the Church and the associated corruption, scandal and exploitation of the common people that contributed to the Reformation during the first half of the 16th century.[16] The advancement of science, technology and industry from this time eventually led to the Enlightenment and the Industrial Revolution of the 18th century. As trade and commerce increased and expanded, the Church that had once been unified by Rome became fractured and fragmented. Protestantism grew through the establishment in the 16th century of Lutheranism in Germany, Calvinism in the Low Countries and Anglicanism in Britain, amongst others.[17] These developments can be seen as attempts to reform religious practices and reconcile religion with the rationalism of the emerging scientific and industrial age.[18] They occurred in a period of rapid scientific discovery, innovation and understanding; increasing applications of science in the development of technology; and expanding use of technology in creating commercial potential at a time of massive urbanization in Europe and colonial expansion abroad.

The scientific revolution and the Age of Reason are not only related to the fragmentation of the Church but also to a diminishment in its influence and power. Western societies, especially those of northern Europe, became increasingly secularized,[19] a process that some argue is still occurring,[20] as well as more individualistic, rationalistic, secular and far more urbanized.[21]

19

These changes established the basis of the Modern Age, which can be taken roughly as the period from the 17th to the mid-20th century. However, by the second half of the 20th century, after 200–300 years of scientific, industrial and commercial developments and expansion, and with two world wars, the horrors of the Holocaust and the atomic bombings of Japan still in the recent past, there arose a need for new ways of interpreting the world and humankind's place within it. The older understandings no longer seemed valid or capable of dealing with questions arising from the existential angst caused by the threat of nuclear destruction, the increasingly obvious environmental damage from industrial activities, and the pluralism of a multicultural and an increasingly mobile global population. Not only had the traditional religions by this time lost much of their relevancy but the Modern worldview that had evolved since the Reformation now, also, was being challenged. During the second half of the 20th century, many new understandings developed and an era that has been termed the Postmodern emerged.

Prior to this, however, there had been many indications that people were concerned with the environmental and socio-economic consequences of the Modern Age. Thoreau's *Walden*, published in 1854, was highly critical of the expanding technologies of the time.[22] The latter part of the 19th century saw the establishment of the world's first National Park[23] and the formation of the Sierra Club,[24] both in the US and both aimed at conserving natural places and wildlife. In terms of social issues, the late 19th century and first half of the 20th century witnessed the introduction of the first social security and health insurance acts and saw some initial activities in changing the prevailing attitudes concerning the rights of women and of homosexuals.[25] However, it wasn't until the later part of the 20th century that many of the environmental and social concerns began to be accepted on a larger scale, which in turn led to significant reform.

The 1960s were a time of considerable unrest, fear and uncertainty, especially among the younger generations of the western countries. The danger of nuclear war triggered peace campaigns in Europe and the US throughout the late 1950s, the 1960s and the 1970s. These extensive protests challenged the position of the establishment and the traditional, conservative bastions of power because it was perceived by many that the very future of the planet was at stake. These fears were not unfounded – in 1963 the world came to the brink of nuclear disaster with the Cuban missile crisis. This pervading threat to the future was evident in books and art of the time. Nevil Shute's novel *On the Beach,* published in 1957, was the story of a world laid waste by atomic war.[26] In the 1960s, works by Pop artists such as James Rosenquist and Larry Rivers contained numerous references to death, war and destruction.[27]

Growing concerns about the actions of human beings and the threat to the future were spurred on by the publication in 1962 of Rachel Carson's *Silent Spring*,[28] which drew attention to the environmental costs of widespread pesticide use; this book is often linked to the start of the environmental movement.

The energy crisis of the early 1970s, caused when the OPEC countries placed an embargo on oil exports, raised public consciousness about energy use and led to developments in energy conservation and the consideration of alternative energy sources, such as wind power. The oil crisis put at least a temporary halt to the production of large, 'gas-guzzlers' in the US, which were replaced by smaller, more modest and more fuel-efficient cars.

Increasing environmental destruction and air pollution and concerns about energy resources resulted in the emergence and expansion of the Green movement in the late 1960s and early 1970s. The Club of Rome was formed in 1968[29] and the US Environmental Protection Agency was set up in 1970.[30] Friends of the Earth[31] in Europe and Greenpeace[32] in Canada were both founded in 1971, and the following year a United Nations conference in Stockholm led to the establishment of the United Nations Environment Programme (UNEP).[33]

Alongside these developments that focused on the environment, there were also advances in social issues and human rights, areas that would also eventually become embraced by the term 'sustainable development'.[34] The Civil Rights movement in the US, campaigning for the rights of black Americans, was at its peak at this time. Martin Luther King delivered his 'I have a dream' speech at a Civil Rights march in Washington, DC, in 1963. During the mid-1960s, race riots broke out in major cities all over the US and in 1969 the US Supreme Court introduced desegregation. Women's emancipation was also on the rise at this time. In 1960, the contraceptive pill was approved in the US,[35] starting the sexual revolution and influencing the progress of the feminist movement. In 1970, Germaine Greer's influential book *The Female Eunuch* was published, which challenged the subservient role of women in a male-dominated society,[36] and in 1973 a woman's right to have an abortion was legalized in the US.[37] This period also saw the beginning of the Gay Rights movement, which has been attributed to a riot that broke out at the Stonewall Inn in New York City in 1969 in response to a police raid;[38] the subsequent decade saw the establishment of numerous homosexual rights organizations.

Therefore, during these years we see a multitude of changes and events occurring throughout the western world that, on the one hand, responded to increased environmental awareness and a recognition of the fragility of the planet and, on the other hand, social inequities and human rights. In 1972 a photograph of the Earth from space, taken by the astronauts of the Apollo 17 mission, reinforced the finite nature of

21

the Earth and its vulnerability.[39] When these many and diverse events are viewed as a whole, we can see that the foundations of sustainable development were laid in the 1960s and the early years of the 1970s.

The publication in 1971 of Victor Papanek's *Design for the Real World – Human Ecology and Social Change*[40] brought the mood of the times to the attention of, and within the scope of, the product designer. Papanek's lambasting of conventional product design and his call to address real needs rather than created wants resonated with many young designers at the time. In 1973, E. F. Schumacher's *Small is Beautiful – Economics as if People Mattered*[41] began to show the relationships among economic enterprise, poverty (especially in developing countries), energy use and environmental repercussions. Schumacher's views on the introduction of appropriate technology in developing countries to allow greater self-reliance paralleled many of the sentiments of Papanek and began to be implemented through the establishment of the Intermediate Technology Development Group in the UK.[42] Buckminster Fuller, who had been developing his ideas for the effective use of technology since the 1930s, came to renewed prominence in the early 1970s. Fuller believed it was possible to combat famine and poverty through the thoughtful and responsible use of science and technology – through an approach he termed 'comprehensive anticipatory design science'.[43] He was one of the earliest proponents of renewable energy sources, and his ideas were very influential on the younger generation in the late 1960s and early 1970s.[44] The work of Papanek, Schumacher and Fuller, amongst others, responded to the environmental and social reforms of the 1960s and presented a persuasive alternative for the product designer. This alternative path was well intentioned and certainly idealistic, but it was none the worse for that. As another way forward, a way that would attempt to circumvent the shortcomings of industrial capitalism, it was perhaps inevitably and appropriately embryonic and optimistic.

Social discontent and fears of nuclear war and environmental destruction were manifested during the 1960s and 1970s in the form of protests and demonstrations and through the creation of special interest groups. From the late 1970s on, however, many of these concerns started to become integrated into the establishment in the form of legislation, agreements and representation. In 1983 the Green Party entered the West German Parliament with 27 seats.[45] In

22

1987 the Montreal Protocol to limit the production of ozone-depleting substances was adopted.[46] In 1989 The Netherlands introduced its first, and at the time the world's most comprehensive, National Environment Policy,[47] and in 1992 the first UN Conference on Environment and Development, known as the Earth Summit, was held in Rio de Janeiro.[48] During these years, further environmental and social issues became evident. Indications of ozone layer depletion over the polar regions and of global warming trends were revealed by scientists,[49] and reports of the debt crisis faced by many developing countries were followed by pictures in the press of mass starvation in Africa, especially in Ethiopia.[50] The gross inequities between rich and poor countries were raised to new levels of public awareness through the Live Aid Concerts organized by Bob Geldof,[51] and, during the mid-1990s there were numerous reports in the western press of the use of sweatshop labour by firms in developing countries that were supplying goods to US companies for consumption in the west.[52] Throughout the 1990s and into the 21st century, attention became more focused on the role of business and its relationship to environmental degradation and social deprivation. In the US, Paul Hawken published *The Ecology of Commerce* (1993),[53] which proposed that business could be a primary mechanism to achieve a more sustainable future. In Europe, Wolfgang Sachs and colleagues offered an alternative approach to development in their book *Greening the North* (1998)[54] and in Canada, Naomi Klein's influential book *No Logo* (2000)[55] was a scathing indictment of the branding techniques of big business, of globalization and of social injustice.

In recent years, more protests and riots have been seen around the world. The targets of these have been the major corporations and political leaders who make agreements that, according to the protesters, exacerbate social inequities and environmental harm. Demonstrations, sometimes violent, were seen at the World Trade Organization meeting in Seattle in 1999, at the G8 Summits in Genoa, Italy, in 2001 and in the following year in Kananaskis, Canada. In 2003, World Trade Organization talks collapsed in Cancun, Mexico, amid further protests and serious differences between rich and poor countries – especially with respect to government subsidies given to farmers in the richer economies which, it is alleged, render produce from developing countries less competitive. Also in 2003, we saw the reappearance of the peace march in worldwide demonstrations against the US-led war in Iraq, which many saw as a ploy to secure oil resources. These were

23

the biggest international displays of protest since the anti-nuclear and anti-Vietnam War marches of the 1960s. In 2004, there were student protests ahead of the Asia Pacific Economic Cooperation Forum in Santiago, Chile,[56] and at the G8 in Gleneagles, Scotland, in 2005 there were further protests and arrests,[57] together with Live 8 concerts across the world, again organized by Bob Geldof, which called for greater social justice for poorer nations.[58]

These diverse events, changes and reforms constitute a significant shift in attitudes and understandings. To a large extent, the Modern worldview has become replaced by a Postmodern worldview, where absolute certainties have been supplanted by more relativistic values. In many cases this has led to greater tolerance and the acceptance of difference, although it also has to be acknowledged that in some areas, especially in some European liberal democracies, there have been signs of a growing intolerance, particularly in the area of religious beliefs.[59] Environmental responsibility, social equity and human rights have now become established in our legislations and in our thoughts and actions. The notion of achieving more sustainable ways of living is held up by political and business sector leaders as something worth striving towards – even if there is little understanding of what a sustainable society might actually look like and even less of how we might get there from our current state of high energy use, resource depletion and consumption.

These changing understandings have affected the product design and manufacturing sectors in a variety of ways. In many countries, legislation now controls air emissions, water pollution and the dumping of toxic substances. International standards such as ISO 14000[60] lay down best practice guidelines for environmental responsibility, The Natural Step[61] and similar programmes have been taken up by a number of major corporations, and tools such as life cycle assessment[62] have been developed to aid companies in designing products that have lower environmental impacts. However, there have also been developments that run counter to understandings of sustainable development. Labour exploitation in developing countries is still widespread and is often associated with major western corporations. The production of very large automobiles with high fuel consumption has returned, especially in the US,[63] and there is massive dependence on road transport in general, rather than on more energy-efficient and more environmentally benign methods such as rail. The links that must be formed between local-scale initiatives and mass production in order to further environmental responsibility and greater social equity and self-reliance have received relatively little attention, and staggering rates of production, consumption and waste generation continue apace.

It seems that the vision of a sustainable society, especially when the population of the world exceeds 6 billion,[64] is far more an ideal than a feasible possibility. In this and in other ways, sustainable development bears all the hallmarks of a mythic story – a story that tries to come to terms with, and provide resolution to, something that is beyond our grasp.

Steiner has explained that the term 'mythology' can be attributed to a body of thought if (1) it provides an idea of completeness – a total picture of humanity in the world, (2) it has a recognizable beginning and development, including key founders and texts, and (3) it develops its own stories, language and scenarios.[65] In sustainable development we have clear evidence of all three. Firstly, its main elements of environment, ethics and economics provide an encompassing view for our physical, moral and socio-economic well-being. Secondly, while the seeds of sustainability may have been sown earlier, it began in earnest during the 1960s and 1970s through the protest movement, social changes such as environmentalism and feminism, and through key authors such as Carson, Schumacher and, in product design, Papanek. These ideas and principles became cemented during the 1970s and 1980s and the term 'sustainable development' was popularized through the publication of the Brundtland report in 1987. Thirdly, scenarios, stories, jargon and language are all rapidly emerging within the field to reify its concepts and ideas. It has its evangelists and prophets who proclaim the new vision and warn of dire consequences if we do not heed their words and change our ways. There has also been a plethora of books that emphasize the dangers of continuing on our current course, document environmental disasters, warn of the dangers to health of air pollution or speak out against the policies of major corporations. Some of these arguments are well founded, while others are more melodramatic but often more tenuous in their assertions. Nevertheless, the body of work that has arisen over recent years to address and begin implementing the ideas contained under the sustainable development umbrella constitute a rich and diverse set of

25

ideas. Furthermore, a lexicon of terms is emerging, such as 'the Natural Step' and 'Factor 10', together with the three Es of sustainability, 'product/service systems' and 'back casting and scenario development', which are familiar to those working in the field.

So we see that sustainable development appears to satisfy all the criteria of 'myth'. It offers an idea of completeness, a total vision. It has a recognizable beginning, identifiable founders and key texts, and it is spawning a burgeoning collection of narratives, terminologies and scenarios. It contains many of the elements of more traditional mythologies and religions, but re-presented in a contemporary, secularized form.

These observations do not negate the value and importance of sustainable development, they simply allow us to see it from a somewhat different, perhaps more philosophical, perspective. While a future, sustainable condition may not actually be physically achievable, its very presence in our consciousness, as a potential goal of sustainable development, indicates a discontent with the current state of things and a need to strive towards something we believe to be better – for the environment, for others and for ourselves. British academic and cleric Richard Holloway has pointed out that down the ages there have been many of these notions of a final, defining destiny aimed at achieving harmony and human equality. He suggests that, while they are never entirely achievable, their main purpose is to spur us towards justice and compassion in a world filled by desire and greed.[66]

In this chapter, I have tried to show that sustainable development encapsulates and represents particular aspects of traditional teachings; it consists of several broad, interconnected themes that address some of the major pragmatic challenges of our time. However, it is often considered a kind of cure-all for today's environmental and social problems – and not merely as an element within a much larger narrative of meaning and significance. But without some greater aspiration or vision of human existence and purpose, it is hardly enough to inspire us, let alone sustain us. Sustainable development yields only a partial and, ultimately, a rather meagre picture of the human condition. It may address some of the important practical issues of environmental stewardship, social justice and economic security, but it is often stultifyingly prosaic. It is largely bereft of ideas that nurture and develop the inner person – the inspirational, the imaginative, the transcendent and the struggle for self-knowledge. These are aspects of our existence that fuel the artist, the composer, the musician and the poet. We have a long heritage of philosophical, artistic, mythical and sacred traditions that can provide us with a foundation on which to base our current endeavours and to address our environmental and social responsibilities. Sustainable development must embrace these vital aspects of human culture if it is to make a meaningful and lasting contribution.

In an age that gives short shrift to religion and the traditional mythical views of the world, it is sobering to realize that we have, in effect, created our own myth for our own time and in language that we can accept. But, as many are now rejecting literal interpretations of traditional sacred texts, we must be prepared to do the same for our own. If the question to ask of the traditional myths is not 'Are they true?' but 'What do they mean?' then we must ask the same question of the evolving myth of sustainable development. We must not ask 'Is it possible to achieve?' but 'What does the creation of this new narrative mean in contemporary society and for us personally in our work and our lives?' By asking such a question we can begin to see sustainable development from a different perspective. It represents much more than simply an analytical approach to environmental auditing or improving business accountability. It also represents a way of acknowledging our values and beliefs and ascribing meaning to our activities. In this sense, sustainable development offers a contemporary way of, at least partially, filling the void left by the demise of religion in public discourse. On the other hand, it must also be acknowledged that sustainable development is both ideological and immature. As such, it has neither the breadth nor the profundity of the traditions that, to an extent, it supersedes. It would seem, therefore, that our contemporary 'sustainable' myth might well be insufficient to sustain us.

27

4
DESIGN PROCESS AND SUSTAINABLE DEVELOPMENT
a journey
in design

Industrial design began in the early years of the 20th century to provide design services for manufacturing.[1] Since then, its role has developed with the industry and today it is often the key ingredient of a company's success. A broad range of expertise, knowledge and skills enables the industrial designer to make important contributions to our modern, globalized systems of product development, production and marketing. However, when we add sustainable development to the mix of issues to be considered by manufacturing industry, the industrial designer is generally ill equipped to offer advice. In addition, a primary concern of manufacturing has to be the economic factor. When sustainability issues are raised, as they have been on an increasing basis in recent years, it is perhaps understandable that many companies are reluctant to deal with them; the issues are complex, company knowledge is often lacking and, perhaps most critically, any action to address concerns about sustainability is usually perceived as being detrimental to the bottom line.

Sustainable development often seems incompatible with conventional priorities and business norms. To develop a more effective relationship between sustainable principles and the creation of our material needs, it may be necessary to take a rather different approach. Instead of trying to 'force fit' sustainable principles into an existing and often unreceptive manufacturing system, it may be useful to approach the subject from the opposite direction, and consider how functional objects might be designed and manufactured to be compatible with principles of sustainable development. This would allow sustainable concerns to be included from the beginning and could provide much needed direction for developing new models of production. To do this requires a change in perspective and for the purpose of illustration I would like to use an analogy. The following comparison of two journeys demonstrates the type of shift in thinking that is required of the designer who wishes to explore the unfamiliar and uncertain territory of sustainable design.

In 1845, Sir John Franklin, an experienced explorer, set out from England to discover a sea route from the Atlantic to the Pacific through the Canadian Arctic – the fabled Northwest Passage. This was his fourth Arctic journey and the most well prepared and well stocked expedition ever mounted to the region. It comprised two ships with 129 men. The ships were fitted with the very latest technologies including steam engines and propellers to supplement the sails, a steam heating system and desalinators to distil drinking water from seawater. They took enough provisions to last three years, with over 60,000kg of flour and 8000 cans of food. They had a library of nearly 3000 books, early photographic equipment, silver plate, mahogany desks, dress uniforms and even a grand piano.[2] Sir John Franklin did not believe in scrimping; he intended to live well and in the manner to which he and his men were accustomed; and that was his undoing. Despite his previous experience in the region, the technology, the planning and the immense supplies, not one crewmember survived: all died of starvation, illness and cold, and neither ship was ever seen again. Subsequent accounts from the Inuit of the region and the recovery of frozen remains have revealed a final struggle for survival of harrowing desperation and indications of cannibalism.[3]

The deaths of Franklin and his men were unnecessary and wholly avoidable. Seventy-five years earlier another Englishman, Samuel Hearne, had already explored the same region and had shown that the

Northwest Passage did not exist in any form that was useful as a trade route. Over a period of nearly three years, Hearne trekked 5000 miles in the area between Hudson's Bay and the Arctic Ocean. In contrast to Franklin's struggle for survival, Hearne was able to maintain detailed journals about the wildlife, the people and the environment; and he spent time making careful pencil drawings of what he saw.[4] Unlike Franklin, Hearne travelled light, and looked to the indigenous people for guidance and instruction. He adopted their ways, their diet, and their modes of travel, and he was not in the least prejudiced against them, even though many of their customs horrified him and on more than one occasion he was cheated, robbed and abandoned.[5] His willingness to learn from the native people not only made him unusual for his day, but also allowed him to successfully live and travel in the region.

The difference in these two stories is that, while both men were exploring new territory, Franklin's approach was impositional, whereas Hearne's was responsive. Franklin brought with him not only tons of supplies but also a set of values and expectations from another context. He tried to force-fit the norms and conventions of 19th-century England into the barren, frozen lands of the Arctic. And it worked for a while, until the supplies ran out, and then the entire expedition perished because they had not learned how to survive in their new environment. Hearne, on the other hand, responded to the new conditions. His lack of egotism and pretension meant that he was able to adapt to his new context and he became competent in the nomadic ways of the native people. In other words, Hearne's approach was sustainable whereas Franklin's was not.

The discipline of design is also about exploring new ground and charting new territory, and if we are to do this effectively and sustainably, we must be fully aware of the new context in which we find ourselves and learn to respond to it in an appropriate manner. We must also consider the baggage, in the form of preconceptions, that we bring along with us.

When we are in the midst of things, it is often difficult to appreciate the context: there are too many details getting in the way. So we must try to obtain a different perspective, and one way of doing this for our current situation is to look at it in terms of its historical development. In the previous chapter, I discussed the key historical events that led to the emergence of sustainable development in the late 20th century. Our

31

contemporary manufacturing systems are quite clearly a culmination of some 500 years of scientific progress,[6] the development of rationalism,[7] the rise of utilitarianism,[8] 200–300 years of industrial capitalism,[9] a century or so of mass production and accelerating consumerism,[10] and perhaps 30 years of the age of information. And in just the last few decades, Postmodern understandings have also begun to permeate society, bringing with them perspectives that often challenge and undermine previously held certainties. Within this relatively recent period, the concept of sustainable development has emerged in response to the detrimental effects associated with our activities. When we look at it from this perspective, as a rather new but systemically challenging and potentially disrupting idea, it is not surprising that our industrialists, economists and politicians are having some difficulty in understanding what it means and how to reconcile it with long-established industrial and economic norms.

What is clear is that many of our conventions and practices are no longer valid for the context in which we now find ourselves. As I will elaborate in later chapters, a multitude of social and environmental indicators make it only too apparent that contemporary production systems and consumption patterns are physically, ethically and spiritually untenable. And so we must move forward into unknown territory and explore new approaches that are more environmentally benign and personally and socially enriching. It is the role of designers, as well as design educators and researchers, to be in the vanguard of this exploration – to visualize new possibilities and offer new responses. As designers, we can set about this exploration in a variety of ways. At one end of the spectrum, we can be like Franklin and retain the practices that have brought us thus far, assuming they will take us further. Most companies and most designers seem to be adopting this approach. They move forward but in a manner that maintains the behaviours of an increasingly outmoded context. It is not unusual for environmental advocates to be viewed as unfortunate irritants or as being against technological advance and progress; one group has even referred to them as 'the new life-haters'.[11] Environmental legislation tends to be opposed at every turn because it is perceived as having a negative effect on earnings. One major company has made much of its use of recycled materials in its products, while simultaneously employing sweatshop labour in the Far East for product assembly.[12] New products are developed but, for the most part, the main intention is to boost sales, increase profits and foster growth. Whether or not the product is capable of making a meaningful and responsible contribution to material culture is often not even a consideration.

It is important to acknowledge that there are now numerous companies making genuine efforts to be more environmentally and socially responsible. But within the current system, where the dominant measure of success is financial profit, with little else of comparable importance, then change is slow and it is difficult to stray too far from convention.

This approach to design and manufacturing is impositional – the practices developed in one context (the Modern) are being applied within another (the Postmodern) that has different requirements. Essentially, it is merely a projection into the future of what has worked in the past. This may have been effective once, but today it is not viable. A central tenet of industrial capitalism is growth, but nothing can grow for ever, and we now seem to be reaching the limits of growth – at least in terms of the types of growth we have valued over the past century.[13] To simply extrapolate from the past and to ignore the evidence around us of the consequences of our actions reveals a blindness to the circumstances, a lack of creativity and a moral failing.

33

At the other end of the spectrum, we can take an approach more like that of Samuel Hearne. This requires an open mind to the new context. We do not attempt to impose our outmoded behaviours but instead learn to adapt to the situation in which we now find ourselves. Only by fundamentally changing our approaches to deal with the new circumstances can we hope to develop new models for design and production that are more compatible with sustainable ways of living. Wrestling with existing models and trying to modify them is not an effective strategy. Progress is frustratingly slow, changes are incremental and acceptance of change is often grudging. By contrast, envisioning and building new models could, eventually, render the old ways obsolete. While improving the existing system is undoubtedly beneficial and to be encouraged, there are many examples showing that a more radical approach can be an effective strategy for instigating more fundamental change. An example from the world of product design would be the calculating machine. Until the 1970s, the basic operating principle of the mechanical calculator had remained essentially the same since the 19th century. However, with the advent of microchip technology those calculators, and the knowledge base and production systems that were in place to produce them, were rendered obsolete within just a few years. Manufacturers had to rapidly revolutionize their approach if they were to operate successfully within a fundamentally new context, or they found themselves quickly out of business. Another, more recent example is the transfer from disc-based formats of recorded music, where a tangible product was purchased from a store along with packaging, to a digital-based format that is flexible, accessible from home and less expensive; a similar revolution has occurred in the transfer from film-based to digital photography.

It is important to acknowledge that, in the case of sustainable development, while we recognize that many of our conventional approaches are unsustainable, we do not know what a sustainable approach might look like. This truly is a journey of exploration. But, like Samuel Hearne, we must leave behind our preconceptions, many of the things we hold dear and many of our expectations. This is not a comfortable thing to have to do; it is disconcerting and the route forward is uncertain – but this is the nature of exploration. It is also the nature of design. To be a designer is to be on uncertain ground.

So let us look at some of the things that, perhaps, we would do well leaving behind, or at least challenging, and then consider how we might begin to take some tentative steps forward.

The imposition of preconceptions on a design project is not only very common, it is also rather unimaginative. When it occurs, we are simply drawing on our existing notions of how objects should be – irrespective of the requirements of the object or the context of use. We just have to look around to see that this type of impositional design is the dominant form today – most cars look virtually the same and they have visual characteristics that are very similar to other products, such as CD players which, in turn, look very similar to vacuum cleaners. There are thousands of designers in professional practice around the world, all trained at universities and colleges to be creative – and yet so many of our products look essentially the same in terms of their overall visual language. Now, one might argue that this is a trivial point, that it is not so important how things look. This is *not* the case. It is critically important how things look – because 'how things look' is a reflection of ourselves, of who we are, of the things that we believe are important and the things we choose to ignore. So the fact that things tend to look the same, that the look of things is geared towards transient trends, fashion and consumerism – these characteristics of products and design are actually very telling; especially when we know, unequivocally, that our current practices are so damaging to the environment and are socially inequitable.

We must ask ourselves why this is so, why do industrial designers tend to design in this way? In my view, it has much to do with the baggage that is brought along. The very term 'industrial design' brings with it a great deal of baggage. It defines an approach, carrying with it a set of expectations, and it represents a particular set of knowledge and skills. Industrial design is closely linked, as a term and as a discipline, with the development of mass production and consumer goods in the early years of the 20th century. It is generally understood as the design of products for large-scale distribution and it is commonly described as a service profession to manufacturing industry.[14] But the characteristics that are inherent to the term industrial design are today highly questionable, as are the characteristics of the industrial system it serves, because many of them are entirely incompatible with sustainable principles. For example, industrial design means the design of mass-produced products, often with an intentionally short life span, for mass markets, whereas sustainable approaches tend to place far greater emphasis on smaller, local-scale initiatives and product endurance. So the term industrial design is not very useful in discussions of sustainable development; the term 'product design', which is used interchangeably with industrial design, has many of the same problems.

35

Therefore, some of the baggage we might leave behind as we explore new, more sustainable directions would be the labels industrial design and product design and our conventional notions of what they imply about the production and aesthetics of functional objects.

A related issue here is the whole notion of the professionalization of design. Professions tend to categorize, separate and distinguish activities, and product design has become a defined, professionalized discipline, which implies certain ideas about material things. By contrast, sustainable development points towards approaches that are holistic and more inclusive and, certainly at this early point in the development of our understandings of the subject, we must encourage diversity and variety, trial and error, and experimentation. The narrowing of our understandings into a specific discipline and within the boundaries of a specific 'profession' is not consistent with the integrative, interdisciplinary and experimental approaches that are needed here. Carl Jung once suggested that one of the roles of religion is to shield us from the religious experience.[15] Similarly, we could argue that one of the roles of industrial design, together with manufacturing industry, is to shield us from a meaningful experience of material culture.

Hence, the terms we use and the systemic characteristics they imply would seem to be a hindrance rather than a help, and it may be useful to drop them from the lexicon of sustainable design – at least for the present. Instead of thinking about design within this conventional frame, we can approach it in fresh ways and think about how to create a material culture that is consistent with, and beneficial to, personal and social well-being, environmental stewardship and economic stability. To do this we must start with fewer preconceptions and improvise as we go.

This might seem rather unrealistic – but let us continue the analogy. If Samuel Hearne had turned to the other 'professional' explorers of his day for advice, he would have received the established view of how to go about Arctic exploration. Franklin took the established view, and even if he hadn't perished, his approach, despite appearances, was far more precarious than Hearne's.

A characteristic of improvisation is that we have to make do with what is available and use limited resources in creative new ways. A priori solutions are less feasible, and a type of design is encouraged that is more sensitive to, and contingent on, context. An important source of precedents of this type of approach is vernacular design. In traditional cultures, there is often a very good 'fit' between material artefacts and the environment, cultural values and beliefs, and ways of life. Traditional cultures can be excellent examples of how to live in more sustainable ways. Objects are often deeply symbolic and meaningful within these cultures, and for this reason they have value over and above functional benefit (this point will be explored in more detail later). We can learn from vernacular design because an important aspect of sustainable development is the 'local' and the specific characteristics of place. Vernacular design can provide us with at least some insights into the diversity and richness of locally appropriate design. We can also learn from the craft and folk design traditions. But it is our challenge to find ways of bringing together the local and the global to create designs that are suited to modern, technologically and economically developed societies. Such an integration would also go some way to bridging the chasm that has grown between craft and design for industry.

To encourage exploration, improvisation and integration, perhaps, instead of trying to be professional, we should become amateurs and dilettantes. These terms are usually taken to be derogatory, but the word 'dilettante' comes from the same root as 'delight', and 'amateur' from the same root as 'amare', meaning love. To be a dilettante and an amateur is to be someone who delights in the diverse beauty of the world and engages in a pursuit because of a love of the subject. Rather than defining objects within strict boundaries, and 'professionalizing' material culture, we need to open up new ways that allow us to delight in the act of creativity, and in the products of creativity – ways that are pursued because of a love of the activity and a love of the environment and the world. Most contemporary products are not expressions of delight, nor are they manifestations of love. It is difficult to feel delight when we know our products are causing enormous environmental devastation, and it is difficult to feel love of a subject that contributes to a system of manufacturing that is permeated by unconscionable social inequities. By contrast, sustainable approaches to design have the potential of not only ameliorating the environmental and ethical concerns associated with conventional practices, but also of helping to create a material culture that truly is a thing of beauty, in which we can find delight because it is a meaningful expression of human values that are responsible, ethical and caring.

37

Another facet of contemporary design is also worth challenging. We often hear that design is about solving problems. Ironically, contemporary design often seems not so much about solving problems as creating them. Marcel Duchamp once said, 'There is no solution because there is no problem'.[16] If there is no problem then what does the designer do? In my view, it is more accurate and more constructive to say that designers create possibilities. We create possibilities of how things could be; but we have given less thought to the question of how things *should* be. When we pass from could to should we introduce an ethical dimension, and this is a key feature of a more sustainable approach.

The concern of this chapter has been the need to reframe how we think about the creation of functional objects in the context of sustainable development; the main points are summarized in Table 4.1. The development of fresh perspectives can be hindered by the terms, conventions and expectations of established practices, and so it seems appropriate to set them aside, at least for the time being, until we have developed a better sense of what sustainable development means for material culture. It is also useful to look at other areas of design, such as the vernacular, to see both the potential and the limitations of placing greater emphasis on 'localization'. However, creativity, imagination and innovation are needed to develop new directions that begin to weave together scales of production, levels of technological sophistication, and diverse cultural needs in ways that are environmentally, socially and economically responsible and desirable.

Table 4.1 **Reframing design:** *A comparison of key characteristics*

Conventional design	Sustainable design
Industrial design	Design of functional objects
Product design	Creation of material culture
Specialization	Improvisation
Conventional	Uncertain, uncomfortable
Professional	Amateur, dilettante
Specific	Holistic, integrative
Instrumental	Intrinsic
Problem-solving	Experimenting
Solutions	Possibilities
A priori design	Contingent design

5
ENDURING ARTEFACTS AND SUSTAINABLE SOLUTIONS
object lessons

A sustainable solution can be understood as one that possesses enduring value in terms of its meanings and characteristics. Therefore, in this chapter I will be considering objects that have existed in one form or another in human society for millennia and which are still made and used today. When objects have been produced over such long periods, spanning diverse cultures, languages and understandings, then we can be sure there are lessons to be learned from them about our relationships with material things and our contemporary efforts to tackle sustainable issues in design and manufacturing.

A perusal of the collections in many of our large national museums[1] reveals that certain kinds of objects have been prevalent in human society since very early times. When considering their endurance, we must distinguish between a specific object and a more general 'object type'. While a particular artefact might be rather ephemeral in terms of its use, its materials, its style or its motif, there are object types that have persisted across very long reaches of time; examples include pottery, tools, weapons, jewellery and statuary. Such objects have been in continuous production for at least 5000 years, and the earliest examples of jewellery were recently estimated to be some 75,000 years old.[2] These types of objects are valued for their utility, their decorative and aesthetic qualities, and/or their symbolic or ritualistic roles. The value ascribed to an object will usually emphasize one of these attributes over and above the others. These object types can rightly be characterized as sustainable; the sheer longevity of their production and use clearly testifies to their enduring importance in supporting human existence or in nourishing human culture. As such, it will be useful to examine some of their general characteristics because these characteristics can be considered in relation to human needs and values, and therefore can inform our contemporary efforts to achieve more sustainable design solutions. Enduring objects, such as those I have mentioned, can be classified into three broad groups:

1   *Functional*: Tools, weapons and everyday pottery are valued primarily for their usefulness. If a tool is ineffective then its value is severely diminished – it would be described as 'useless'. Similarly, a weapon is judged by its usefulness in hunting or in affording protection, and a ceramic pot by its ability to hold liquid. These objects are designed to accomplish practical tasks; design considerations focus on effectiveness, safety and user comprehension.

2   *Social/Positional*: Jewellery items such as necklaces, earrings and bracelets; products such as cosmetics and tattoos; and badges, brooches and medals are all non-utilitarian. While they serve a purpose, they are not practical implements or utensils. Instead, they are used to express identity, to be decorative, to enhance one's appearance, or to indicate one's rank, achievement or affiliation. Their chief characteristics are their social or positional qualities;[3] they serve as social signifiers that can enhance one's sense of self-esteem, one's social acceptance or indicate one's social standing.

3   *Inspirational/Spiritual*: This category includes religious statuary and icons, and fine art objects. All these things refer to or convey inspiring, sacred or spiritual ideas; they are physical expressions of profound understandings and beliefs, and because of this they are considered deeply meaningful. They often have religious, magical or talismanic associations and can serve as reminders or touchstones for our most deeply felt yearnings.

40

These categories represent three very significant object types because each has stood the test of time and held its place in human society irrespective of culture, class, beliefs and language. We can therefore conclude that such objects are non-trivial and, at least in terms of their continuous presence and use in human society, sustainable. We can infer that they fulfil important human needs. Indeed, when we consider their characteristics in relation to our understandings of human needs, such as the modified version of Maslow's Hierarchy of Human Needs[4] and Hick's natural, ethical and religious meaning,[5] it becomes clear that, taken together, these three sets of product characteristics correspond to a broad and comprehensive range of human needs. *Functional* objects allow us to fulfil our physiological and biological needs as well as our safety needs, such as ensuring personal security or fending off danger. *Social/positional* objects refer to our need for love, belonging and social acceptance; our standing within a social group; our ethical awareness; our sense of achievement; and self-esteem. And *inspirational/spiritual* objects refer to our need to know, our search for meaning, our aesthetic sensibilities, personal growth, our spiritual needs, and our need to reach out beyond ourselves to help others attain their potential.[6]

41

However, many objects are not adequately described by just one of these categories. Instead, they bridge two or even all three. These more complex cases reveal that some combinations are highly problematic, both environmentally and socially, while others hold important lessons for the design and manufacture of sustainable goods. We can identify objects that have both social/positional and inspirational/ spiritual qualities, others that have functional and social/positional characteristics, and still others that have functional, social/positional and spiritual/inspirational characteristics. Objects that have only functional and spiritual/inspirational characteristics are probably not feasible.[7] Let us now briefly look at examples that combine these various characteristics:

- *Social/Positional + Inspirational/Spiritual*: This category includes things such as ornaments, commercial art pieces, souvenirs, home décor items, and statuary or art objects that have social/positional meanings attributed to them, such as status, esteem or personal identity. This can also include items based on traditional cultures and religions such as

the commercially produced Haida Masks of the Canadian
west coast. These types of sculptures are produced today for
the tourist or collector markets and in the process changes
occur. Some of these changes can be positive, creating new
opportunities for artistic expression while simultaneously
opening up new avenues for economic development and self-
determination. The changes can also be negative, especially
when the objects become modified, clichéd and stereotyped
in order to serve the market.[8] When these non-functional
objects become commercialized, their religious, ritualistic
or cultural significance is no longer relevant, they become
primarily decorative and there is a danger of them becoming
a pastiche or falling into kitsch. In terms of sustainability, these
object types do not pose much of a problem – on the contrary,
their production can be a valuable contribution. They are
generally 'low tech' and are frequently handmade at the local
level, employing local skills, cultural and aesthetic sensibilities,
and perpetuating cultural ties, albeit in some cases in a new
and often diluted form; but if taken to extremes this last point
can become destructive to a culture's heritage. Nevertheless,
opportunities for local employment using local materials and
local designs are often socially and economically beneficial,
and environmentally of relatively low impact. Furthermore,
the handmade and personal or cultural significance of these
artefacts means that the people who buy them will often keep
them for a long time – even passing them down from one
generation to another. They are often regarded as precious
personal possessions and they may have a heritage value,
which in turn prevents them entering the waste stream.

- *Functional + Social/Positional*: This category includes
consumer goods such as automobiles, watches, music
equipment, footwear and designer-labelled goods. All these
possess positional value in addition to their essential utility.[9]
These are functional products that set one apart from the
crowd and in terms of sustainability they are, by far, the most
problematic. To a great extent these are mass-produced
goods which are promoted and distributed globally; they drive
consumerism and are the cause of many environmental and
social ills. These objects not only combine functionality with

42

positional value, they also become quickly outdated. There are two main reasons for this: firstly, both their functionality and their positional value are intimately connected to advances in technology, and secondly, their positional value is tied to changes in fashion and styling. Within our contemporary market-driven, mass-production system, the linking of technological progress and/or styling with social status has become an extremely potent combination. Today virtually all our utilitarian goods have the potential to be positional, from cars and audio products to refrigerators, kettles and bathtubs. When this occurs an object's value is determined not simply by its ability to properly function, but also by its ability to convey social position, aspiration or affiliation. However, the positional value of these types of objects is inevitably short-lived because technology is always advancing and styling is always changing. These factors spawn the upward spiral of consumerism that is so environmentally and socially problematic.

- *Functional* + *Social/Positional* + *Inspirational/Spiritual*: This category includes objects related to religion and particularly to forms of prayer, for example a Muslim prayer mat, a Buddhist prayer wheel or a Jewish prayer shawl. Each of these articles serves a functional purpose: the prayer mat defines a space for prayer, every rotation of the prayer wheel represents a prayer's recitation, and the prayer shawl is a mnemonic.[10] Inseparable from these functions, each has a symbolic religious or spiritual significance, and each is a signifier of social identity and, potentially, each may also be associated with social status or position. These are important religious and cultural artefacts that all pertain to our inspirational or spiritual understandings, and each is 'used' in an active, functional way that is quite different from a religious statue or painting. These types of artefacts are considered precious because of their sacred associations and their design and use are steeped in tradition. Consequently, they are not simply discarded when a newer model or style comes along. They can therefore be described as sustainable; they have a long history in human society, they are highly valued and they have profound meaning.

43

These examples, the prayer shawl, prayer wheel and prayer mat, are each specific to a particular religious culture. There is, however, a similar object that is found all over the world and in most of the major religions. I would like to consider this artefact in rather more detail because it holds important lessons for our understandings of sustainability and material culture.

Imagine an object that is used today by rich and poor, young and old, healthy and sick; an object that fulfils a prosaic, utilitarian role, and has a deeply spiritual significance; that can be decorative and highly aesthetic; and has for its owner a profoundly personal value that is inherent to that *particular* object, independent of price, quality or materials. Imagine, too, that such an object has a wide variety of designs and manifestations, that it can be mass-produced for a few pennies or, for a similar cost, made at home. Perhaps the contemplation of such an object would allow us to see anew some of the failings of our contemporary, rather limited approaches to product design and production, and offer some pointers for a more sustainable and more inclusive future.

44

In the tragedy of Baghdad a man scarred with the wounds of conflict holds this object.[11] High in the Himalayas a young boy uses it to keep a tally. A smaller version can be seen in the fingers of an old man in a café in Athens. In New York it may be found in the pocket of a business suit or in a fashionable Gucci handbag. In many a Chinatown a stall can be found bursting with different versions in all shapes, sizes and colours. It is an object that crosses boundaries of time, belief, gender, culture and class. The year October 2002 to October 2003 was dedicated to it.[12] In December 2003, 500 of these objects were used by British artist Mark Wallinger to decorate the Christmas tree at Tate Modern in London.[13] It is variously known as the *mala*, the *tasbih*, the rosary or simply as prayer beads, and through the centuries it has carved out a unique place in human culture as an object that ties the physical or outer person with the inner, contemplative and spiritual self. The widespread and enduring use of prayer beads, together with their fundamental relationship to the human search for meaning, make them an important artefact for consideration by the product designer seeking to better understand the relationship between sustainability and material things.

At their most basic functional level, prayer beads are used for keeping track of repeated chants or prayers. Their most common form is a simple circle of beads or knots on a string, ending in a tassel or religious symbol. They are thought to have originated in Hinduism about 3000 years ago.[14] Buddhists have also used them since very early times;[15] the Muslim *tasbih* dates back to about the 9th century[16] and the Catholic rosary to the 15th.[17] The Orthodox churches use knotted prayer ropes and the Baha'i faith uses a version similar to the *tasbih*. An Anglican rosary was introduced in the late 20th century in the US,[18] and there are secular varieties known as 'worry beads'.

The uses and meanings of prayer beads are many. In fact, it is this rich diversity that makes prayer beads such a significant object for consideration in a discussion about sustainable design. Its uses and meanings include:

- *A Tallying Device:* A bead, representing one prayer in the cycle, is held in the fingers whilst the prayer is recited. In this respect, prayer beads serve as a simple functional tool.
- *An Aid to Concentration and Meditation:* Essentially, prayer beads are a device to assist concentration while praying or meditating.[19] The fingering of the beads is a repetitive activity that can be done without thinking; importantly it is an activity that occupies the physical body. Pascal talked of using such routines to allow us to act unthinkingly and mechanically, in order to subdue the machine and the power of reason.[20] This is a critical aspect of prayer beads; the repetitive action produces a quieting effect.[21] We see similar mechanical routines practised all over the world because they are associated with spiritual growth. For example, the spinning of the prayer wheel, the raking of a Zen garden,[22] and the rocking action of orthodox Jews during prayer. These practices are thoughtless or 'unreasoned' actions; they facilitate meditation and, potentially, inner growth. It is this fundamental purpose that raises prayer beads above the merely mundane and functional. The simple string of beads is an instrument of synthesis – an aid in bringing together the inner and outer, or the physical and spiritual.[23] Thus, prayer beads are profoundly meaningful, which, as we shall see, is relevant to our understanding of sustainable design.

45

All the major spiritual traditions are expressed, on the one hand, through teachings and practices that are often somewhat esoteric and difficult to grasp and, on the other hand, through popular understandings and customs. In this respect, prayer beads have various other meanings that add to their widespread appeal:

- *A Talisman:* Prayer beads are often regarded as a lucky charm.[24] In some religions losing one's prayer beads is an ominous sign,[25] and in Catholicism, even in recent times, the rosary has been associated with apparitions and miracles.[26] It is commonly viewed as an object of comfort,[27] and in many Latin countries it is a ubiquitous adornment of a car's rear-view mirror. Such associations are deeply rooted in the human psyche and, despite scientific and technological progress and our rationalistic outlooks, they are still very much present in modern, secular societies. Other common examples include the omission of row 13 in aircraft by major airlines in some of the world's most scientifically advanced countries,[28] and the commonly held superstition that walking under a ladder brings bad luck.

- *A Touchstone:* Prayer beads can serve as a 'remembering object'. It is not a mnemonic in the usual sense. Rather, it serves as a benchmarking device, a 'reminder object', similar to a souvenir, but for a person of faith it is a reminder of that which is true and meaningful.
- *Jewellery:* Prayer beads can also be worn as jewellery. In this case, they are valued for their decorative and aesthetic qualities.
- *A Badge of Identity:* In various ways throughout their history, prayer beads have been used as an outer sign of one's religion, denomination or vocation.[29]

So far, I have discussed the object in terms of its use and meanings, but it can also be considered in terms of its physicality and materiality:

- *A Physical Expression of the Accompanying Prayer Cycle:* In Catholicism the name rosary is actually the same as the name of the prayers that accompany its use. The design of the rosary, a circlet of beads attached to a pendant with a crucifix, is essentially a tactile map and visual diagram of the prayer cycle. Hence, its physical design is an indicator of its use and meaning.

- *The Physical Qualities of the Object:* These include the size, weight, colour and texture of the beads, whether they are warm or cold to the touch, and how they sound when they are picked up and used. These are key aspects of one's aesthetic experience of the object. Prayer beads can be of plain wood or of precious jewels, simple or elaborate. The reasons for such variety can range from a genuine attempt to achieve an appropriate expression for a devotional object, to a choice that has more to do with social standing. Simple wooden beads can be an authentic expression of simplicity and humility, or a disingenuous outward expression of piety. A costly, bejewelled set of beads can be an entirely appropriate object for use in religious practice, or it can be a sign of wealth and social standing.[30] Hence, the physical appearance of prayer beads can be diverse, variously interpreted and used to express a broad range of values.

- *Varieties of Manufacture:* Prayer beads can be handmade from the simplest of materials or batch-produced in larger numbers by local artisans. They are also commonly made by mass-production processes. How it is made, what it is made from, and where it is made may have a bearing on the value ascribed to it by its owner. However, a cheap, mass-produced set of beads can be as precious to its owner as a set made from rare and expensive materials. Moreover, prayer beads often include an emblem identifying the place where it was purchased, such as a pilgrimage site. This adds a souvenir quality to it, but also a particular sacred association.

47

From this brief overview it is apparent that there is a wide range of meanings associated with this object. They span the utilitarian, the deeply reflective and contemplative, the talismanic, the emblematic and the decorative. Prayer beads can also serve as a touchstone of values and an indicator of social status. For these reasons, this object can acquire an exceptionally intense and highly personal quality of possession-ness; it is an object that one tends to really 'own' in a very intimate way[31] regardless of the fact that it may have cost very little and be made from mass-produced plastics.

There are two more aspects of prayer beads to bear in mind when considering sustainable design:

- *Evolution Over Time:* Neither the prayer beads as artefact nor the cycle of sayings that accompanies its use were 'designed' as such. Rather, both evolved over a long period into the forms we see today. These forms are the result of both popular (or bottom-up) practices and institutional (or top-down) approval and modification.[32]
- *Evolution Among Different Traditions:* The different forms of prayer beads around the world demonstrate that is easily adapted to diverse cultures and traditions, becoming a symbol of both belief and identity. Hence, its flexibility allows it to become acculturated and this contributes to its continued but varied use and meaning.

To this point, I have considered various types of enduring objects, and categorized and discussed them in terms of human needs and values. One object in particular, the prayer beads, warranted more detailed analysis because it is an important example that spans the various categories I have introduced. We can now look to the lessons this object might hold for sustainable product design, bearing in mind that we cannot necessarily draw any firm, generally applicable conclusions from the characteristics of just one object. Nevertheless, from the foregoing we can make the following observations:

- *The Physical and the Meaningful:* It seems that a very powerful sense of personal possession-ness can be attributed to an artefact in which there are strong, interwoven relationships between the object, physical activity, tactility, visual understanding, aesthetic experience, meaning, inner growth and allusions to the numinous. The object discussed here, prayer beads, is fundamentally profound in its conception as a thing, and this is articulated through its physical design, its use and its meaning to its owner. It is a deeply evocative artefact that is neither trivial nor trendy, nor is it based on transient technological novelty or styling. For these reasons, it is not susceptible to many of the factors that render so many contemporary products short-lived and unsustainable.
- *The Heart of Sustainability:* It is an object that relates to a broadly acknowledged set of human understandings that are independent of culture, religion, language or era; what Leibniz called the *philosophia perennis*[33] and Lewis referred to as the

evangelium eternum.[34] This undoubtedly contributes to its enduring and widespread use. However, a ceramic pot also spans culture, religion, language and time. So what is it that distinguishes one enduring artefact from another and makes the prayer beads such an intensely personal and precious possession? Objects that have a wide range of characteristics and meanings, including the profound, greatly surpass those of basic, utilitarian goods and this is what makes prayer beads, and not pottery, so important for our understanding of sustainability. Many, if not the majority, of our contemporary material goods also exceed basic utilitarian needs; they possess layers of additional meanings. Yet, to a large extent, contemporary artefacts are readily discarded and are clearly unsustainable in their conception. By contrast, the prayer beads have been conceived in response to our *highest* needs, which have been termed self-actualization, transcendence[35] and religious experience,[36] and which refer to attaining one's potential and relating to something beyond the ego.[37] In addition to these higher intentions, prayer beads can also reference other needs, such as social standing and identity.[38] And they also serve a basic function and have a variety of meanings related to popular culture. Thus, they can be understood, used and acknowledged in many different ways.

- *An Essentially Personal Object:* The intimate personal-ness of the ownership of this object is a rare but very important characteristic to bear in mind when considering the nature of sustainable objects. When we value an object in a deeply emotional and personal way, then it becomes precious to us and worthy of our care.

- *A Challenge to 'Localization' and its Link to Sustainability?* There has been much discussion about the need for increased 'localization' to contribute to sustainable approaches in product design and manufacturing.[39] To an extent at least, prayer beads would appear to challenge this claim. It is certainly true that in many parts of the world this object is made at the local level and of local materials such as plant seeds. It is also mass produced from inexpensive 'anonymous', unsymbolic materials, and yet can still hold a profound meaning and an intimate sense of possession-ness for its owner. This is because

49

the locus of this sense of ownership is related more to what
the object represents, or to that to which it points, rather
than to what it actually *is* in terms of its materials or mode of
manufacture. Any detrimental reaction resulting from its cheap,
ubiquitous 'thing-ness' is overcome by its iconic associations,
so that it can still be a deeply meaningful personal possession.
This is perhaps the most important lesson for sustainability.
The meaning of an object, even a newly manufactured,
mass-produced plastic object, can provide a deep sense of
ownership and value and can eclipse the specific characteristics
and any physical shortcomings of the object.

From this it seems reasonable to draw a further conclusion. At its most
basic, utilitarian, 'undesigned' level, we could say that a functional
object is capable of fulfilling an identified human need. When we go
beyond this basic utility and introduce 'design', to give the product
market appeal, then we start assigning to the product attributes that
will, ostensibly, satisfy a range of other human needs, such as 'a sense
of belonging' and 'self-esteem' needs. Objects designed to appeal
to these needs (i.e. 'functional, social/positional goods') are often
rapidly outdated and unsustainable. Beyond these 'middle-level' needs,
however, there are the higher needs such as aesthetic and spiritual
needs. Products conceived to refer to these can appeal to our highest
potential and in doing so, the very factors that spur unsustainable
practices in objects are overcome. In the one example of prayer beads,
at least, we have a product that is inherently sustainable, more than
simply functional, and ubiquitous. This example demonstrates that this
combination is at least possible to achieve. The challenge is to see if it
is possible in more common, everyday products.

At this point, we may try to take a few steps beyond the example of
prayer beads to include some less explicitly religious products that are,
at least to some extent, simultaneously functional, social/positional
and inspirational/spiritual. It is difficult to give such examples, and
any selections will inevitably be subjective and perhaps contentious.
However, they might include some of the work by Philippe Starck, such
as his Juicy Salif lemon squeezer of 1990 for Alessi. This product, which
looks a like a pointed metal egg on three spindly legs, may not be
especially functional, and its prime role would appear to have become
positional, but it is also a strikingly sculptural and perhaps inspirational

design. Similarly, the designs of Daniel Weil, Ron Arad and the Droog designers are not merely functional, nor are they simply a combination of function and social/positional characteristics. Their sculptural and aesthetic attributes tend to endow them with inspirational/spiritual qualities.

These examples are perhaps not ideal: their durability has yet to be tested and, in some cases, it is often difficult to get beyond their strong positional associations. However, they do provide some indication of direction. They combine the various product characteristics discussed in this chapter and encapsulate meanings, beauty and sculptural qualities that allow them to rise above the mundane.

Many of our contemporary products surpass basic utility: they include a multitude of technical features and styling and aesthetic considerations. The vast majority of these products are short-lived, unrepairable and, by any measure, unsustainable. Given this state of affairs, we are faced with the question, 'Is it possible to have an object that is more than merely functional, but which can also be understood as sustainable, and if so, what would be the characteristics of such an object?' This discussion has attempted to answer this question and has revealed that sustainable product design is not to be found simply in the physical definition of an object, in the types or scales of manufacturing, or even in the nuances of the design. It also suggests that sustainability does not necessarily *require* a return to local production, the use of natural materials or high-value materials, craft processes or even high-quality production. Instead, once basic utility is surpassed, we enter an area of design that deals with the social and positional aspects of material culture and it is this area, when added to function, that appears to stimulate consumerism, disposable products and unsustainable practices. However, beyond the social/positional lies another area of human understanding, the inspirational/spiritual, that seeks and brings higher meaning to our endeavours. When this level of understanding informs our material productions, the destructive tendencies within the social/positional can be overcome, leading to objects that are, in their fundamental conception, deeply meaningful. And it is only by attempting to make our material culture meaningful that we can hope to contribute to a sustainable future.

51

6
REASSESSING 'GOOD' DESIGN

objects as symbols of beauty

At the beginning of the last century, many of our possessions, such as furniture, rugs, clothes, tools and hardware, would have been produced locally or regionally, or at least within our own country. Many of them may even have been created by our own hands. Products were generally built to last and the idea of 'disposable' products was virtually unknown. By contrast, at the beginning of the 21st century few products are made locally. A large proportion are imported, with different components being manufactured in various countries, brought together, assembled and distributed. Furthermore, the number of products we own has increased enormously; many products are now disposable and the useful life of so-called consumer durables is often just a few years.[1]

This shift has caused a severe detachment from our material world, a detachment that has not only contributed to socio-economic disparities and environmental degradation, but has also resulted in a lack of understanding and a devaluing of material culture. A reassessment of physical products is required, together with a creative re-engagement with 'things', if we are to find lasting meaning and value in our material world whilst simultaneously alleviating the damaging consequences of contemporary consumerism. *Design* can be a key component in this; how we design products, the assumptions we make and the preconceptions we have when we design, as well as our notions of good design, all have to be questioned.

Reconfiguring our notions of material goods and the nature of functional artefacts is a complex and fascinating design challenge. We have the opportunity today to design products in new ways that not only address critical environmental and social issues but also allow us to restore depth and significance to our material world.

The notion that we have become disassociated from our possessions may not be very obvious. After all, we are surrounded by hundreds of material things that we use everyday, from furniture to technical equipment to appliances. We find these products useful and beneficial, and many of them tend to make our lives easier. Indeed, in numerous ways we have become dependent on products to live effectively in modern society – for example for communication, transportation and entertainment. But despite our dependency on them, there exists a chasm between the products we own and our ability to determine, contribute to, and understand them.

As I said in Chapter 4, the manufacturing sector in general, and industrial design in particular, have professionalized material culture and in doing so have usurped our participation. We buy products that are predefined, pre-packaged and presented to us as a fait accompli. This professionalization of the processes of design and making has provided us with functional products that often have considerable instrumental value, but it has made relatively few contributions to the evolution of an inherently meaningful material culture, by which I mean a material culture that is not only economically viable, environmentally responsible and socially equitable but also culturally and personally enriching. Our inability to participate in the creation of our material goods is critically related to these notions of meaning. In terms of our material world and our possessions, when we are unable to contribute we become reduced to mere consumers. Our lack of involvement in the design and making of objects, and our consequent gap in understanding, undoubtedly affect how we value them. We become increasingly divorced from an intimate connection with things – their meaning, their source, their formation and their maintenance. This has reached a point where, today, it seems almost absurd to suggest that we might play a substantive role in the definition and creation of our possessions. However, such participation is not only consistent with the broad environmental and social principles of sustainable development, it is also essential, on a more intimate and personal level, if we are to imbue our material culture with meaning and value.

It is often difficult to maintain interest in large, long-term, rather nebulous aims such as those of sustainable development unless they touch us emotionally and are continually 'made real' to us at a personal level in our everyday lives. Therefore, if we are to rethink our approaches to material culture, we must see the value in it not just as a means towards some distant, somewhat hazy notion of a sustainable society, and not simply in terms of rationalized steps towards 'the social good' or 'environmental conservation'. A new approach to design and making must also be seen as an end in itself, as an improved, more meaningful rendition of materiality that enriches our lives at a deeper, emotional level, in addition to the utility of the object, the economic benefits of its production, and the inclusion of environmental and social considerations. This requires a greater understanding and a more profound relationship with our material world, which, it seems, can be best achieved at the local level. Numerous authors have suggested a strong connection between achieving more sustainable ways of living and smaller-scale, local initiatives:[2]

55

> **The most beautiful house in the world is the one that you build yourself.** (Witold Rybczynski, 1989[3])

While it might seem rather unusual to suggest that we should be more involved in the making of our functional goods, in other areas of our lives this is quite normal. For example, many people take an active part in the design and details of their homes. They modify and upgrade them over time, as needs and tastes change, and they personalize them in a variety of ways. To facilitate this, there is a supply chain infrastructure in place, in the form of home hardware stores, which allows people to purchase basic components for home repair and decoration. People can do much more than simply choose from predetermined and pre-designed schemes. The availability of the basic elements enables people to participate in the design of their homes in ways that are creative, fulfilling and affordable. Moreover, a large variety of books, manuals and magazines are available, not to mention numerous television programmes, which teach techniques and illustrate possibilities. As a result, a house can be transformed into a specific home that reflects the values of the owners and is instilled with personal significance, meaning and value.

Another example is the preparation of a meal. Again, a supply chain infrastructure is in place to provide people with the necessary ingredients, and information, techniques and recipes are readily available. Preparing a meal, particularly a meal for sharing with others on a special occasion, is an endeavour that is steeped in ritual, ceremony and meaning.[4] Opportunities for creativity in preparation and presentation are limitless. By comparison, a frozen TV dinner, where all the elements of the meal are laid out on a segmented tray, is a commodity that has been predetermined and is anonymous; it allows no opportunity for the purchaser to be creative. The TV dinner might be convenient but, beyond satiation of appetite, it is bereft of many of the qualities that render a meal meaningful. This is why it would seem insulting if we were to invite guests for a meal and we placed TV dinners on the table. In most societies around the world the time and care one puts into preparing a meal, especially one for sharing with others, is an important and culturally significant undertaking.

When we consider home making and meal preparation, we place greater emphasis on the intentions, the effort and the meanings behind the decisions and actions, rather than focusing solely on the end result. We can appreciate that a home or a special meal reflects the person who has created it, and the values and priorities of that person. While the end result might not conform to our personal notions of beauty and might not be to our taste, nevertheless it *can* be seen as being beautiful because it is a symbol of the hospitality and generosity of the person who created it.

Unlike homes and meals, we do not generally make our own products. While some people might make a chair or a lamp, products such as music equipment, radios, hairdryers and appliances are not things we generally think of making ourselves. Consequently, these types of products, purchased off-the-shelf, offer no opportunity for us to participate in their creation or to gain a sense of personal accomplishment. These products can be seen as the consumer-durable equivalent of TV dinners – predefined and pre-packaged. They can be valued for their function and, perhaps, for their appearance as an object, but they generally have little inherent meaning for us. Today, we are inundated with such products. Mass manufacturing, often carried out using high levels of automation and usually in factories located in countries with low labour costs, means that these products are relatively inexpensive to purchase, but not cost effective to repair; and we have little compunction in discarding them when they cease to function, indeed we have little other choice.

By contrast, something we have created ourselves, or that a loved one has created, has a different kind of value for us. Such an object will be valued *despite any lack of skill evident in its creation*, and whether or not it actually functions well or as intended. It is valued over and above function and appearance. Its value for us is inherent to the thing itself as an expression of one's creativity, or because of the personal association that it represents, rather than solely in its utilitarian merits or aesthetic attributes. Like the prayer beads discussed in Chapter 5, its beauty lies in its meaning and the intentions it symbolizes and is part of its essential nature. Hence, its value is inherent rather than instrumental, and its beauty is intrinsic rather than extrinsic. For these reasons, if such an object becomes damaged or ceases to function, we would probably attempt to repair it, rather than simply discarding it. And if we had a hand in its creation, we would be more able to effect a repair because we would already have an understanding of the object – what it is made from, how it is made and how it works.

57

Examples of such artefacts would include furniture items made in a hobby class, a handmade quilt or sweater or a model aeroplane made from a construction kit. But the electronic products and appliances that we use everyday are not created in this way and consequently are bereft of qualities that make them intrinsically meaningful to us. It is these types of products that we dispose of so readily and which are clogging our landfills. For example, in the Greater Vancouver region of British Columbia, Canada, 13,000 tonnes of small appliances and 8000 tonnes of computer equipment ended up in landfill in just one year, and a recent European directive was introduced to reduce the 6.5 million tonnes of electronic and electrical equipment that is annually discarded.[5] Hence, these types of products are a major area of concern and must be reconsidered and re-conceived if we are to seriously address sustainability within the field of product design.

This line of thought suggests that there is a fundamental and irreconcilable disparity between our conventional notions of beauty – what might be termed 'outer' or extrinsic beauty, and sustainability. The word sustainability evokes ideas of longevity, continuity and endurance. 'Outer beauty', on the other hand, is perishable and transient. It exists only for a short period, but fades with time. We speak of 'the ravages of time', by which we mean the inevitable erosion of outer beauty as occurrences over time besiege its perfection. Thus, the splendour of the rose wilts and the loveliness of youth sags into old age.

So too with products – the modern product encased in its fashionably styled injection-moulded casing is polished and perfect. But its flawlessness is, and can only ever be, temporary. With the passage of time its fashionable colours and lines lose their appeal, its surfaces become blemished, and its once à la mode desirability weakens until it disappears altogether. At which point it will probably be discarded and replaced, and the cycle begins again. Hence, waste is increased, consumption is promoted, the principles of sustainability go unheeded and our material world is devalued.

58

At this point, it might be helpful to offer an example of an alternative approach. The *dhoti* is a long, loose-fitting loincloth traditionally worn by Hindu men in India; Mahatma Gandhi is probably the most well-known figure to wear this garment. Gandhi's *dhoti* was made from cotton he had spun himself. From a perspective where business suits and western fashions were the norms associated with power, social position and wealth, the *dhoti* could be readily dismissed as unsophisticated, coarse and undignified. Indeed, in the newsreels of Gandhi's visit to Britain in 1931, the predominant tone of the commentary is condescending and disparaging. The reporter makes numerous remarks about Gandhi's clothing and refers to him as a 'bizarre little man'.[6] For Gandhi, however, the *dhoti* was much more than a simple article of clothing; the spinning wheel and homespun clothing had social, political, economic and even spiritual importance.[7] The *dhoti* was a distinct and conscious breaking away from the 'western' business suit, which he had worn during his earlier career as a young barrister, and as such it was deeply symbolic. The *dhoti*, and more generally homespun cloth or *khadi*, represented self-determination, self-respect, creativity, cultural restoration, independence, and a political and economic statement against colonial rule. Seen in these terms, the *dhoti* becomes an extraordinarily dignified, meaningful and beautiful piece of clothing, a physical embodiment of a philosophy and set of values.

Similarly, the beauty of the 'local' product lies in what it means, what it represents and what it aims for, rather than simply in its outer appearance as a physical object. To appreciate these aspects of a product, we must have some insight and understanding of why the object is articulated in the way that it is. If we maintain our preconceptions, and look at and judge such objects from conventional (i.e. unsustainable) notions of beauty and taste, then they can be easily ridiculed and rejected. However, our perceptions of an object can change once its basis is more fully understood.[8] What may have been regarded as ugly, crude or undignified can then, potentially, be seen as beautiful and an embodiment of meaningful values. And, of course, the converse is also true.

> **Delights from external objects are wombs of suffering. In their beginning is their end and no wise man delights in them.** (Bhagavad Gita[9])

Like many of the world's major sacred teachings, the Bhagavad Gita warns against finding pleasure in worldly objects, because such pleasures and delights are seen as distractions and obstacles to deeper, more profound understandings (this theme will be explored further in the next chapter). However, we *can* find delight, not in the objects themselves, but in their potentially enriching and virtuous meanings – what they embody in terms of individual or collective creativity and the provision of healthy, meaningful employment; personal accomplishment; and equitable and ethical work practices. A functional object can become the culmination, physical manifestation and symbol of 'good' works – in its intention, design, making, use and disposal. Thus, we can understand the beauty of an object in a different way. Beauty can be captured in the object through what it *represents*, and not simply through its appearance.

Unfortunately, most of today's mass-produced products are not representations of 'good' works. Their superficial, fashionable façades too often disguise a hidden world of resource depletion, pollution and social disparity and exploitation. If, in its design and manufacture, the associated environmental, ethical and socio-economic issues are ignored, then the object can become symbolic not of beauty but of ugliness and harm.

7
DESIGN, SUSTAINABILITY AND THE HUMAN SPIRIT

how the
other
half lives

Long ago it was said that 'one half of the world does not know how the other half lives'. (Jacob A. Riis[1])

In the 19th century, Jacob Riis wrote about the other half of society – the weak, the disadvantaged and the under-represented. In modern society, in the contemporary worldview and in the process of design itself, there exists a similar division – but in this case, the other half is not to be found externally, as a particular sector of society, but internally, as a facet of ourselves. The other half of who we are – the creative, the imaginative, the ethical and the spiritual – is also weak, disadvantaged and under-represented, compared with the rational, instrumental side of our nature. The emphasis on utilitarianism, economic efficiency, pragmatism, aggressive competition and the idea of progress in today's societies and today's world of design has limited and often eliminated the poetry, the elegance and the creative austerity of our other side. The suppression of this other half has led to what many see as a materially abundant but spiritually impoverished world. While this notion of two halves or aspects of our personhood should not be overstated or taken too literally, it is nevertheless a useful mechanism for considering further the nature of our thoughts and activities in relation to design.

There are many references to two halves or two sides of the human condition. These two sides have been characterized as inner and outer, higher and lower, physical and metaphysical, and body and soul.[2] This image of two facets of ourselves can be expressed not only as a duality between our material or physical side and our spiritual or metaphysical side, but also as a distinction in our ways of thinking and knowing, such as subjective/objective, intuitive/rational and holistic/analytical. There are also dualisms recognized in traditions such as Chinese Taoism, with its inseparable and complementary yin–yang relationship, yin representing emotion, the feminine and the passive, and yang reason, the masculine and the active. The yin–yang relationship also represents the inner/outer, heavenly/earthly or higher/lower aspects of our humanness.[3] Also, distinctions have been made between what might be termed our 'scientific experience' and our 'aesthetic experience', the former being characterized as transitive, transparent, homogeneous, specific and sequential, and the latter by their respective opposites – intransitive, opaque, heterogeneous, totalized and rhythmic.[4]

62

It has been said that attention to the development of the rational, scientific, logical and verbal side of our nature tends to prevail in our educational systems,[5] and it has certainly become dominant in contemporary societies – overwhelmed as they are by advances in science and technology, utilitarianism, economic rationalism and consumerism.[6] In a world dominated by such reductionist thinking, it is perhaps not surprising that the other side of our nature, the side that seeks meaning and higher purpose, has been neglected, suppressed and ill-developed in recent times, not to say disdained. The public school systems in North America effectively ignore our spiritual side,[7] with often little or no reference to the teachings of the world's great religious or spiritual traditions. Spirituality, however, is seen by some as not just an additional element but as the central tenet of a more holistic approach.[8] Moreover, and as I will discuss further here, art and aesthetics are closely associated with intuitive ways of knowing and spiritual development, but education in these areas is either absent altogether or frequently the first to be eliminated when financial constraints lead to the paring down of curricula in schools, colleges and universities. Today, the business world, higher education, modes of working and our ways of life are dominated by the rational, the temporal, the scientific and the analytical, and often by predominantly *outer* concerns for material gain and physical comfort. As the British philosopher Iris Murdoch has pointed out, 'Metaphysical problems now reach the popular consciousness in the form of a sense of loss, of being returned to a confused pluralistic world from which something "deep" has been removed.'[9]

The 'inner' side of us includes self-awareness[10] and, beyond that, a cognizance of what might be termed spiritual awareness. Traditional wisdom teachings tell us that constant attention to, and development of, this side of our nature lead to true happiness, wisdom and enlightenment. However, this whole concept of higher and lower or outer and inner dimensions to our humanness has become increasingly foreign to us over the past few hundred years, as utilitarian, rationalistic understandings have developed and expanded. When the inner or vertical dimension is neither recognized nor understood, then inevitably we will, and do, choose to seek purpose, fulfilment and happiness through other means – focusing on such things as increasing comfort and pursuing enjoyment through physical or sensual pleasures. Cultivation of the higher faculties, the seeking of meaning, deeper understandings and spiritual development, and striving towards what Taylor calls a moral ideal,[11] become anathema and, to a considerable extent, this has occurred in our contemporary world.

These observations link directly to products and product design. Once our physical needs have been met, we seek further products and experiences that provide us with comfort, convenience, enjoyment and distraction. Television, DVDs, computer and video games, hobby products, theme parks and the like are the sophisticated contemporary tools of existential distraction, their prime purpose being, in addition to the economic imperatives of the producers, to provide entertainment and transient pleasure. This emphasis on seeking diversion and pleasure through objects and acquisition is not only closely associated with spiralling consumerism, waste production and environmental degradation, our desire for such products also indicates that we seek fulfilment via these sensual *outer* means, and not through the pursuit of the *inner*. In turn, these activities are capable of occupying our minds so completely that they effectively thwart any tendencies towards an *inner* course.

63

It is important to consider how things might be if we attempted to redress this imbalance and gave more attention to the side of our nature that contemplates purpose and seeks meaning. Such an understanding would permit a more even-handed approach to our activities, one that is urgently needed as we strive for more sustainable modes of living. For the designer, of course, this raises many questions about the relevance and nature of products. If our present lifestyles and the products that support them derive from an over-emphasis on our 'outer half', then how would we live, what products would be important and how should they be designed if we placed greater emphasis on our other half – the intuitive, the holistic, the aesthetic, the heterogeneous and the 'inner'? How *would* this other half live?

This inner aspect of our humanness – which, we are told, can be continually cultivated to seek and appreciate the ethical, the virtuous and the spiritual – is also the part of us that is imaginative, creative and aesthetically sensitive. Furthermore, because artistic endeavour relies upon these characteristics, it could be said that good art originates from, and is expressive of, our inner or higher side. Murdoch has said, 'Art makes places and open spaces for reflection, it is a defence against materialism and against pseudo-scientific attitudes to life ... Great art inspires because it is separate, it is for nothing, it is for itself. It is an image of virtue.'[12]

We see that both metaphysical and psychological discussions (see reference to Maslow in Chapter 5) point to an inner aspect of our being that is associated with virtue, goodness and higher potentials. It is a direction that is closely related to artistic endeavour and aesthetics, and tends to be seen as somewhat separate from our everyday *outer* activities. As such, it can provide something of a counterbalance to our more worldly, materialistic pursuits.

Like art, the discipline of design also calls upon our imagination, creativity and aesthetic sensitivity. Design, however, is not art. To suggest that it is, or can be, is to demean the discipline of design by failing to acknowledge its particular and distinct role. Kant defined art in terms of 'purposiveness without purpose'[13] – it has no empirical, practical or utilitarian intent. Design, on the other hand, is driven by a combination of social and economic motivators, and the products themselves are designed to be purposeful. Even though that purpose might often be trivial, the utility of the object together with the purposeful intent behind its conception are what distinguish design from art. However, it must also be acknowledged that while design is not art, there are often commonalities in techniques, processes and thinking that bring the design and artistic processes close together. It is this proximity that allows us to consider design as a process of 'thinking and doing' that calls upon both the inner and outer sides of our nature. Good design is neither art nor purely instrumental device, neither wholly artistic nor wholly utilitarian, but an inseparable union of the two. Hence, design can be regarded as an activity which, potentially, bridges the two sides of our nature, and when it does so it becomes a holistic endeavour that looks towards our inner self to bring meaning and aesthetic balance to the creation of functional objects. If genuinely and honestly pursued, this will inevitably include an ethical component and even a spiritual element. When the inner aspect is acknowledged, developed and brought to the design process, it can have significant implications for how we go about designing and how we think about the nature of our material objects. Conversely, a functional object created without such a holistic approach will remain a prosaic device devoid of qualities that reflect our full humanity.

A more balanced approach to design allows us to consider both the quantitative and qualitative aspects of material goods in relation to inner/outer accord. After basic needs have been met, the quantity of material possessions an individual might see as desirable will be a function of many factors, including societal norms, but it is probably not too far off the mark to suggest that beyond a certain point, further acquisition can start to detrimentally affect one's ability to develop inwardly. Too many material goods, or a preoccupation with them and the 'benefits' they offer, can distract us from inner attention – this is a teaching of many traditions.

65

Regarding the design of functional objects, it is important to reflect on what our 'inner' side can tell us about how we might define their qualitative characteristics. This is critical if our material culture is to express and support our higher potentials. This qualitative concern is not simply a question of high or low quality – but one of fitting quality, such that the object is congruent with our inner nature. Another way of thinking about this is in terms of 'appropriate concern'. It would be reasonable to suggest that beyond a certain point, material goods can start to occupy a position of excessive importance in our culture and our lives. Therefore, there would seem to be a level of appropriate concern to be found in the design of objects – where decisions about materials, form development, features and detailing reflect an adequateness without being immoderate, indulgent or excessive.

This notion of appropriate concern for material goods is essential if we are to take a more balanced approach – one that affords greater recognition of our inner selves and that begins to address sustainability issues at a deeper, more fundamental level. To appreciate more fully the basis of appropriate concern it is necessary to look a little closer at our inner or other half.

> **His room was at the top, right under the roof, low-ceilinged, with thick stone walls, a single bed, a prie-dieu, and a rough wooden armchair. There was a basin for washing and the usual crucifix on the wall, near a narrow slit of window which gave a partial view of the monastery's belltower.** (Brian Moore, The Statement, 1995[14])

To understand something of how the other half lives, we have many sources from history and around the world. From these we can gain an impression of how a life dedicated to inner development tends to regard material culture. This is not to suggest that we should all seek the life of an ascetic, but it does allow us to see our contemporary lifestyles in the economically developed countries from a different perspective.

Probably our most extensive sources that indicate the nature of the inner life and its response to outer concerns are the texts and traditions of the world's major religions. While there are many examples of great opulence in religious artefacts and shrines, there is an important distinction to be made between artefacts of ceremony, ritual or devotion and those for personal use or comfort. If we look at the more ascetic traditions, where the pursuit of the inner, contemplative life is perhaps more fully embraced, we see that material comforts and possessions are often kept to a minimum. Consideration of these distinctive characteristics can give us some indication of how the other half tends to regard the place and nature of material goods.

Many teachings suggest that material goods, and especially a mind that is preoccupied with such things, hamper inner development. From the spiritual traditions of India we are told that the person seeking the inner path must seek it alone, free of aspirations and possessions.[15] Buddhism regards possessions and attachments as a form of bondage that prevents enlightenment.[16] In Judeo-Christian texts there are many passages that declare the necessity of eschewing material possessions and personal wealth.[17] The Islamic faith tells us that, 'It is difficult, for a man laden with riches, to climb the steep path that leadeth to bliss.'[18] The spiritual traditions of China exhibit similar attitudes, for example, the Tao Te Ching tells us that indulgence in fine clothes, foods and possessions places one far from the inner way.[19]

We see that for thousands of years, in many cultures, the pursuit of inner understandings has suggested a reduction in the importance and quantity of material goods. Monastic 'rules' are often quite categorical about the dangers to spiritual progress of private ownership, preferring to share possessions.[20] Similar views on shared goods, simplicity and material austerity are expressed by other intentional communities that dedicate themselves to the spiritual life, such as the Shakers,[21] the Amish[22] and the Hutterites.[23] Such communities not only tend to minimize the quantity of artefacts, they also tend to reject decoration and embellishments, regarding unadorned objects more fitting to spiritual pursuits.[24]

67

It becomes evident from various teachings and sources that inner development can affect one's attitudes to both the quantitative and qualitative aspects of material culture and, ipso facto, environmental stewardship and sustainability. From the designer's perspective, the qualitative implications are perhaps the most interesting and the more important because it is the qualitative characteristics that fall under the designer's purview.

This gives us some indication about directions and approaches to product design that are consistent with inner priorities and the wisdom teachings of many traditions. There is, of course, no single, definitive 'right way' for product design, but we can derive some impressions that might be helpful in our search for more balanced, moderate and sustainable ways forward; ways that encompass both the outer imperatives and the inner potentials of the human condition. The notion of 'appropriate concern' is an essential element for developing this more comprehensive approach. Wittgenstein considers a similar idea when he discusses inconsistencies among the four Gospels. He argues that the inconsistencies are preferable or even necessary and gives a theatre scenery analogy: '... a mediocre stage set can be better than a sophisticated one, painted trees better than real ones – because these might distract attention from what matters.'[25] Hence, the details of the tangible (i.e. the physical or the historical) are not so important. The respective artefact or account is, in each case, necessary, but only in a rough or approximate form that is sufficient to provide the background or the basis for what really matters. In the theatre example this is the play itself, in the case of the Gospels it is 'the putative transcendent reality' to which all sacred texts point.[26]

Schumacher, who pioneered the whole notion of appropriate technology, with its inherent idea of adequateness, expresses a similar view when he says:

> To enhance our Level of Being we have to adopt a life-style conducive to such enhancement, which means one that grants our lower nature just the attention and care it requires and leaves us with plenty of time and free attention for the pursuit of our higher development.[27]

In addition to the traditional texts I mentioned above, numerous contemporary figures such as Mahatma Gandhi and authors such as Murdoch, Schumacher and Taylor tell us that the most critical feature of being human is our potential for seeking meaning, higher purpose or Truth. In this endeavour the place and relevance of material objects, in terms of their quantity and quality, are somewhat ancillary. The least necessary to fulfil the essentials becomes enough, so that we can get on with the 'essential decisive thing' – more than this would be distracting and an obstacle to inner development. Adequateness is not regarded as simply tolerable, but as preferable and necessary.

The re-orientation of product design and production to achieve a more balanced, holistic approach would also have pragmatic repercussions. The two sides of our nature are inseparable and complementary and so greater appreciation of our inner potentials would inevitably affect and benefit many aspects of our outer activities. A shift toward adequateness in the quantity of goods has the environmental benefit of reducing resource and energy use, reducing production of waste and pollution, and preserving habitats. A sense of adequateness in the qualitative characteristics of products has various implications for design, and is also relevant to more sustainable ways of living. Firstly, adequateness can be considered at a product's inception. The fundamental concept of the product, what it is, can be scrutinized with reference to inner as well as outer requirements. For example, I previously referred to products such as televisions and video games that are inherently and often excessively distracting to inner development. The conceptual framework of a product can therefore be examined with respect to its ability to create conditions that support and enhance our full potential.

Secondly, adequateness can be applied to a product's physical and qualitative characteristics; that is, how the product is designed and defined. An adequate or 'good enough' approach to product definition suggests a quite different set of priorities than we have come to expect in the fields of design and mass production. Functional convenience, precision, high tolerances and perfect finishes are constantly strived for, and are promoted as better and more beautiful – but these are the priorities of a design and production system that is, by and large, unholistic, driven by economic rationalism, severely detrimental to natural systems and often ethically questionable. These ideas of appropriate concern and adequateness can similarly challenge the approach of the Shakers, who also sought high precision and minute attention to detail in their products through dedicated craftsmanship. This approach, although emanating from a deep commitment to things inner, could be criticized as reflecting an excessive attention to material goods and their definition. Of course, a counter-argument here could be that the mode of work itself is a form of contemplation and its product a manifestation of inner pursuits. It does, however, pose intriguing questions as to the relationship between inner development and outer expression; and it is perhaps a particular irony that products from a group dedicated to the inner life now command extremely high prices and often become objects of status. A similar example might be the products produced in the 19th century by William Morris, with the best socialist intentions. Because of the attention to detail, craft and perfection, the products had to be sold at relatively high prices, thereby negating the egalitarian principles at the heart of their conception.

Hence, the precision and pursuit of perfection in mass production and in high-quality craft would appear to be, in many cases, contradictory to the evolution of conditions of adequateness so critical to inner development. In certain applications, precision is, of course, necessary to ensure that a product will properly function. However, precision and perfection are frequently unnecessary and they can be counter-productive for both inner development and sustainability.

69

A quite different approach to design and production is possible. The idea of 'rough' products, of imprecision and of adequateness in the making of everyday functional artefacts would seem to be more in line with the general direction of achieving an inner/outer balance and sustainable ways of living. 'Good enough' products can reduce concern, both in the making and in the use and ownership of products, to a level more conducive to inner development. The principles of sustainability point us towards a greater emphasis on local production and the provision of fulfilling, local employment. This contributes to environmental stewardship, by evolving a locally based industrial ecology, and to social equity, which is an essential element of sustainability and of spiritual teachings. Production that employs and values people rather than machines also implies a qualitatively different type of product. A machine aesthetic is obviously inappropriate. The human hand can produce beautiful qualitative characteristics but high tolerances and reproducibility are not its forte. Similarly, surface finishes that are uniform and precise are well suited to automated production – whereas multifarious or even unfinished surfaces are often more appropriate and more achievable when using natural materials and human labour. Moreover, because of their variegated, 'rough' qualities, such objects are able to absorb the marks of use more effectively without detrimentally affecting the overall appearance – this obviously contributes to product longevity and sustainability. Potentially, the production of such products at the local level, employing local people, can be an economically viable alternative to today's mass-produced, largely unsustainable products. The 'adequate' product can, because of its nature, and should, because of its intent, be relatively easy and quick to produce, making it an economically feasible alternative. Its viability and acceptability are, however, crucially dependent on imaginative, challenging and innovative design.

Such a direction for design has the potential to embrace and support our other half in the creation of our material world, as well as making a fundamental contribution to the goals of sustainability. It also has the potential of making our material world far richer, multifaceted, locally appropriate and culturally significant, which, compared to the global homogeneity arising from today's mass-produced objects, is a prospect to be welcomed.

8
FASHION
AND
SUSTAINABILITY
the attraction of opposites

Fashion is merely a form of ugliness so unbearable that we are compelled to alter it every six months.
(Oscar Wilde)

A conspicuous aspect of contemporary manufactured goods is that they have become objects of fashion. To promote fresh sales in an already saturated market, the appearance of products is regularly reworked and updated. This strategy kindles new interest and encourages what we might term the aesthetic obsolescence of previous models. There would seem to be irreconcilable differences between this notion of fashionable products and the principles of sustainability. Sustainability requires a drastic reduction in our ecological footprint,[1] and increasing a product's useful life has been regularly advocated as a way of contributing to this goal. Fashion, on the other hand, suggests a passing trend or fad – something transient, superficial and often rather wasteful. It represents the opposite of longevity and, as such, would appear to be an impediment to sustainability.

Even though 'fashion' tends to be regarded in this way, and consequently is often frowned upon by those working in the field of environmental design, it need not be in conflict with sustainable principles. Indeed, it may even be a key element in working towards more sustainable ways of living. It is a mistake to discount fashion per se. There are positive as well as negative aspects to this influential aspect of modern culture. If we approach it in the right way, and ensure that we are discerning and receptive to the aims of sustainability then, perhaps somewhat paradoxically, fashion in design can prove a valuable ally in the evolution towards more ecologically and socially responsible ways of producing material products.

The term fashion is applied to that which is currently popular – it is commonly used in the context of clothing design, but there are also fashions in customs, manners, music and, of particular importance here, in styles of products and material goods. It is a term that implies change, something that is in fashion now will shortly be out of fashion because something else will have superseded it. Therefore, inherent to the notion of fashion is time (a topic I will return to in Chapter 12). As time passes, fashions change – things become old-fashioned and consequently no longer desirable. The rate of such change is now probably greater than it has ever been – which is often seen as a good thing for economic competitiveness and market stimulation, but a bad thing for resource conservation and environmental stewardship. However, these negative connotations pertain only to the way in which fashion is manifested and used. Change itself is inherently neither positive nor negative – it is the nature of the change that is important.

> **Every generation laughs at the old fashions, but follows religiously the new.** (Henry David Thoreau[2])

If we consider some of the pros and cons of fashion we can, perhaps, discern where it can begin to help or hinder our progress towards sustainability. On the 'pro' side we can say that fashion in design fosters creativity and the exploration of new, previously untried solutions. There is a vitality and a freshness in much fashion-oriented design that piques our interest and keeps our material world 'alive' with an energetic and often light-hearted joie de vivre. Fashion-oriented design captures our aesthetic interest and imagination, sometimes even despite ourselves, and allows us to take pleasure and momentary delight in its originality, newness and creative distinctiveness.

Fashion is a particularly appropriate, powerful and well-used tool in a free-market economy – which constantly demands new solutions to stimulate the market and to create competitive advantage. In such an economy, fashionable solutions can bolster sales and prevent company failure – thus maintaining market viability and workforce employment. Such competitiveness requires and encourages ingenuity, imagination and innovation. In markets without such competition, as was the case in the former USSR, there is little incentive to be creative and to progress, not just technologically but also in terms of social development and environmental care. Without an incentive to be innovative, it seems, 'fashion' becomes less important and there is a tendency towards economic, technological, aesthetic and social stagnation, which, because of outmoded technologies and approaches, can also be severely detrimental to the environment. Thus, while there are innumerable problems created by the free-market system, a non-competitive system can result in a rather lacklustre and dull milieu that is damaging to the environment and to human welfare.

The 'cons' of fashion in design are primarily associated with how it can detrimentally affect our values. Without some form of restraint, the emphasis on newness, novelty and innovation can become equally, if not more, damaging to people and the environment than a system that stagnates. An emphasis on the latest fashions in clothes, cars, electronics and home appliances, if unmoderated by something deeper, can foster bogus values – values that over-emphasize materialism as a way of finding fulfilment and happiness. This is clearly prevalent today in the economically developed countries. Advertising and marketing techniques are used continually to encourage consumerism by promoting it as a way to find success and happiness; and this is fed by fashion. This dominant message is patently false and, as I discussed in the previous chapter, is contrary to the teachings of the world's major wisdom traditions – all of which warn of the dangers of concerning oneself too much with material wealth and possessions.

Fashion-oriented design is thus closely linked to free-market economics – but when a company's prime emphasis is on profit, when this becomes its raison d'être, then human welfare and environmental responsibilities become unnecessary impediments to the maximization of profit and growth. Unmoderated, the fashion-oriented, free-market system becomes greedy – over-utilizing resources, creating immense

73

environmental damage, and deliberately and constantly creating dissatisfaction through morally questionable marketing techniques. It is starkly apparent that our predominant concern with profit and growth (and thus the processes we use, the nature of contemporary products and our aesthetic preferences) reflects a grossly imbalanced and 'unsustainable' paradigm.

However, if we are to move towards sustainability in a timely manner, development and change will be essential. It is unlikely that there will be an abrupt, systemic shift in the ways we live and work which will suddenly align us with sustainable principles. It is more plausible that changes will occur incrementally and, hopefully, become increasingly congruent with sustainable thinking. An evolution towards sustainability will require many small, progressive shifts that bring us ever closer to our goal. Inherently, such an evolution requires innovation, change and creativity. Therefore, if we are to transform our ways from the 'unsustainable' to the 'sustainable', we need to employ those approaches that are precisely characterized by 'fashion'. The transition will be achieved by stimulating incremental changes in the right direction – each consequent step being an improvement over the last so that we swiftly progress towards more responsible, sensitive and holistic practices. Hence, fashion in design can be used as an important tool, if done with care, for generating timely and positive transformation.

In contrast to short-lived, fashionable products, the design of long-lasting products is commonly seen as an appropriate means of encouraging more sustainable practices.[3] While this argument has merit and is appropriate in some instances, it also has significant shortcomings. So many of our current understandings and modes of designing and producing products are inherently antithetical to the principles of sustainability. Therefore, one of the dangers of promoting product longevity is that it could simply prolong an unsustainable system while simultaneously adversely affecting employment opportunities. In many cases, to promote product longevity from our current standpoint would be ill conceived and premature. From where we are now, if we produce long-lasting products they will be products conceived by a mindset that is still steeped in, and only just emerging from, a century or more of product design, development and production that is unequivocally *unsustainable*. To think that we have the ability, at this point in our history, to design long-lasting products that fully address the

74

complex, multifarious issues inherent to sustainability could be seen as arrogant, not to say foolhardy.

Instead of relying on product longevity, we should be exploring design with humility, and assume that whatever we design for today will *not* be appropriate in the future. Whatever we produce should be designed in a way that places little burden on the planet, in its production, use and disposal, while also providing healthy and fruitful work.

Sustainability is, as yet, beyond our grasp and its meaning beyond our full understanding, and so an appropriate way forward would be to take small, evolutionary steps in what we consider to be the right direction from our present position. As we do so, our understandings will develop and our course will be continually modified. Thus, the carefully considered use of fashion in design can be regarded as a useful mechanism to stimulate interest and progress in directions that begin to embrace and articulate sustainable principles. If the economically developed nations are to advance towards a less materialistic society, to a more culturally advanced, meaningful understanding of how we live, then we will need many innovative approaches. To find new ways forward that satisfy the complex interrelations among the three main tenets of sustainability, we will need to try new things, and as we struggle to find better ways, we cannot expect these trials to be 'correct', at least not wholly. The task is so large that the transition will generate many blind allies, many incomplete solutions and will require constant refinement and improvement. Therefore, we could say that many, if not all, of these trials will be transient, will last for a while before becoming superseded. They will, then, be akin to 'fashion'.

An important consideration when directing fashion in design towards sustainability will be a balanced approach that embraces economic viability, social well-being and environmental gains, or at least environmental neutrality. Economic viability requires the maintenance of fresh product lines and cost-effective production. To achieve this in a socially and environmentally responsible manner, sustainable principles point to a more locally based manufacturing system which emphasizes the development of local employment, the local economy, locally relevant and appropriate designs and the development of a cultural identity attuned to place.[4] Social well-being is obviously closely linked to economic security, and also to the ways products *could* be designed. Thus, it becomes necessary to develop a design approach that, to

75

some degree, utilizes locally available materials, short production runs and changing designs, and that employs a local, skilled, flexible production workforce. This could provide good quality employment opportunities within a community and in doing so would provide people with economic security, community wealth and a sense of personal worth and contribution – while also creating a stimulating, aesthetically vibrant and evolving material culture. The environmental gains of a more locally based emphasis can also be significant – allowing local repair, reuse and recycling in order to constantly improve and enhance products while simultaneously attending to environmental concerns. The integration of more locally based approaches with our current mass-production techniques for the manufacture of economically viable, socially responsible and environmentally sensitive fashionable products can provide a way forward that sustains a vigorous market economy while ensuring development and change towards practices that are both socially and environmentally responsible.

We must also consider what such a direction implies for the future of design, in terms of the nature of our material products, aesthetic norms and how we judge design. The key to achieving sustainability in product manufacturing is design excellence, but, as I discussed in Chapter 6, the criteria by which this is judged will likely be quite different from our conventional notions of good design. Designers will be challenged to balance and integrate, in thoughtful and creative ways, the various, often conflicting issues of sustainability. We must learn to use less and to use what is available, rather than always creating specific, new components and materials that require more energy and resources, and thus have a greater detrimental impact. Design which achieves all this will probably be quite different from our current notions of good design – so to judge it by outdated criteria would be to do a disservice to the integrity of the design intent. Contemporary aesthetic norms are based in capital-intensive, highly automated, unsustainable procedures. These procedures tend to reduce the potential for fulfilling employment and often ignore social and environmental losses. We can deduce, therefore, that products produced within a more sustainable paradigm will be aesthetically quite different from those which we have come to regard as meritorious. An aspect of the transition towards sustainable product design, therefore, will be to explore new aesthetic possibilities which are true to, and expressive of, new sensibilities.

76

There is no one correct way and no right solution – approaches and directions will always change as time progresses, as generations change and as tastes evolve. This is not necessarily a bad thing – it allows us to hone our approaches, to stay on our toes and to keep things fresh, vital and joyful – which is what fashion is surely all about.

9
THE
APPLICATION
OF THEORY

experiments in
sustainable
product design

It is a fruitless task to try to define sustainable product design
– there is no common essence and it is inappropriate to try to find
one. Sustainable product design encompasses a great diversity of
approaches that will vary with place, time, environment, culture and
knowledge. No one knows what a sustainable society will look like,
we can only speculate on possibilities. However, as we work towards
it, our knowledge and understandings will increase and our vision
of development that is, in some sense, sustainable will evolve – the
goalposts will keep moving, as it were. Sustainability is thus a fluid,
dynamic, unfocused goal – and this is how it has to be; any attempt to
define a vision of a sustainable society will always fall short. Similarly,
any one approach to sustainable product design will be incomplete.
Some current approaches focus on product life cycle assessment,
others on product longevity, design for disassembly or the use of
recycled materials. All these can make a contribution but all, in and
of themselves, are inadequate. I have made my own attempts to
translate ideas about sustainability into product prototypes. These too

are inadequate, but it is the attempt to interpret abstract, theoretical ideas in the creation of tangible objects that is important in this type of investigative design work.

The designs presented in this chapter are centred on the notion of local production which, as I said earlier, has many environmental and social benefits.[1] To explore what sustainability might mean for product design, I have used the three principles of environmental stewardship, social equity and economic development rather than continual growth,[2] together with work done by urban planners in envisioning sustainable community scenarios.[3] The examples here are some initial, experimental designs of everyday functional objects. Their creation makes use of commonly available materials, off-the-shelf parts, simple tools and local labour, rather than highly mechanized production. They are not conceived as commercially viable products which can compete in today's market place. Rather, they are explorations in which the design process is used to develop and articulate functional objects for local use, repair and recycling within a general notion of a sustainable community scenario. In pursuing this kind of design work I take the view, held by many design academics, that exploratory design is an appropriate form of design research within the university and a constructive alternative to professional practice.[4]

The resulting designs are not readily classified. They are not typical product designs for mechanized production – that is, they are not industrial designs. Nor are they craft designs – little or no traditional craft skills are required to produce them. These artefacts represent a hybrid category that draws on elements of mass production, semi-mechanized production and hand fabrication. Mass-produced parts are combined with locally produced components, reused items and/or recycled materials. Again, this seems entirely appropriate when we talk about sustainable product design. In working towards sustainability, we should be drawing on many existing procedures and techniques and modifying them and adapting them, but not necessarily rejecting them wholesale. Many of the negative consequences of our current, evidently unsustainable, approaches are not necessarily the result of inherently harmful methods but the lack of moderation in their use.

The thesis of sustainable development recognizes that labour is relatively expensive, but it also points out that current automated production methods fail to include the so-called 'externalities' in the economic models (e.g. pollution, resource depletion and the social consequences of unemployment). Because of this, the costs, and in turn the retail prices, of current mass-produced products can be kept artificially low; critical factors for achieving sustainability are simply not taken into account. Local production that employs local materials and produces products for local use allows reductions in transportation and packaging, facilitates recycling, reverse manufacture and the cyclic use of materials and parts, and local maintenance and repair. It also allows products to be adapted to local needs and to reflect local or regional aesthetic preferences. This, in turn, contributes to cultural and community identity – 'community' being an important aspect of sustainability.[5] Consequently, localization can be inherently far more sustainable than our current system of mass manufacturing and product distribution.

These design explorations therefore represent a shift in the way we think about product manufacturing in terms of our scales of production, the provision of fulfilling employment, social responsibilities and use of materials. The resulting products also tend to challenge our preconceptions of aesthetics – which, in contemporary product design, are closely linked to the notion of newness. Sustainable product design explores reuse of materials, re-manufacturing and product longevity. If we begin to create long-lasting, but repairable and upgradeable products made from reused materials and parts, we will have to reassess our ideas of products and the value and place of the 'new', the glossy and the perfect. A product which bears the marks of time and use and its own history could, potentially, have a richness lacking in many of today's squeaky-clean but rather barren products; but to appreciate this richness we will have to readjust our value system and our expectations of product aesthetics.

In these 'experiments', various elements of sustainable design have been explored:

Inventiveness of necessity

Sustainability demands resourcefulness and restraint. New solutions have to be found which require less. In the Arc Light, Figure 9.1, the flexibility of movement was attained using a simple arc of wire over a fulcrum. The arc, which shifts the balance point as the lamp head is raised or lowered, replaces the relatively complex friction or spring mechanisms often found in task lamps. The motion is wide-ranging and flowing, and the action is delicate, poised and bird-like. Construction is from bamboo garden canes, a small food tin for the lampshade, a water pipe and two corks for the counter-weight and a cast concrete base. Electrical parts are standard, off-the-shelf components which, at the end of their service here, can be readily reused in other applications.

Other lighting examples are shown in Figure 9.2, Lather Lamp, a task lamp that makes use of a soap bottle, and Figure 9.3, Wire Light.

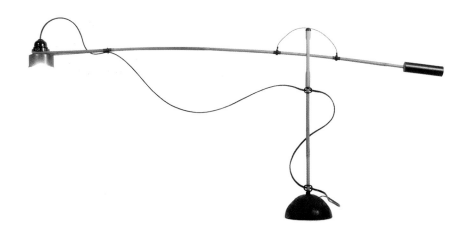

Figure 9.1
Arc Light:
Bamboo canes, wire, water pipe, corks, concrete, tin can, standard electrical parts

Figure 9.2
Lather Lamp:
*Soap bottle, wire rod, concrete,
standard electrical parts*

Figure 9.3
Wire Light:
*Wire rod, concrete, standard
electrical parts*

Improvisation and spontaneity

The constraints of limited resources at the local level in terms of materials, processes and tools, combined with a realization that most contemporary products are actually a physical manifestation of unsustainable practices, can create a liberating environment in which to reconsider the nature of objects. The Kind-of-Blue Chair, Figure 9.4, is an exercise in improvisation, spontaneity, making-do and the inclusion of chance.

Figure 9.4
Kind-of-Blue Chair:
*Reused wood, screws,
nails, glue, acrylic paint*

I believe there is a strong relationship between intuitive, extemporized, rough design work and sustainability. Meticulously considered, honed design may have a certain kind of beauty but, in many respects, it is a sterile, lifeless beauty that represents only one side of our nature. We can appreciate the precision but there is often little sense of empathy or resonance. The intuitive gesture, the spontaneous, the improvised – all have a vitality that is unavoidably lacking in highly rationalized work. And, when a product is being put into mass production for world markets, everything *has* to be very carefully planned and controlled: there is simply too much capital invested for it to be otherwise.

Here, then, is another reason for reconsidering scales of production. Smaller-scale manufacturing for local markets allows us to adopt approaches that permit these aspects of design, and our selves, to be reintroduced. This helps ensure a wholeness in the creation of our material environment and it enables products to be a more complete expression of our material needs – needs that extend far beyond the utilitarian. Indeed, John Ruskin held that rough work allowed energy, vigour and the mark of our humanity to become manifest.[6]

In the case of the Kind-of-Blue Chair, the individual pieces of wood, comprising off-cuts or found pieces, were used as they came to hand, in the form and size they happened to occur. Fastenings are nails, glue or screws, and the geometry of construction ensures stability. Similar examples are shown in Figure 9.5, Low Chair, and Figure 9.6, Square Chair.

85

Figure 9.5
Low Chair:
*Reused wood, screws,
nails, glue*

Figure 9.6
Square Chair:
*Reused wood, screws,
nails, glue, acrylic paint*

Aesthetic longevity and 'surface'

Many contemporary products rely on shiny, highly polished, new surfaces for their visual appeal. Automobiles, audio equipment, kitchen appliances and furniture are common examples. However, monochromatic, glossy surfaces on painted metals and moulded plastics are delicate and highly susceptible to marring. Any bumps, scratches or dents are immediately obvious and the accumulation of tiny scratches, caused when using or cleaning the object, will eventually dull the surface. And it is usually a difficult task to maintain or repair such a surface once it is marked. This deterioration of surface quality can cause a sense of dissatisfaction in the owner or user. Even though the product might still work well, the appearance can seem scruffy and drab. The lack of opportunity afforded by the material to maintain or repair the surface can compound this sense of discontent and the product will often be replaced because it has become prematurely aesthetically obsolete due to its surface qualities.

There are various ways to address this issue. Earlier, I discussed rough work from the point of view of spontaneity and improvisation. However, rough surfaces can also contribute to aesthetic longevity. Surfaces that are unfinished or created from reused parts or recovered materials – as in the Kind-of-Blue Chair – are often able to absorb wear and tear in ways that do not detract from the overall appearance of the object. One more scratch on a variegated, irregular surface that is an integral part of the object's design will be unlikely to cause aesthetic dissatisfaction. Hence, reused materials can be employed in aesthetically sensitive ways to create objects whose surfaces are able to absorb abuse. But it should be emphasized that the aesthetic qualities of such surfaces will be quite different from those of the artificially distressed surface, which is often applied to create the impression that the object is older than it really is. The spurious quality of such surfaces suggests an affectation or pretension and the resulting objects lack authenticity.

Another, related way of addressing the issue of aesthetic durability is to provide a complex surface that is easily maintained. In the Cable Radio, Figures 9.7 and 9.8, the casing is constructed from a coarse particleboard, which yields a randomly patterned surface when polished. This surface can withstand scratches and knocks without detracting from the appearance of the object, and the surface can be easily maintained by the owner and revamped with a cloth and polish.

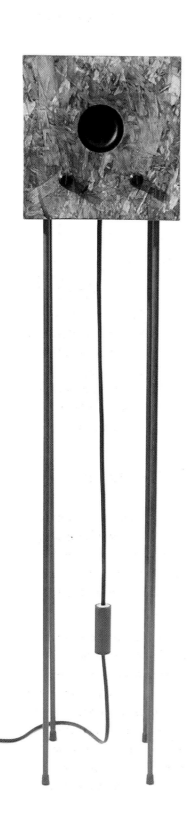

Figure 9.7
Cable Radio:
*Reused electrical parts, steel
rod, chipboard, water pipe*

Figure 9.8
Cable Radio detail

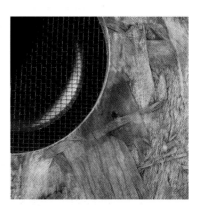

Energy use

Miniaturization of electronic components over the years means that we now live with a profusion of small, portable, battery-driven products. The widespread use of portable radios, personal stereos, digital cameras, motorized toys and so on means that vast quantities of batteries are being discarded, often after only a few hours of use. Even if rechargeable batteries are substituted for disposables, the inefficiencies in recharging still represent a rather immoderate use of energy. Such wasteful and harmful practices are a common feature of product design.

The Cable Radio is a design for a mains-powered radio. Part of the design challenge was to resolve two seemingly contradictory elements. On the one hand, the small size of components and circuitry allows the product envelope to be quite small. On the other hand, a mains-powered, and only mains-powered, product is not a portable object. It is therefore important to convey this idea – that it is non-portable and requires a 'place'. Together, the inclusion of the long legs and the use of the power cable as a visual element articulate this requirement. The housing for the electronics and speaker is relatively small and is positioned at an appropriate height for ease of operation and for listening.

Local manufacture – forms and fastenings suited to basic tools

All the designs presented here can be manufactured at locally based, generally equipped production facilities that are capable of producing a range of products in relatively low quantities (batch production) for local or regional markets. The design of such products is, of course, influenced and constrained by the economic, environmental and social considerations of the local production scenario.

Today, capital- and energy-intensive techniques are widely used to produce complex, moulded product casings. These parts, which are commonly defined by the industrial designer, require no further fabrication, and integral fittings, for holding internal components, allow assembly times to be kept to a minimum, a process that is often labour-intensive. Almost all the design precedents for electrical and electronic products rely on high-quantity production techniques such as polymer injection moulding. Most historical and contemporary telephones and virtually all personal computers, PDAs[7] and portable music equipment feature injection-moulded casings made with automated equipment. These processes, used to produce goods for international markets, are not appropriate, desirable or economically viable at the local level. The local approach requires the development of alternative techniques that make use of knowledge, skills and materials in new ways and in unconventional applications.

The Plaine Telephone, Figure 9.9, is made by attaching the components to a single piece of plywood, thus avoiding the need for the fabrication of a casing. All cuts and drilled holes are at right angles for ease of manufacture with basic equipment. The dial keys are simple cylindrical pegs, the 'handset' utilizes a reused bottle cap and some wire and is set on pads fashioned from a rubber inner-tube, an off-the-shelf toggle switch replaces the switch that is normally activated when the handset is replaced, and the circuitry is simply screwed to the underside of the board. The intent here was to create a usable telephone by employing the simplest of local techniques – it represents an exercise in looking for alternatives to precedents, rather than any suggestion of a definitive local design. The Wall Phone, Figure 9.10, follows a similar idea, but the circuitry is exposed on the front of the design and has been coated in latex paint for protection and to provide colour contrasts. In this case, the circuitry is a decorative element in the design. The Solar Calculator, Figure 9.11, also features exposed circuitry rather than styled enclosure. Here the materials and components are bare and undecorated; the intent was to allow the texture and natural hues of the piece to provide aesthetic interest.

90

Figure 9.9
Plaine Telephone:
Reused electrical parts, plywood, reused rubber, dowels, mild steel wire, tin lid, acrylic paint

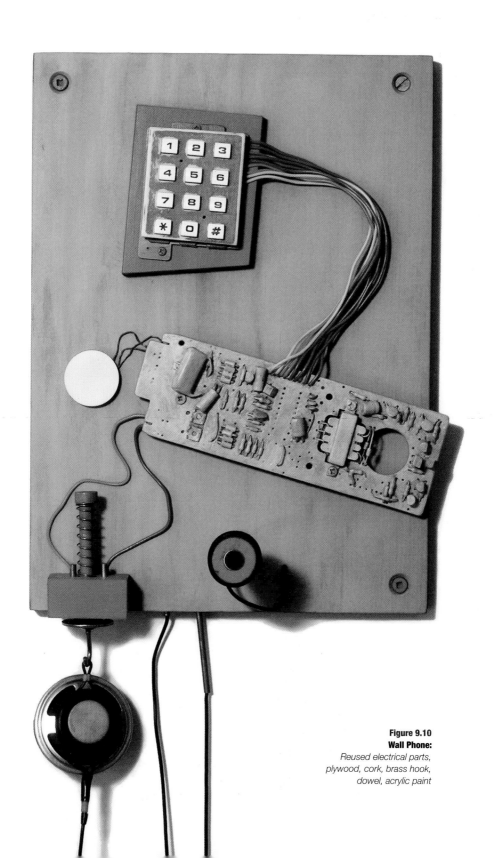

Figure 9.10
Wall Phone:
Reused electrical parts,
plywood, cork, brass hook,
dowel, acrylic paint

Figure 9.11
Solar Calculator:
*Reused electrical parts,
recovered mahogany,
cardboard, paper*

Integration of scales – mass-produced plus locally made parts

An important but little explored aspect of sustainable product design is a reassessment of our scales of production so that products can be made, repaired and reused within an industrial ecology of cyclic resource use at the local or regional level. Where appropriate, products and parts could be made using locally available resources, but there would remain many components that would be more appropriately manufactured in high quantities. For example, light sockets, bulbs and electronic parts would be difficult to manufacture at the local level and it would be inappropriate to do so. It is important to retain standardization of these types of components for safety reasons and to ensure compatibility. Sustainable product design must, therefore, combine and integrate scales – using locally and regionally produced parts from regional materials in combination with mass-produced parts. If the mass-produced parts are designed so that they are not specific to a particular product, they can be recovered and more easily reused in other applications. A standard, mass-produced lamp socket can be used in a variety of lighting designs; similarly, a length of threaded rod, electrical cable or a keypad has many possible design applications. On the other hand, a specialized moulding produced for one particular product application might be difficult to reuse.

93

The Lumière Floor Lamp, Figure 9.12, is a simple design that illustrates this integration of scales. It utilizes a number of off-the-shelf, mass-produced components, including a lamp socket, a mini fluorescent lamp, cable, a floor switch, threaded rod and fasteners, together with locally produced and found components – reused hardwood components for the cross-arms and base, a sheet of locally made paper as the shade and a large pebble for the base weight. Packaging and shipping of components is reduced to a minimum. Fabrication of several parts and product assembly is done locally and the basic design can be modified and adapted to suit local requirements. In addition, the design is such that its construction is explicit and easily comprehended – this facilitates repair and disassembly for replacement or recovery of parts. Reuse is encouraged by the fact that all mass-produced components are standard, off-the-shelf parts. Another design that combines a mass-produced part with a locally made base is shown in Figure 9.13, G-Clamp Nutcracker.

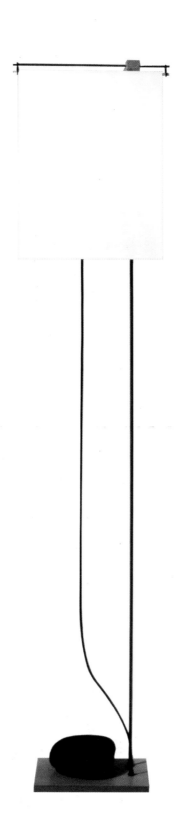

Figure 9.12
Lumière Floor Lamp:
Threaded rod, recovered
ash wood, handmade paper,
steel rod, pebble, standard
electrical parts

Figure 9.13
G-Clamp Nutcracker:
G-clamp, concrete

Elegance and empathy through design

When developing products within the limitations imposed by locale, processes, techniques and human skills must be used imaginatively to convert often uninspiring or non-ideal materials into elegant forms that contribute in a positive way to our material culture.

The Remora Box, Figure 9.14, is a legged, leaning chest constructed from recovered planks with screw fastenings and threaded-rod legs. Here an attempt was made to bring an element of finesse to an otherwise prosaic item constructed in an expeditious and rudimentary fashion from commonplace materials. An additional feature of this approach is that the simplicity and evidently basic means of construction allow a certain empathy with the object that is based on an understanding of what the object is made from and how it is constructed. The materials and finishes bring a character to the piece, which can contribute to its sustainable value. Many contemporary products lack this sense of connection because they are made using processes, materials and fastenings that are unfamiliar to the user or owner. This lack of understanding of one's material environment not only hinders product repair and maintenance, it also distances us from the objects we use. Without a greater sense of rapport with our material surroundings, we tend to value products only for their functional convenience but not as material things. Consequently, when products fail to perform their intended task they are discarded and replaced rather than maintained, repaired or upgraded.

These examples represent an approach whereby environmental and social considerations inherent to the notion of sustainability can be made relevant to the discipline of product design. These initial explorations were conducted through direct engagement in the creative activity of designing itself, rather than through investigation of technical issues, which can inform, but are not central to, the design process. It suggests that a reassessment of our approaches to product manufacturing is both necessary and feasible. A greater emphasis on the local could start to transform our infrastructures, our economy and our attitudes, and begin to align them with the principles of sustainability. Large manufacturing plants located in industrial zones and producing a limited number of models of new products in large quantities would be replaced by the local production and re-production of a variety of products in smaller quantities for local consumption.

Figure 9.14
Remora Box:
Recovered wood, hinges,
threaded rods

97

This could be accompanied by the evolution of a more service-oriented economy where products could be maintained, repaired and upgraded, and parts could be reused and recycled. Consumers and users of local products would have the assurance that their products could be maintained within the local region. Smaller-scale, less-intrusive, production facilities could be located closer to residential areas, thereby reducing the need for commuting. Furthermore, the production of products that have aesthetic and cultural attributes, which raise them above the merely functional, can help reduce emphasis on consumerism and 'the new' and begin to foster attitudes of responsibility and care. However, it is the designer who must put the flesh on the bones of this potential. It is through design that we can envision and demonstrate how 'things' could be, how products can be redefined for local and regional conditions, how a diverse and thoughtful variety of routes could bring a richness and depth to the creation of our material culture so that it is not only environmentally and socially responsible but also aesthetically expressive of the ethical core at the heart of sustainability.

10
TACIT KNOWLEDGE IN DESIGN
visual myths

we can know more than we can tell (Michael Polanyi[1])

Creative pursuits such as design draw on many different ways of thinking and employ a wide variety of techniques. There has been much written about the creative process, and methods have been introduced to help stimulate creativity – such as lateral thinking,[2] problem-solving exercises,[3] and brainstorming techniques.[4] In design school we use two-dimensional and three-dimensional design projects to introduce the student to ideas of making, craft and composition.[5] However, in my own experience as teacher and designer, I have found that these exercises, useful as they are, fail to address an important element of the creative process. This is the part of design that is unique and personal to the designer and deeply rooted within the individual. This aspect of the creative process is rarely addressed or even recognized but is, nevertheless, important to our understandings of design, our design outcomes and ourselves as designers. In the context of sustainability, I think it is especially important for this to be more fully acknowledged. A designer is not merely an anonymous cog within a service profession we call industrial design. A designer is an individual who gives part of him- or herself during the creative act – a part that must be valued if design is to become more humane and more sustainable.

In this chapter, I will consider this aspect of design and suggest a means to express, and thereby gain a deeper understanding of, the sources of our creative and aesthetic judgments. Such an understanding can enhance the designer's awareness of the creative process and contribute to its growth and development. Also, by acknowledging the basis of our design decisions and attempting to understand their meanings and implications we are better able to question our assumptions and challenge precedents. This, in itself, may be justification enough for exploring a little more deeply our prevailing approaches to design. However, given the myriad social and environmental problems associated with product design norms,[6] it is particularly important today that we reflect on our actions and reconsider how we regard material objects. Fresh insights are urgently needed; contemplating and communicating the bases of our design decisions can, hopefully, contribute to our understanding of these issues. In addition, conveying something of the background behind a design to the purchaser or user of the product can be beneficial from a sustainable perspective, because the story or intention behind an object can affect our appreciation and aesthetic experience of it,[7] and thus affect how we value it (see Chapter 15, where I discuss this point further).

The ideas expressed here emerge from my personal experience of the creative process and have evolved, primarily, by reflecting on the experimental design work introduced in Chapter 9. Ostensibly, these designs responded to the environmental, social and economic issues inherent in the notion of sustainable development. At the conscious, rational level, there were logical explanations for the various design decisions and justification in terms of the principles of sustainability. However, while engaged in the process of creating these designs, and perhaps especially when reflecting on them later, I became aware of something more, which existed below the surface, beyond rational explanation. An underlying but barely acknowledged sensibility pervaded *how* the conscious, sustainable agenda was actually being addressed in the design process. This subconscious aspect of design may be difficult or even impossible to fully understand and effectively describe. Nevertheless, it was an important, perhaps even the major, influence on the work – almost to the point where the declared, rationalized agenda becomes inconsequential by comparison.

Others, outside the world of design, have discussed this type of thinking,[8] whereby the knowledge that characterizes the 'self' is acknowledged as that from which we discover or design or interact in other ways with the everyday world. When this aspect of our thinking is recognized, it becomes apparent that many of the ways in which we rationalize our intentions and justify our design work may reveal only a partial picture of what the work is really about, and this may be the less significant aspect of the work. The rationalized argument does not reveal the essential, aesthetically defining quality or feeling of the work because this is indefinable, subjective and largely subconscious; nevertheless, it is critically important to the activity of designing.

To gain a better understanding of this intuitive core at the heart of the design process, it is necessary to find some means other than rational argument and discussion. To this end, I have attempted to develop a way of acknowledging and expressing ideas about the roots of our design decision making, which I have called 'visual myths'. These visual myths are supplementary to the designed object but can provide a useful and appropriate means for expressing what Buchanan has termed, 'personal visions infused into a rhetorical art of communication'.[9]

> **The faculty for myth is innate in the human race ... It is**
> **the protest of romance against the commonplace of life.**
> (W. Somerset Maugham, 1919[10])

Duchamp held that we should not attempt to analyse the creative act, which is a subjective, intuitive process.[11] The scientist-turned-philosopher Michael Polanyi discussing the nature of discovery also suggests that the subsidiary or *tacit* knowledge from which we draw cannot be fully justified or explained.[12] While analysis and rational explanation may be inappropriate, it is still important to gain some insights into the roots and meanings of our design judgments and aesthetic preferences. Only by doing so can we hope to more fully comprehend and evolve our creative ideas and processes. Reflecting on our decisions and creative work is fundamentally meaningful, and essential to the development of a more responsible rendition of material culture. Only by seeking a deeper understanding, which includes becoming more cognizant of the meanings of the intuitive aspects of our creative decisions and interventions, can we act and respond in ways that we believe to be appropriate. And, as Hick has said, for an object to be meaningful it has to be intelligible to us, and this enables us to 'behave appropriately (or in a way that one takes to be appropriate) in relation to it'.[13]

Therefore, rather than attempting to analyse the creative act, an intuitive, imaginative approach is proposed here to express something of the basis of the design thinking. To illustrate this approach a selection from the experimental 'sustainable-design' projects, some of which were described in Chapter 9, form the *starting* point. Reflecting on this work led to a series of impressions that were then expressed through composite visual imagery, resulting in a set of images that constitute recollections, contemplations and meanings related to the original designs. They are not analyses, but rather visual stories, or visual myths, which at one level are constructed fictions but, at a deeper level, begin to reveal aspects of the original design thinking. Hence, the visual myth is an attempt at comprehension where one does not have the answers in advance; indeed, there are no definitive answers as such. It is more a process of manifesting intimations of tacit knowledge through the acts of doing and expressing. The essential element is the tangible, visible expression, which contributes to reflection through the development of a reciprocal process of thought and action. This manifestation becomes the medium of communication to the designer and to others:

102

- The process of creating a visual myth becomes a form of reflection – it is a dialogue with the self, reflecting back to the designer his or her thoughts and intentions. As in any creative process, the designer then responds by changing, adding to and altering the work until a satisfactory resolution has been achieved. Throughout this process, thoughts and intentions are being filtered, rejected, reflected upon and combined. Eventually, the visual piece is judged to be an appropriate rendition of an essential ingredient that was fundamental to the aesthetic definition and character of the original design to which the work refers. (This process is not finite because, potentially, one could create a second visual myth to express something of the first, and so on; but the law of diminishing returns would quickly come into play.)

- The finished piece provides a way of communicating to a third party. When seen in conjunction with the object, it adds another layer of information that, hopefully, makes the object itself more intelligible and allows us to 'behave appropriately ... in relation to it'.[14]

The creation of the visual myth can be understood as a contemplation of a designed object through the creation of referential visual imagery. It is complementary to the product design process and is, in effect, an extension of it. It can allow the designer a way to articulate insights about his or her design process and sources of aesthetic discernment. This is achieved in a manner that is very familiar to the designer because it is itself a creative act and calls upon intuitive, subjective decision making. Hence, it would seem to be a more appropriate process than some form of structured, analytical technique. As Buchanan has said, 'There can be a discipline of design, but it must be different in kind from disciplines which possess determinate subject matters. Design is a discipline where the conception of the subject matter, method, and purpose is an integral part of the activity and the result.'[15] Therefore, the approach presented here is aesthetic rather than analytical, and presentational rather than discursive.

103

The *visualizing* of tacit knowledge that is inexpressible by rational explanation is a particularly appropriate means of expression and communication for the designer. Polanyi gives the example of the police Identikit picture, whereby a witness remembers a face and attempts to create a likeness by choosing from different elements – eyes, mouths, noses etc. It may be impossible to describe in words what a person looks like in a way that is sufficiently accurate or useful. However, by employing a method of visualization, the witness is able to draw out his or her *tacit* knowledge of the person's likeness.[16] In a similar way, but with the advantage of a training in visualization techniques, the designer can draw out and express the tacit knowledge that pertains to his or her own design work.

We will go on producing myths, ways of explaining ourselves to ourselves. (Richard Holloway, 2001[17])

The word 'myth' properly applies to stories that reflect a *collective*, cultural, subconscious understanding and expression;[18] this is the way I used the term in Chapter 3. Here, however, I am using it to refer to the intuitive understanding and expression of an *individual*.

The notion of the 'personal myth', which is not without precedent,[19] refers to an imaginative expression that employs metaphor to convey its meaning. Related to this, there have been important connections made between creativity and the spiritual experience, and the latter has a long history of expression in terms of metaphor and myth. Campbell and Yeats have both spoken of the creative artist taking over the role previously filled by priests.[20] Andy Warhol, who presented a rather hedonistic façade to the world, nevertheless drew from a deeply felt spiritual commitment that has been described as 'the key to the artist's psyche'.[21] Frankl has drawn connections between the search for meaning, the spiritual and creativity.[22] Campbell tells us that the spiritual experience is an intuitive realization that transcends verbal description and he links artistic, creative expression with the creation of new myths.[23] Murdoch has linked artistic creativity, mythology, the spiritual and intuitive realization.[24] Together these authoritative voices lead one to an understanding that creative expression, in its process and its appreciation, is essentially aesthetic, intuitive and experiential, that it is closely related to the spiritual experience, and that it can be appropriately expressed in terms of metaphor and myth.

104

Using the language of myth we can point to meanings, but these meanings will be ambiguous and open to interpretation. This vagueness is entirely appropriate for, as Campbell has said, 'If we give that mystery an exact meaning we diminish the experience of the real depth.'[25]

When we use the symbolic language of metaphor and myth, outer appearance means very little, it is what lies behind the appearance that matters. The meanings of metaphor and myth are not literal or explicit, but require interpretation. With this form of expression, psychological or inner meaning is conveyed obliquely via a literal or outer meaning.[26] As I said in Chapter 3, the question to be asked of a mythical story or image is not 'Is it true?' but 'What does it mean?' Heinrich Zimmer has put it this way, 'Symbols hold the mind to truth but are not themselves the truth.'[27] This indirect form of expression is used because, as I said above, intuitive realizations, such as the creative act and the spiritual experience, defy direct description.

Therefore, the visual myths presented here are imaginative works that give an impression of the original design thinking and sources. This impression is conveyed through the aesthetic experience, which is holistic, ambiguous and open to multiple readings. Each visual myth can be regarded as a self-contained work that is independent of, and in addition to, any rationalized explanation of the creator's intentions (in this case the conscious, formal agenda related to issues of sustainability and product design).

Thus, the approach is not rationalistic, but a contemplative act that allows the ideas to be expressed in a format that is appropriate for the appreciation of creativity – that is, through the aesthetic experience. By this means, these visual myths can initiate, in both their making and their presentation, a reflective discourse about the original designs; this is their purpose.

This dialogue between the designer and the work, and the designer and a third party is itself developmental. Part of the process of evolving one's thinking and ideas is finding a means to externalize and articulate them. In this regard, the key is to find a means of expression that is appropriate. The visual myth provides a way in; it allows a deeper understanding by adding to the dialogue already started by the original design work. Thus, the visual myth:

- is supplementary to the designed objects;
- refers to, and potentially provides insights about, the creative process behind the designed objects;
- is impressionistic, ambiguous and holistic and as such, should not be subjected to rationalized analysis or explanation;
- refers to, but does not explain, a creative experience, in the same way that the language of scripture, myth, fable and parable are symbolic. The literal meaning loses importance; it is the metaphorical meaning that matters.

The distinguishing feature of a visual myth created by the designer of the original object, compared to other supplementary imagery that often accompanies designed objects (such as theme boards or advertising posters), is that only the designer can reflect on and express the sources of his or her design decisions. Others might create visual myths that refer to objects, but only the designer can attempt to express the tacit knowledge from which his or her design was drawn.

Creating such images can enable us to better understand our own creative work because, reduced and abstracted as they are, these images are expressions of otherwise vague, unarticulated, and therefore perhaps unrecognized, thoughts and knowledge. It is the very act of expressing that brings a deeper level of realization, and only when this intuitive realization becomes part of our perception can we begin to respond to it and thus develop and grow. Thus, the visual myth, in its making and completion, is a vehicle for reflection. It is not a *necessary* part of a designer's approach, but it can be a valuable supplement that encourages contemplation of one's activities and, as Socrates once said, 'the unexamined life is not worth living.'[28]

Six examples of visual myths are presented here, without explanation, together with the original objects to which they refer (Figures 10.1–10.6). As I said in Chapter 9, the original design issues of sustainability were an important focus of the work and, with a particular concentration on electronic products, the vehicle chosen for purposes of exploration was the radio. Therefore, the objects presented here are, for the most part, radio designs; one furniture piece is also included.

The visual myth images are all works created for academic/educational purposes only. Where existing images have been adapted and incorporated, sources have been acknowledged, referenced and, where appropriate, are reproduced with permission of the copyright holders. Every reasonable effort was made to secure permission to use existing images.

B1   GOA GAZETTE   Thursday, June 14th

TRAVEL

Island of the Roc holds ancient hi-tech secret

The descendants of Sinbad still produce 'radios' according to a tradition that goes back at least three hundred years.
SHAHRIYAR SHAHZAMAN has been there.

The Isle of Salahbah, according to legend, was once the home of the great Roc, the mythical bird that carried off Sinbad the Sailor. Today, it basks undisturbed in the tropical sunshine. It has been spared the usual tourist invasion largely because it is almost impossible to get to. There is no airport and no regular ferry. Eight hundred kms east of Yemen and a thousand kms southwest of Bombay, it rarely sees tourists. The most determined travellers, with plenty of time on their hands, can negotiate a passage on a fishing boat from Trivandrum in southern India. The journey can take up to three weeks – but the rewards are many. Perfect natural beauty is encompassed by white sand beaches and fringed with palms. Accommodation is simple and sparse in one of the two hostelries on the island.

The handicrafts of this seafaring principality are of great variety and worthy of special mention. They can be divided into two main groups: those of the coastal towns, especially the towns colonized by the Portuguese; and those made by the Kerber tribes of the central mountains.

Crafts in the coastal areas include fabrics, leatherwork, jewellery that often recalls that of both medieval Europe and east Africa, and most curiously, a primitive form of wireless receiver. This latter is perhaps the most puzzling handicraft to be found in this entire region. The Salahbariis, it seems, were familiar with the principles of transmitting radio waves for at least two centuries before Marconi's discovery in Europe at the end of the 19th century. The best quality Salahbar radios can be found in the ancient souk of Risfah, some 30kms west of the capital on the coastal road to Yibri. There, it is possible to see the 'Salahbah Radio' craftsmen at work, usually aided by young apprentices who are learning the ancient skills. Despite the influx of inexpensive mass-produced radios and other modern products, the traditional radios still dominate, inherent as

Fishing boats at Yibri: these provide the only means of getting to and from the island

they are to the cultural and spiritual identity of this island people.

The arts of the mountains exhibit a severe geometrical decoration and are less refined in both technique and expression. Weaving is perhaps the most celebrated of the mountain crafts, especially the mats of alfa-grass from the area surrounding the village of Mahoud. In the North the chief handicraft is pottery which is made, without a wheel, by the women; it is unglazed but elaborately slip-painted with contrasting hues of the diluted clays. Earth tones combined with the blackening from firing in open furnaces result in a crude but not unattractive utilitarian pottery that is becoming much sought after by collectors from the United States.

One of the many Salahbah 'radio' makers

See SALAHBAH, PAGE B9

Figure 10.1
Crystal Radio:
Newspaper Article

Source:
Photographs by the author. Text inspired by and partially adapted from: Boulanger, R. (1966) Morocco (trans. by J. S. Hardman), Hachette Publishers, Paris

Figure 10.2
Cable Radio:
Family Memorabilia

Source:
*Digitally modified photograph and
assemblage of other images adapted from
the collection of the author. Text page
adapted from* The Imitation of Christ – A New
Translation, *by Thomas Á. Kempis, (translator
not attributed), Burns and Oates, London,
ca. 1900, p6*

RADIOS AND RADIO LISTENING

An Introduction

to this most popular hobby

by W. Stuart

YOU may often have admired the smooth, steady performance of well-designed, well-balanced radios and possibly wondered what is the secret behind their success. Actually there is no special secret. Radio designing and listening is actually quite simple, once you know the basic principles which govern how a radio will perform.

If you have yet to build your first radio, don't be put off by thinking that a lot of expensive tools and equipment will be needed. Far from it, even quite advanced models can be made with the aid of some razor blades, a few pins, pliers and sandpaper. Later on it will help if you extend your collection of tools to include a fretsaw, hand drill, small hammer, modelling knives, soldering iron and a small vice – but in the early stages all you need are the few simple items previously mentioned. An old kitchen table, drawing board or even a smooth unwarped plank will provide a fine building surface.

As with most hobbies, success and enjoyment from radio building and listening depends to a large extent on getting off on the right foot. It's a waste of time and money simply to buy a bundle of materials haphazardly and then start building something that vaguely resembles a full size radio.

Only simple tools are needed to build a radio. Plywood is available in sheets of various thicknesses.

In time, practical experience will provide you with sufficient knowledge to enable you to design your own radios, but in the first instance you should start off by building a simple wooden box for an existing radio circuit than can be salvaged from a used radio. Perfectly serviceable radios can be purchased for a few pennies at your local church or scout jumble sale, or ask your dad if you can have the radio circuit from his gramophone equipment.

The best way to understand radio design is to look at the various types of radios and see what proportions are necessary for successful designs. It is quite a simple matter to make up a number of radios of different types and try them out. They need not cost very much for most of the materials required can be obtained for a shilling or so. And radio listening itself can be grand fun.

Figure 10.3
Boy's Own Radio:
Children's Annual

Source:
Drawing of radio by the author. Text inspired by and adapted from: Colbridge, A. M. 'Kites and Kite Flying', pp97–101, and Dean B. 'How to Build Model Planes', pp115–120, Eagle Annual No. 3, edited by Marcus Morris, Hulton Press, London, ca. 1952 (publisher not traced). Drawing of boy's head adapted from 'Sammy and his Speedsub', Swift Annual No. 2, edited by Marcus Morris, Hulton Press, London, ca. 1955 (publisher not traced)

Figure 10.4
Kind-of-Blue Chair:
From a Cabin Wall

Source:
Photographic image of collage by the author. Inset photographs modified from images in Old Ebbw Vale in Photographs *by Keith Thomas, Stewart Williams Publishers, Barry, South Glamorgan, Wales, 1979, pp1, 158. Use of images with permission of both the author and the publisher. Partly revealed postcard of* Nuestro Señor Crucificado *by Diego Velasquez. Text by Bill Evans quoted from the liner notes of the compact disc* Kind of Blue *by Miles Davis, Sony Music Entertainment Inc., 1997, reproduced from the original 1959 LP*

Radio à la Provençale

For this version of the traditional radio, the ingredients consist of a circuit recovered from leftovers of other products, approx. ½ sq.ft. of board such as pine, plywood or chipboard, a 6v transformer – the circuit should have this with it, or you could ask your appliance repairer for a spare one (alternatively, in a pinch you can use 4 rechargeable 1½v dry-cell batteries, depending on local availability, but you will need to make a battery container), a variety of screws and bolts, some strong adhesive tape (duct tape is ideal) and an old wire coat-hanger.

Attach all the ingredients together by fixing them to the board with screws and wiring the circuitry, speaker, and transformer or batteries. Use the tape to attach awkwardly shaped components. The coat hanger can be fashioned into an FM aerial. Place the whole on a table or shelf in a light, visible spot for about three days. Contemplate your creation and consider how it could be enhanced.

Meanwhile, accumulate some finishing materials such as sandpaper, white-spirit, paints, polishes, brushes and rags. Disassemble your radio. Thoroughly clean all the ingredients. Coat the board in an application of your choice – wax, paint, wood-stain or simply a clear coat to prevent finger marks. Paint circuit components if desired – this is up to you. Reassemble.

Pour a glass of wine – a Bordeaux or Cabernet Sauvignon goes particularly well with this design. Tune the radio to your favourite program and sit back and relax.

Figure 10.5
Hermit Radio:
Recipe

Source:
Image drawn and digitally modified by the author. Text inspired by French Country Cooking *by* *Elizabeth David, John Lehmann* *Publishers, London, 1951*

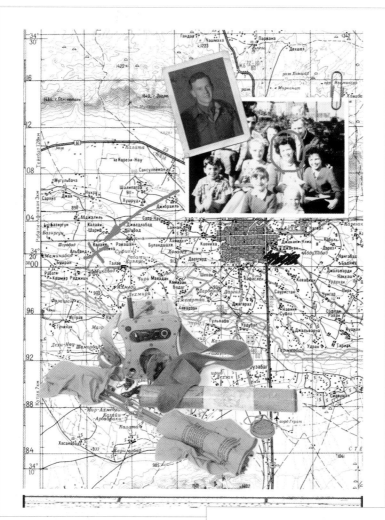

Figure 10.6
Tin Radio:
Resistance

Source:
Russian map of Afghanistan adapted from:
www.lib.utexas.edu/maps/middle_east_and_asia/
herat_1985.jpg, accessed 4 March 2002. (Public
domain, see www.lib.utexas.edu/maps/faq.
html#3.html) Photograph of 'Gibson Girl' radio
transmitter adapted from an image in The Book
of Kites by Paul and Helene Morgan, Dorling
Kindersley Limited (publishers), 9 Henrietta St,
London WC2E 8PS, 1992, p11. Reproduced with
permission of Dorling Kindersley Images. Other
images adapted and modified from photographs
in the author's collection

11
REFRAMING DESIGN FOR SUSTAINABILITY

unmasking the object

Whatever one thinks about the continual growth model of today's capitalist economies, there is no doubt that technological development and product manufacturing have both positive and negative effects. Alongside their ability to create wealth and provide a wide variety of benefits, there are enormous costs. Even though modern manufacturing facilities employ very sophisticated technologies, the fundamental approach to product design, production and distribution has remained essentially the same for a century or more. Resources are extracted from the earth, refined, formed into parts and assembled into products using mass-production processes; these products are then widely distributed, sold, used, discarded and replaced. This system, which has become increasingly automated over the years, is mainly unidirectional in terms of its flow of resources and energy. For most consumer products, post-use processing such as repair, refurbishment and redistribution, and retrieval of materials and components, are economically marginal and relatively rare; effective and widespread maintenance infrastructures only exist for the more expensive products, such as automobiles and white goods.

Here, I would like to consider the relationship between these unsustainable practices and the aesthetic qualities of the manufactured product. To a great extent, the aesthetic qualities of a product are a function of the system that produces it. It follows that the aesthetics of most consumer products are, in fact, the aesthetics of immoderate waste and environmentally and socially damaging practices.

If, as a society, we are to reframe our notions of material culture, we must first recognize the problem and do so in ways pertinent to our own individual roles and contributions. An important aspect of the designer's role is product aesthetics, and therefore the relationship between aesthetics and unsustainable production practices warrants further consideration.

One way to more fully explore this relationship is to create an *aesthetic typology* for contemporary, unsustainable products. Such a typology would enable the designer to recognize the links that exist between the aesthetic qualities of products and the unsustainable practices by which they are produced. This can then provide a basis for change.

A typology of this sort requires the development of aesthetic identifiers that, collectively, are capable of characterizing[1] certain kinds of consumer goods, such as small appliances, electrical products and power tools, which are produced, distributed and discarded in ways that are unsustainable and increasingly out of kilter with the zeitgeist of our post-industrial society. An aesthetic typology is not based on product function, but on visible and tactile traits of form and finish, traits that can be linked back to modes of production that are problematic. This kind of typology would:

- provide a means of differentiating unsustainable products;
- help reveal the relationship between the aesthetic features of a mass-produced object and the unsustainable production techniques and material specifications of its manufacture;
- challenge the dominant conceptions of products and product design that help to prolong unsustainable practices.

Thus, an aesthetic typology is a means of stating the problem in terms of design. In effect, an aesthetic typology for contemporary consumer products would reveal what *not* to do. It then becomes our challenge to develop alternative, more benign directions for design.

To construct an aesthetic typology, certain aesthetic identifiers can be proposed that are common to many consumer goods and which, *collectively*, may be useful in distinguishing unsustainable practices. We can begin by simply looking at consumer products and discerning some general features and traits. These can then be related to understandings of sustainable development. Appropriate products for this exercise would include the many small, relatively inexpensive consumer goods that are in such widespread use today but which are difficult or economically unattractive to repair (compared to the purchase of a new replacement product). These would include:

- personal music equipment such as 'Walkman' type CD, cassette, MiniDisc and MP3 players;
- televisions and radios;
- telephones and cellular phones;
- music equipment such as 'boomboxes' and lower-end home stereo products (higher-end music equipment can usually be economically maintained and repaired);
- small electrical appliances for the domestic kitchen such as electric whisks, food mixers, food processors, liquidizers and filter coffee makers;
- power tools for home use such as electric drills and saws;
- electronic products such as digital clocks and calculators;
- video and computer game products such as handsets, joysticks, game cards and control boxes.

115

These products are mass produced for worldwide distribution. The same products with the same designs are available in London, New York, Hong Kong and Buenos Aires. Few, if any, of these products are designed for a specific place or culture – instead, their design is aesthetically and culturally neutral. We might compare them with the example of prayer beads, discussed in Chapter 5. Prayer beads are also widely available and commonly mass-produced and yet are still capable of being adapted to culture, belief and place.

Most contemporary products, such as those listed above, are defined in terms of outer casings, which enclose the working parts. Commonly, casings are made from injection-moulded plastics such as the co-polymer acrylonitrile butadiene styrene (ABS). They often have highly polished, smooth finishes with rounded edges; such finishes are readily achieved by injection moulding. Plastic flow is more effective and expulsion of the part from the mould is less problematic with such forms. The outer casing effectively contains and protects the working parts, but has a relatively fragile surface that is easily damaged. Moreover, materials such as ABS are not generally familiar or easy to maintain or repair. By contrast, wood products can often be readily repaired by non-specialists using commonly available items such as glues and screws; wood can also be maintained with fillers, scratch removal products and polishes.

In addition, the vast majority of consumer products are manufactured via highly automated mass-production processes, often in countries with low-wage economies. This enables the unit cost of the product, and hence the retail price, to be kept relatively low. In turn, because of their low price, products can be readily replaced when fashions change. Indeed, styling changes by manufacturers are frequently the drivers of product replacement.

These observations provide a basis for constructing a preliminary aesthetic typology for common consumer products. To this end, the following initial set of aesthetic identifiers is suggested:

- culturally neutral or bland;
- pristine, polished and fragile;
- concealing and disguising;
- cold or remote;
- curved, rounded and smooth;
- fashionable or showy;
- complete and inviolable.

Each of these can be linked to unsustainable practices, which are described in Table 11.1. Collectively, they constitute an aesthetic typology that allows us to differentiate products produced by an inherently and manifestly unsustainable system. All the common products listed earlier can be distinguished using this typology; they are mass-produced using automated (low labour) techniques, they are energy-intensive in their manufacture and international distribution, and they are not usually repaired or repairable. By contrast, a locally made object for local use, such as a crafted wooden box, might exhibit some but not all of these typological identifiers. It might be curved, rounded and smooth, and pristine, polished and fragile, but it will not be cold

Table 11.1 **An aesthetic typology for contemporary, unsustainable products**

Aesthetic identifier	Description	Relationship to unsustainable practices
Culturally neutral or bland	This is a function of mass production for global distribution. Cultural or regional preferences and distinctions are generally omitted from the design because the same product has to be acceptable to users all over the world	In their design and production, products which exhibit such aesthetic neutrality often fail to respond to the particularities of place that are so important to the notion of sustainable development (Van der Ryn and Cowan, 1996)
Pristine, polished and fragile	This is dependent on capital- and energy-intensive production processes and usually a 'one-time use' of finite resources to achieve faultless forms and surfaces	With everyday use the 'perfect' appearance quickly becomes scratched and damaged – which can engender user dissatisfaction and premature product disposal and replacement. In addition, delivery to the market of such products requires a heavy reliance on packaging. Thus, the flawless but delicate surface design of many contemporary products helps stimulate unnecessary consumerism and contributes to waste production
Concealing and disguising	The exterior of the object is perceived as an 'envelope' or casing. It is usually a moulded or press-formed shell that has little bearing on the function or form of the inner workings of the product	This is a barrier to product comprehension. It not only hampers product repair, it can also contribute to a lack of resonance with, and attachment to, our material possessions because we do not understand them and we cannot engage with them, except in a very superficial way
Cold or remote	The materials and finishes of many contemporary products are unfamiliar and remote in terms of the general user's understanding	This is also a barrier to product comprehension. This quality can contribute to a lack of ease or comfort with one's material possessions and consequently can affect how one values (or fails to value) them. In turn, this can contribute to a lack of regard for material objects and an increase in their disposability

117

Aesthetic identifier	Description	Relationship to unsustainable practices
Curved, rounded and smooth	The exterior forms of many contemporary products, often made of plastics, are distinguished by forms that can be readily injection-moulded. Consequently, hard edges are eliminated, corners are rounded and forms become smoothed	This 'moulded' aesthetic is indicative of energy- and resource-intensive mass-production processes that are environmentally damaging and frequently socially problematic. Production is often done in low-wage economies with poor worker conditions and lax environmental policies. Hence, this aesthetic characteristic can be indicative of environmentally and socially unsustainable practices
Fashionable or showy	Many so called 'consumer durables' are designed in ways that both pander to and spur short-lived trends – through unnecessary updates and changes in form and colour	When such 'permanent' products, which are problematic in terms of their disposal, are designed in ways that quickly become outdated, then it is indicative of irresponsible practices, a lack of respect for the environment and profligate use of finite resources. Such designs foster premature 'aesthetic obsolescence', waste and consumption
Complete and inviolable	This aesthetic quality is a function of the overall presentation of the object in terms of its sophisticated forms, finishes and materials	Most products demand passive acceptance by the user; there is little or nothing to be added or contributed by the user. Even the repair of a simple scratch or break is not invited and it would be difficult to achieve a satisfactory result. Thus, the user cannot truly 'own' the object if he or she cannot engage with it, understand it (except on a very superficial level) or maintain and care for it. Again this can foster a lack of valuing of the object and lead to its premature disposal. This feature is related to the 'professionalization' of design and the fact that the physical descriptions of our material goods have effectively been taken out of the hands of ordinary people and local or regional communities

118

or remote nor will it be complete and inviolable; its materials and constituent parts are familiar and understandable, it can be easily cared for and repaired, and its particular use can be determined by the owner. Taken together, these identifiers differentiate the mass-produced, unsustainable object from a more sustainable object produced by different means. Thus, for these examples at least, the proposed typology seems to be effective. The main point here, however, is not that these specific identifiers are necessarily the most comprehensive, but that through the use of identifiers such as these we can start to recognize the relationship between product aesthetics, the production system and unsustainable practices. The unsustainable nature of the production/distribution/disposal system is revealed through the aesthetic qualities of the products created by it. Therefore, the typology helps the designer to recognize the problem *in the language and terms of design itself* – and it is this recognition that provides the foundation for developing more responsible practices.

The proposed aesthetic typology is based on general observations of common consumer products, and linking these to typical manufacturing and product distribution practices that are, in many respects, unsustainable. In making these connections between aesthetics and sustainable development, however, it is important to acknowledge two critical factors. Design is, to a large extent, subjective, intuitive and normative. Therefore, general observations related to product aesthetics are simply that – general and based on observation of certain kinds of current products. Exceptions and counter-examples can be put forward, but the majority of small appliances and other consumer products do tend to exhibit the aesthetic characteristics described above. There may be other characteristics that would also be useful, but for demonstrating the principle, this list is sufficient. In addition, sustainable development cannot be defined except in very general terms. We do not know with any certainty what a modern sustainable society might actually look like; indeed, as I suggested in Chapter 3, sustainable development can be understood more as *contemporary, secular myth*, rather than a definitive process or state. For these reasons, we can understand an aesthetic typology that is linked to unsustainable practices as a reasonable and, hopefully, useful tool to help us discern undesirable aspects of contemporary products and practices, and these in the terms of design itself. As such, these propositions are not, nor should they be,

119

scientifically based or subject to quantitative or reductionist scientific justification – this would be entirely inappropriate.

The creative and visualization abilities of designers give them a unique and potentially influential role in the process of reframing objects so that in their materials, manufacture and appearance, they are in accord with, and expressive of, sustainable principles and meaningful human values. We can infer from this that *sustainable* objects will be markedly different from existing products and will be identified through a rather different aesthetic typology.

In attempting to reframe design to address today's priorities, we can identify the problems with our existing modes of operation and propose new directions that might well satisfy a broad range of sustainable principles. However, this is quite different from knowing what a new, sustainable design approach actually is, and the design criteria that such an approach must fulfil. If we try to pin down the approach and the criteria too soon then we risk constraining and curtailing what is, in reality, a dynamic, evolving and complex area of concern. Instead, a variety of design approaches must be explored in order to bring together and synthesize often competing priorities. The aesthetic typology introduced here is an effective way of summarizing, in terms of design, and revealing, in terms of visual qualities, the unsustainable system behind a contemporary product. Once this link is established, designers can begin exploring approaches that clearly differ from current models and seem to be in accord with an ethos of sustainability. These explorations will contribute to our ideas of sustainable design and enable us to view the issues from a broader perspective. With this in mind, I offer the following topics for consideration because they are given little attention in mainstream product design and production.

Encountering versus experiencing objects

McGrath, referring to the work of Martin Buber, explains that our view of nature, emerging since the Enlightenment, has been an 'I–It' relationship – it is a subject–object relationship by which we *experience* things, including human-made artefacts. Viewing things as so many 'Its' fosters 'an ethic of alienation, exploitation, and disengagement' and is exemplified by 'mundane acts such as mass-consumption, industrial production, and societal organization'.[2] The alternative, proposed by Buber, is an 'I–You' relationship – which can occur between people.

The 'I–You' relationship is mutual and reciprocal and is characterized as an 'encounter with' rather than an 'experience of'. It is Buber's contention that if we learn to relate to the world and nature in terms of an 'I–You' relationship it would lead to a more profound, unmediated knowledge of the world. An 'It' is known in terms of specifications such as dimensions, weight and colour; a 'You' is known directly.[3]

This notion has important implications for how we think about the design of sustainable objects and about the relationship between ourselves and the objects we create from the resources of nature. Seen as a mutual encounter, our exploitation and immoderate wasting of natural resources becomes an intolerable violation – a realization that can inform our design work and foster a more restrained and more respectful approach. I will return to this subject in Chapter 15 to explore its relevance in the creation of some specific design examples.

Direct deed

In being professionalized into the distinct discipline of industrial design, design has become constrained by its own conventions – I briefly touched on this point in Chapter 4. However, an important element in this narrowing of vision is the 'mediated' manner by which today's products are defined. The creation of functional objects has become an activity in which the yet-to-be-created object is visualized through sketches, renderings, digital models and physical models. The transition from the folk arts to the world of professional design is a transition of process. It is usually accompanied by a *distancing from* the intimacies and nuances of place, materials and many of the ingredients of an authentic, more visceral experience of the world. This *removal of awareness through process* can be seen as a contributing factor in the development of many unsustainable practices associated with modern manufacturing, such as labour exploitation and pollution: practices that are insensitive to the realities and needs of people and the natural environment. The architect Christopher Alexander, a critic of much contemporary architecture, has similarly spoken of the problems of designing by means of abstracted drawings and blueprints, rather than engaging directly with the tangible issues and qualities of materials and place.[4] The work of Christopher Day, also an architect, is particularly sensitive to locale. He has developed a process of designing buildings that is rooted in place and culture. Through the use of local materials

121

and his engagement with people during the making, his designs bear witness to this more sustainable approach – the process is revealed through the aesthetic experience of the buildings.[5]

In contrast to conventional approaches to product design, objects created through direct deed may be less precise, less fashionable, less efficient and less profitable but they often possess qualities that speak of spontaneity, intuition, local knowledge, moderation, and a more complete awareness of place, materials and three-dimensionality and a deeper and more immediate appreciation of their effects. We need only compare the Djenne Mosque of Mali with a glass office tower: both are 20th century designs but the former is particularly responsive to place. Like Christopher Day's buildings, it respects local architecture styles and is built and maintained from local materials. By contrast, the glass office tower is largely independent of its location and utilizes mass-produced 'placeless' materials. Likewise, we could compare a handmade sisal shopping basket with a plastic carrier bag to appreciate the nature of these important qualitative differences. In another sphere, the jazz pianist Bill Evans also referred to the relationship between direct deed, improvisation and inner reflection, and its relevance to creativity – and it is evident in his groundbreaking extemporizations.[6] The results of direct deed are also seen in the ad hoc improvisations of the poor and others who spontaneously create functional solutions to satisfy immediate needs.[7]

There is an important lesson here. The activity of designing can either reveal or obscure, depending on the approach and techniques chosen, and a direct approach would seem to offer insights and outcomes that are of greater relevance to sustainability, compared to the mediated approaches currently prevalent in industrial design.

Necessity – the mother of invention

The British academic C. S. Lewis once wrote that it is 'scarcity that enables a society to exist'.[8] With abundance, we do not need to concern ourselves too much with the notion of society – with the manners and mores of living alongside others. To a large extent, we can behave as fairly autonomous individuals. When everyone owns a TV we do not need to form an orderly queue outside the cinema, or agree to keep quiet during the film. Similarly, we do not have to cooperate with others to make our own entertainment in the form of games or music. With

Figure 11.1
Local designs 1:
Purses fashioned from the ring-pulls of drink cans, market stall, la Rochelle, France

Source:
Photograph by the author

Figure 11.2
Local designs 2:
Small metal suitcase made from misprinted food can stock, metal workers market, Nairobi, Kenya

Source:
Photograph by the author

scarcity we have to be inventive, to create something useful from very little. An example of this from a time of shortage is the 'Make do and mend' slogan issued by the British Board of Trade during the Second World War,[9] which encouraged people to create new clothes from old so as to avoid demand for new fabrics, which were in short supply.

There are not just environmental benefits to treading more lightly by repairing things and reducing our dependence on acquisition. There are also, potentially, benefits for community and society, and benefits to the individual, by learning how to more effectively understand our material world. The creations that result from such an approach are diverse and often refreshingly serendipitous, original and aesthetically surprising; some typical examples are shown in Figures 11.1 and 11.2.

Making use of what already exists can be the basis of effective and more benign design. Castiglioni's Toio lamp[10] and the more recent work of the Droog designers[11] exemplify this approach.

Challenging the notion of styling

Styling can impair an object's durability because it inevitably becomes unfashionable. In the areas of consumer goods and clothes, designers strive for their work to be à la mode or to align with competitors' models. Many companies employ scouts to provide them with information about trends among young people. This information is then used to produce goods that resonate with current sensibilities.[12] This concentration on up-to-the-minute styling is an effective way of stimulating consumerism but it is often highly problematic in terms of sustainability. However, there are examples of art and design that stand outside this styling milieu. These examples can be useful reference points when it comes to reframing our notions of design for sustainability:

- The untrained Cornish artist Alfred Wallis painted for his own pleasure and he was unaware that he was breaking conventions. His paintings, often rather crudely executed on irregular pieces of cardboard, are naïve but compositionally strong and strikingly original.[13]
- In one of his last works, the *Stations of the Cross* for the Chapelle Du Rosaire in Vence, Henri Matisse managed to overcome his recognizable style. Due to infirmity, he painted the mural while lying in bed, with the brush tied to a long bamboo pole. Consequently, the painting is crudely executed and the hand of Matisse is not evident.[14]
- In a rather different way, Marcel Duchamp's 'readymades' are also examples where artistic style has been eschewed. Duchamp simply selected items, such as a bottle rack or snow shovel from a hardware store and, sometimes with minor modification, presented them as art.[15]

125

- In the 1970s, Italian designer Riccardo Dalisi worked with
  street children who were thought to be unspoiled by cultural
  influences.[16] The spontaneous street designs of necessity are
  examples of artefacts that do not respond to the affectations
  commonly associated with styling.[17]

These are examples where contemporary preferences and expectations
are of little or no importance in the created work. They do not play
the styling game and consequently they are indifferent to the fleeting
inclinations so prevalent in current design practice.

Designer as artist

There has been much written in recent times about collaborative design
approaches, the need for greater consultation with users, the use of
focus groups and the role of designer as facilitator.[18] In professional
practice, these are undoubtedly useful techniques and can aid the
designer in understanding user needs and the requirements of product
production and marketing. Discussion and consultation are also
essential in furthering our understanding of sustainability and post-
industrial design. However, these approaches are not always useful
when attempting to reframe our notions of functional objects.

In our embrace of cooperative and consultative techniques, we must
not forget another, critically important part of creative studies. This is the
more solitary, contemplative approach that is removed from everyday
pressures, the particulars of user needs, and the more mundane 'real
world' practicalities. There is a need to think deeply about the nature of
objects and their potential relationships to people and the environment.
When, as individuals, we engage in this kind of private contemplation
during the creative practice of designing, new understandings about
functional objects can be forthcoming. It requires time, silence and
solitude. Like the act of artistic creation, this is a way of designing that
requires and commits the whole being of the designer. It is through
such commitment that, according to Buber, we can hope to realize a
relationship with things rather than merely an *experience of* them.[19]

It seems that this kind of design may be best explored within academia
– separated as it is from the pressures and pace of private sector
practice. There will be time later for dealing with the implications and
practicalities of implementation, and this is when a more consultative
approach again becomes useful.

126

Design as critique

Functional objects do not always have to be all that functional. They do not have to be efficient, effective, economic or even acceptable. Mass-produced products have to be all these things because there is so much capital invested in their production; they have to be profitable. Therefore, the tendency is to play safe and stay with the tried and true. Understandably, change tends to be incremental and cautious. There are, however, other ways of considering the creation of functional objects, and one of these that is especially useful is 'design as critique'. Design itself can be used as the vehicle of critique and as a means of communication for drawing attention to the inadequacies of current assumptions. This approach has been used to effect in the 'unreal products' created by a number of contemporary designers to challenge norms and expectations.[20] Critique is also implicit in Kawakami's light-hearted *Chindogu* designs, or 'unuseless inventions' where the apparent benefit offered by the object is outweighed by the inconvenience of actually using it.[21]

Acknowledging diversity

Sustainability not only implies diversity, it demands it, because sustainable approaches are so strongly associated with the specifics of place, region, climate and culture. Sustainable development is a kind of development that is rooted in and grows from these infinitely varied particularities.[22] This would seem to be at odds with the overwhelming 'globalization' of corporations, communications and manufacturing that has been occurring in recent times and the homogenization of culture and products that accompanies such a development. It would perhaps be understandable for those promoting 'localization' for sustainable development to become rather despondent, given the apparently unstoppable momentum of globalization. However, the indiscriminate ideological rhetoric associated with the term globalization is misleading.[23] Properly defined, the term refers to an intensification of global social interdependencies accompanied by a growing awareness of the relationships between the local and the international.[24] Hence, globalization can and should acknowledge the value of the local, the diverse and the particular. Unfortunately, as historian Eric Hobsbawm has pointed out, contemporary manifestations of globalization have three significantly unsustainable features. Firstly, globalization combined with market capitalism limits the ability of the state to act. With respect

127

to sustainable priorities, this limits a government's ability to serve as a moderating influence on corporate aims in the interests of the common good. Secondly, it turns the citizen, who has rights and responsibilities, into the consumer, who has only rights. Thirdly, it enables enormous wealth to become concentrated in the hands of the few, which results in burgeoning social inequalities.[25]

Alongside corporate aspirations of unfettered exchange across a worldwide free market, and the growth in power of transnational corporations that stand outside the democratic process, we have also seen a renewed emphasis on national sovereignty. For example, with the fall of the Berlin Wall many former Soviet states quickly asserted their independence. And in recent years the US has chosen to remain outside a number of international agreements and jurisdictions, such as the Kyoto Protocol on climate change and the International Criminal Court.[26] Thus, despite undoubted trends towards 'globalization', it would be too simplistic to presume that progress means an unswerving road to cultural homogeneity and a dissolution of regional and national diversity. The situation is infinitely more complex and dynamic. There are elements of globalization that actually nourish localization,[27] many indications of a growing emphasis on national statehood, and many examples of resistance to the global ambitions of private corporations.[28] Nevertheless, the overall effect of increasing globalization does appear to be counter-productive in terms of sustainable development.

For the designer, the assumptions of mass production for global markets – as the principal model for contemporary products – can and should be challenged. Potentially, designs can be developed that are adaptable to place, create good work at the local level, use local resources as well as mass-produced components, and are expressive of local cultural preferences and norms. It is the designer's challenge to envision functional objects that are technologically sophisticated and appropriate for modern, developed economies, and environmentally responsible, socially enriching and economically viable in their creation, use and disposal.

A recognition in design of the appropriate place of objects

Perhaps one of the most significant factors hindering the progress of sustainable development is simply that we may be giving far too much prominence to material goods. This does not just apply to the acquisition of goods, but also to their design. From certain perspectives, the emphasis placed on the detailed design and perfection of form of mundane objects can be seen as unwarranted, unseemly and misguided.

With the advance of digital communications technologies over the past few decades, we have moved from an economy based on producing and selling goods to one of producing and selling information, services and entertainment. The former was an industrial economy, the latter is a post-industrial economy or, as Gray has suggested, an entertainment economy,[29] in which the primary commodity is the information, service or entertainment being delivered, rather than the actual product that delivers it. Furthermore, the technology within the physical product is only relevant for the short period that it is useful – and the rapid pace of technological development soon renders it obsolete. It follows that the design and aesthetics of the physical product become rather inconsequential and beside the point. In fact, the product as a whole, including its engineering, becomes secondary – a mere conduit for the delivery of services. This is especially the case for electronic products such as televisions, music equipment and computers.

In addition, in his book *Secularization*, Edward Norman argues that we live in 'an age which sets welfare and material security as the objects which, it is supposed, describe the real purpose of life on earth'. [30] If this is the case, and there are many signs to support this assertion, then it is not surprising that the design of material goods has taken on a disproportionate importance. However, if such an emphasis is actually an impediment to individual growth, as I suggested in Chapter 7, then a quite different approach to the design of functional objects is called for.

Whether product design becomes less significant in a time of information and entertainment, or for more profound reasons, a question is raised about the appropriate emphasis to be given today to the design of a functional object. For both the above reasons, as well as for purposes of sustainable development, it would seem more fitting to acknowledge the relative unimportance and fleeting nature of products, and to develop a responsible approach to design that is in accord with this understanding. Perhaps it is time to view functional objects in far more humble terms – as simply basic useful things that are transient, unadorned, unambiguous and unimportant.

129

I have attempted to apply these ideas in the design of some illustrative electrical and electronic objects. These examples are created from reused mass-produced functional parts combined with rudimentary components made locally from readily available materials. An emphasis has been placed on *divesting* the objects of conventional notions of styling and 'good' design and, as in previous examples, on revealing the working components, rather than masking them with styled casings. Fastenings, materials, processes and finishes are all basic, familiar and easily replaceable. Compared with the examples discussed in Chapter 9, the approach here is even more rudimentary, with less concern about 'styling' and more emphasis on 'making do' with things that are available.

Divested Design 1 (Figure 11.3) is an ad hoc torch; the design has been stripped of considered or applied 'styling' and quickly fashioned from recycled parts mounted on unfinished plywood. Similarly, Divested Design 2 (Figure 11.4) is a remotely operated doorbell that has been rapidly made from scrap materials and electrical parts. Minimized Design (Figure 11.5) is another remotely operated doorbell but made entirely from functional components with no other materials or parts added. Having largely stripped these designs of aesthetic considerations, in Ensemble Design (Figure 11.6) I start to reintroduce some aesthetic concerns. This design is a CD player/radio that makes use of circuitry recovered from a discarded cassette player/radio and from a personal CD player – both products were still working but no longer fashionable in terms of their outer appearance. The components have been mounted on various recovered objects – a wooden crate, a set of TV legs, a piece of discarded wood and a bamboo cane. Ensemble Design brings together these disparate, discarded objects and gives them all a renewed useful life by re-contextualizing them as a new, functional object. More attention has been paid here to visual coherence through the application of finishes, so this design is somewhat more refined than the earlier examples although conceptually the same in terms of the design process and use of materials.

Figure 11.3
Divested Design 1:
Ad hoc torch

Figure 11.4
Divested Design 2:
Ad hoc remotely operated doorbell

Figure 11.5
Minimalized Design:
Remotely operated doorbell,
uses only functional parts

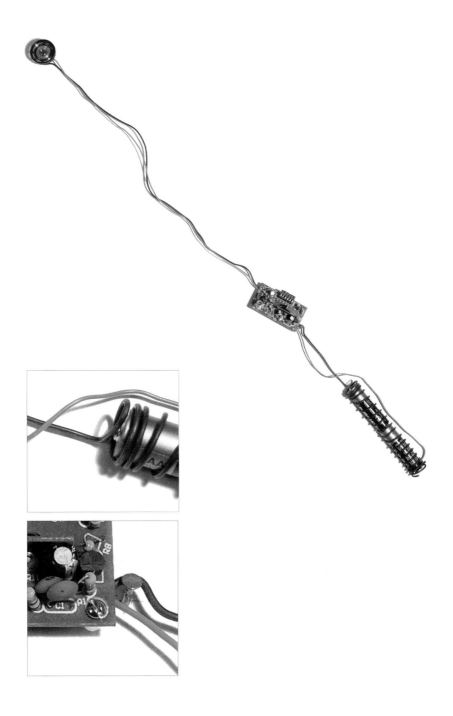

Figure 11.6
Ensemble Design:
Ad hoc CD player/radio

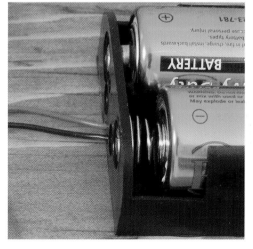

All these propositional designs incorporate the ideas discussed above:

- they make use of functional parts that are normally discarded because the casing of the product becomes old-fashioned;
- aesthetic interest is derived from the functional circuitry rather than the design of an outer casing;
- the processes used in their creation can all be achieved at the local level;
- they have been designed by 'direct deed' rather than mediated through drawings and models;
- they are made from materials that are locally available;
- they are not styled in a conventional sense and implicitly they challenge notions of outer, applied styling;
- they are designed as transient objects – to be used for a short period, after which components and fastenings can be readily disconnected and reused;
- they combine recovered, functional components with re-contextualized parts and, when brought together, both are given a new, useful life.

136

These examples illustrate the potential implications for product design of a number of critical aspects of sustainable development. These include the development of integrated scales of production to address socio-economic and environmental issues at the local level, and a rejection of design factors such as aesthetic perfection and fashionable styling that foster consumerism and waste. In these designs the working parts are revealed, the construction is explicit and the materials are familiar – they could be termed 'unmasked objects'.

In this chapter, I have proposed an aesthetic typology as a way of characterizing the aesthetic qualities of many contemporary consumer goods, and design traits associated with unsustainable practices. I have also suggested reframing design by considering a number of relevant topics. However, the real conclusions of this discussion are the propositional designs. These are not definitive designs, merely steps along the way to sustainable design. They are functional, electronic objects that have been stripped of conventional notions of 'good' design and the usual expectations of industrial design. I believe this eschewing of convention is a necessary step in the process of rebuilding our material culture for sustainable development. While these objects are, by the very nature of creative design, personal interpretations, they do serve to illustrate the potential implications of the discussion for the alignment of product design with sustainable principles. Functional objects tend to become less important and are defined in very basic ways. They are no longer objects of consequence – they are not trendy, stylish or compelling. Instead, they become explicitly transient and unadorned; they are no longer seductive 'objects of desire'. As such, they are perhaps instructive in demonstrating just how far we have to shift our ideas from our current ways of producing material culture if we are to seriously confront sustainable development in the spheres of product design and production.

137

12
TIME AND
DESIGN
crushed
before the
moth[1]

Sustainable development implies a kind of development that can continue over a prolonged period. Hence, time is an essential ingredient of our notion of sustainable development. In this chapter, I would like to consider our understandings of time and their relationship to sustainable product design.

Products are by their very materiality transient; their usefulness is, unavoidably, a function of time. They become obsolete for a variety of reasons, all of which help fix a product in a specific time frame, which is usually a relatively short period ranging from just a few minutes to perhaps a few decades (see Table 12.1). Products appear on the market, are used for a while and pass into history. And, while products have always come and gone, the last 50 years or so have witnessed a burgeoning in the rates of product-related waste – many so called 'consumer durables' have irresponsibly brief life spans, and product production has expanded enormously.[2] As I discussed in previous chapters, these developments have coincided with changes in societal values and beliefs. The past half-century, with the ascendancy of Postmodern thinking, has seen a falling away of traditional values and notions of truth, and the emergence of an increasingly relativistic outlook.[3] Older beliefs and certainties have become less secure, and a culture with greater doubt has developed.[4] Concurrently, education and work patterns have changed, with significant social effects. People have moved out of their communities to find work or to attend post-secondary education. Long-established continuities have become fractured and society has become more atomistic and individualistic.[5] These social and cultural transformations reflect changes in our understandings – changes that are intimately related to our notions of time and our attitudes to material culture. A reflection on how we think about time can be useful in revealing how we conceive and create our material world, and can lead to other ways of considering the design of functional objects. Here, I would like to consider two quite different conceptions of time, namely secular time and sacred time. A distinguishing feature of these two understandings is how we regard the

Table 12.1 **Factors contributing to product obsolescence**

Disposability	Products are explicitly designed to be short-lived and disposable for a variety of reasons – including financial, hygiene, safety etc. Examples include razor blades; packaging; paper cups, plates and cutlery; and medical supplies such as syringes, scalpel blades etc
Wear	Products wear out; this can be for a variety of reasons such as technological, for example disposable batteries. However, the life of a product is often prematurely curtailed because components are of poor quality and they are easily broken. Examples might include inexpensive music equipment, children's toys and low-quality appliances
Non-repairable	Many mass-produced products are designed in ways that make them difficult or not cost-effective to repair – inexpensive electrical and electronic products such as power tools and personal stereos are often less expensive to replace than to repair
Functional obsolescence	The function for which a product is intended is no longer required and the product has become redundant. For example, in some countries the number of people who smoke tobacco has reduced significantly in recent years – and so the requirement for tobacco-related paraphernalia has also been reduced – ashtrays for homes, restaurants and cars, cigarette cases, cigarette holders etc
Technological obsolescence	Technology is always developing and therefore old technologies are constantly being superseded – for examples phonograph cylinders were replaced by records which in turn were replaced by compact discs
Aesthetic obsolescence	A product's appearance becomes outmoded and, even though the product might still function perfectly well, it may be replaced because its outer appearance is no longer new and perfect, or because its 'look' is no longer fashionable

present. In secular time, the present is but a fleeting moment; in sacred time, it is eternally now.

Generally, we regard time today in terms of secular time – the time of duration; time that passes; the time of clocks, schedules and agendas. It is chronological, linear and unidirectional. We can imagine it as a line drawn from the dark mysteries of the past, progressing forward into the vast potentials of the future. On this timeline we place periods and incidents that we consider important – geological epochs, eras and episodes in human history and significant events. With clocks and calendars and timelines we categorize and order our lives, our thoughts and our knowledge. In this concept of time, the past is seen as something that is over and often of little consequence to everyday life or contemporary business.[6] Henry Ford summed up this view with his famous dictum, 'history is more or less bunk'.[7] But in secular time the present is also of little importance; it becomes reduced to a momentary occurrence – it has no duration, it is simply the ever-reducible instant between that which is over and that which is yet to come. And so we see that with exclusively secular, sequential notions of time, the past becomes largely irrelevant and the present is condensed to a brief moment. It is hardly surprising, then, that our society tends to place great emphasis on the future. We plan for the future and forecast future trends, we set our sights on achieving next year's performance targets, and developing the next generation of technologies. We hanker after the latest models and the most up-to-date fashions, we strive to be on the leading edge, and we fear being left behind. We can buy next year's model today, we can buy now and pay later – the future is here, as the advertisements so often tell us.

This view of time and our focus on the future are perhaps inevitable developments of the Modern Age. Over the course of the last 100 years, western societies have undergone vast expansions in industrialization and capitalist economics – expansions based on the idea of continuous growth. These changes have spurred developments in technology, promoted 'the new' and 'the latest', and escalated the production of increasingly short-lived products. In fact, they have helped promote all the criteria of product transience I have identified in Table 12.1. This system has created enormous advances, variety and benefits, but has also led to unparalleled rates of resource depletion and waste production, and significant social disparities. These are all logical

141

outcomes of our contemporary market system – and our notion of time is inextricably caught up in these developments.

Industrial design was born of this milieu. From its earliest days it was a discipline strongly connected to advertising and marketing[8] and its first practitioners were hired to give new looks to products to stimulate consumer interest.[9] In fact, the major contribution of industrial design has always been to define the outer appearance of products. While the inner workings, based on developing technologies, do change over time, outer casings can be defined more subjectively and can be updated much more rapidly, making the previous model seem old-fashioned and less desirable.[10] And so, while products are discarded for a variety of reasons, it is the industrial designer who, often intentionally, creates aesthetic obsolescence.

The aesthetics of a product can be very powerful because they are a key factor in creating an emotional tie with the object. Aesthetics can help transform a product from an uninteresting and unusable collection of functional components into a useful and attractive object that provides a meaningful benefit to people's lives. Unfortunately, in our contemporary market system, product aesthetics are often reduced to the superficial styling of an outer casing that gives the impression of newness and progress, even though the hidden, functional parts remain unchanged. We see these ever-shifting stylings in most consumer products; they do little to improve the usefulness or quality of our material culture, but they do stimulate consumerism.

Rapid changes in product appearance, intimately connected as they are to our production and economic systems, are a function of how we conceive our world; they reflect our ideas of progress, our values and our understandings of time. They tend to support the contention that our thoughts, and indeed our lives, are focused on the future and the next thing, and that we have reduced the present to a fleeting moment. But there is another way of understanding time, another way of conceiving past, present and future. Before our modern, secular, chronological time, there was a quite different perspective.

In a world dominated by chronological time, the word 'eternal' is generally taken to mean a very, very long time, but this is a misconception. Eternity is beyond time.[11] Eternity encompasses all time. It embraces the past, the present and the future. Eternity does not progress or have duration, it simply is. Eternity means the eternal now.

Wisdom teachings from many cultures have taught us to live in this idea of the 'now', the present moment, rather than dwelling on the past or worrying about the future. According to these teachings, it is only this present, enduring 'now' that is real and where we find meaning and fulfilment. 'Now' does not exist in time.

When chronological time comes together with the eternal now, a different understanding of time results, that of sacred time.[12] Sacred time is the cycle of time. It is characterized by the cycle of birth, growth, death and renewal. It is the unchanging cycle represented by the seasons of the year and the monastic day. It is the basis of all sacred calendars and it has been recognized in most cultures and traditions throughout the world.[13] It is this conception of time that is important for our understanding of sustainable design.

In contrast to the linear progression of chronological, secular time, sacred time presents us with a circular view of time, with repetitions and recurrences; it can be regarded as an endless repetition of eternities.[14] Sacred time acknowledges both the physical and the metaphysical, the body and the soul. Physical existence in chronological time is balanced with metaphysical or spiritual awareness that, in many traditions, has meaning and significance beyond time. The philosopher Jacob Needleman has explained that we can only understand the meaning of our lives by attempting to reconcile these two realities, what Kirkegaard expressed as the finite and the infinite, the temporal and the eternal.[15]

143

The essential point for the purpose of this discussion is that the secular, chronological aspects of life, which are so dominant in contemporary society, are utilitarian and find expression in the language of utility, whereas the sacred is expressed in terms of poetry and symbolism.[16] Consequently, if we wish to create a more meaningful and a more enduring material culture, one that not only mitigates the detrimental effects of our current methods, but is also a more complete articulation of human values, then traditional understandings of sacred time and the symbolic expressions that emerge from these understandings can provide us with clues of how we might proceed. A few examples of sacred symbolism will help to illustrate how these forms of expression weave together the physical world with spiritual understandings.

There is much symbolism in the design of a traditional Christian church. The entrance, generally found in the west side, symbolizes that a person is leaving the secular world and entering the sacred. Close to the entrance is the font, the place of baptism, representing the beginning of one's spiritual journey, which leads to the east. The journey to the east, the journey of one's life, leads to the altar, which is located in a physically and (symbolically) spiritually higher place at the east end of the church and represents the gateway to God.[17]

Medieval maps employ similar symbolism. The 13th century world map known as the Mappa Mundi, in Hereford, England, is a good example.[18] On this map, a line drawn in an easterly direction from the spiritual centre of the earth, represented by Jerusalem, leads to the Garden of Eden, beyond which lies God (i.e. east of Eden). Like the symbolism in a church, the journey to the east is, again, the journey towards spiritual truth. Unlike modern maps, which represent physical space at a particular moment, the Mappa Mundi represents both space and time.[19] It depicts the world in all time, from creation to the end of days.[20] It is a map that acknowledges both the physical and the spiritual, the secular and the sacred.

These dualities of the human condition are also evident in the Yin–Yang of eastern thought, and in the battlefield dialogue between Krishna and Arjuna in the Indian sacred text, the Bhagavad Gita.[21] And, in the book of Job, a line of which provides the title of this chapter, the moth symbolizes the passage of time.[22]

These brief examples offer a glimpse of the symbolism inherent to the world's sacred traditions. So why, we may well ask, is symbolism used in these traditions, and why is it relevant to our understandings of sustainable development? Symbolism is so prevalent in the religious and wisdom literature of the world because our apprehension of the eternal and the sacred defy direct description or depiction; instead, we can only inadequately allude to them. Today, living as we do in a more secular age, many of these symbolic meanings are lost on us and are of little general interest. Despite this, there remain traces of the sacred in our culture, and there are new expressions of the sacred and the metaphysical constantly being developed by contemporary thinkers and artists. This is inevitable because, even in an age that tends to reject formal religion, we still seek meaning in our lives and struggle with the same dualities that have preoccupied humankind for millennia. No matter how much we may have desacralized our culture, we never entirely eliminate religious-type behaviours. For example, we still give special significance, or what might be seen as quasi-religious status, to certain places and events – the place of our birth or particular locations from our childhood.[23] Visser has explained that the dining table represents a 'sacred' area in a house. It is a place where certain types of behaviour are expected and deemed appropriate. It is a place where cleanliness is very important and a place that must not be defiled. In the process of being laid for dinner, the dining table becomes ritually set apart; and the most formal dining table is one set with a white linen tablecloth, on to which the spotless cutlery and dishes are laid;[24] the white tablecloth defines a pure, inviolable 'sacred' space.

We see this idea of ritual separation, of setting things apart, in other contexts. The white wall of the gallery or museum is an unblemished area on which works of art are exhibited. The white gallery plinth, used to display sculptures, has a similar role. It designates a space that is set apart for an object deemed worthy of respect because of its beauty or its artistic contribution. Major exhibitions at the world's foremost galleries and museums acquire almost semi-religious status, drawing large crowds to view the works of art and to pay homage to the artists.

In recent times many artists have attempted to express ideas of the sacred, but in less traditional, often abstract forms. Kasimir Malevich was an early proponent of non-representational expressions of the metaphysical; his austere compositions, of which Black Square of 1913 is perhaps the best known, were intended to counteract more utilitarian forms of art that were representational. For Malevich, art transcended everyday life. The canvas represented sacred space, a space set apart,[25] and he regarded white as a mystic colour representing inner space. It has been suggested that his White on White painting of c.1918 was meant to convey something akin to enlightenment or a state of nirvana.[26] Similarly, Ben Nicholson seems to have been attempting to express metaphysical qualities in his White Relief paintings of the 1930s,[27] and the American abstract expressionist, Mark Rothko, was striving to create works that were symbolic of the eternal and the spiritual without being either denominational or representational.[28]

Today, when the grand narratives of western culture are considered by some as no longer credible, many Postmodern artists have ostensibly chosen to reject profundity and meaning in favour of surface, superficiality and distraction. Nevertheless, when it comes to exhibiting their work, many of these same artists still seek to separate their creations from the everyday, secular world – and they rely on

145

convention to create this 'quasi-sacred' distinction. Damien Hirst encases his suspended carcasses in pristine, white-bordered tanks, and Gavin Turk's works are presented in glass cabinets on white plinths or in white-bordered frames.[29] Also, despite the alleged rejection of traditional artistic concerns that sought meaning and depth, the struggle to convey ideas about the sacred remains a constant theme up to the present day. Chris Olifi's controversial painting *The Holy Virgin Mary*, 1996, which features balls of dung and shapes cut from pornographic photographs,[30] and Hirst's 2003 exhibition *Romance in the Age of Uncertainty*, which represented Jesus, the disciples and various martyrs in the form of filled glass cabinets and the encased heads of cows,[31] are but two examples.

This brief overview of two quite different ways of understanding time illustrates how the 'sacred' employs symbolic modes of expression to convey something of our higher or spiritual apprehensions. By contrast, the 'secular', concerned as it is with those things that are worldly and prosaic, is expressed through the utilitarian. If our endeavours are to be more meaningful and enduring, both these facets of human understanding have to be acknowledged. However, over the past century it is clear that in the field of product design and manufacturing the overwhelming emphasis has been on the utilitarian priorities of business expansion and economic growth. This lack of balance has resulted in the unprecedented levels of production and has contributed to our contemporary experiences of environmental and socio-cultural degradation.

All physical artefacts will sooner or later decay and be discarded, but their meaning and value can remain relevant by ensuring that they are founded on more holistic approaches that somehow bring together the utilitarian with the poetic and the symbolic. Of course, one could argue that this is precisely what industrial designers have always endeavoured to do – to combine utility with aesthetic sensitivity. But, it can also be argued that in contemporary product design, aesthetics, symbolism and poetry are merely exploited to meet the functional and commercial priorities of business. The purity of the aesthetic is cheapened, becoming a seductive and ultimately tawdry façade that belies, on the one hand, the scientific genius and technological brilliance of the modern product and, on the other, the ugly and damaging world of human exploitation and environmental violation that frequently accompanies its production.

146

The wonder of our modern world is not that we can purchase a music system in hi-tech style, retro style or wood veneer but that we can purchase such an extraordinary thing as a music system at all. Choices of styles are not only trivial compared to the marvel of the product itself, they also detract and distract one from the beauty, ingenuity and sheer inventiveness (and also from the true costs) of manufactured products. This devaluing of our material world is only too evident today. The eye that has seen too much becomes the tired, bored and inattentive Postmodern eye, the cynical, discontented eye that takes momentary interest in the idea of being able to own a powerful, multimedia computer in strawberry, blueberry or lime, but fails to see the wonder in being able to own a computer. This state of affairs would seem to call for a fundamental reassessment of product design. It suggests a direction forward that would seek to re-enchant the world of our material productions – rather than continuing to offer irrelevant choice to a distracted eye that is already saturated with excess. At the same time, it suggests a direction that would responsibly acknowledge the costs of our endeavours and the transient nature of many of our solutions. And it seems that an appreciation of 'sacred time' and 'sacred space', terms that encapsulate the mystery and wonder of life, the poetic and the spiritual, and so many things that are omitted from our efficient, rationalized, business world, would be the way to do this – a way of counterbalancing and enriching our industrial, economic and utilitarian prowess.

However, while efforts can be made to pursue such a direction, any attempt to fully integrate the sacred with the secular might be misplaced. Eliade has explained that there exists an unbreachable barrier between the sacred and the profane, describing the division as an abyss; and Malevich held that the scientific, technological and utilitarian were totally different from, and irreconcilable with, artistic endeavour. Whether these two expressions of human experience are quite so divided and incompatible is, of course, a matter of debate. Nevertheless, our modern attempts to combine them within the design of manufactured products would suggest that an effective integration remains problematic. The many environmental and socio-cultural consequences of our production activities make this only too clear.

In order to take the ideas discussed here as a point of departure for the development of products, it will be useful to reiterate some of the main points:

- Secular time is chronological and temporal, it is congruent with particular understandings of progress, it emphasizes the future, and its expressions are utilitarian.
- Sacred time concerns the eternal, recurrences and the present, and its modes of expression are symbolic.
- Traces of the sacred are never completely eliminated even in ostensibly secular settings.
- In western societies, white is a common convention used to indicate a sacred or quasi-sacred space – a space set apart.
- The integration of sacred, artistic and poetic expressions with the secular, utilitarian and temporal appears to be problematic.

It is now necessary to illustrate how these considerations can affect our approaches to the design of functional objects. I have made some attempts to do this, and the resulting propositional designs are presented in the next chapter, together with further thoughts that inform the design process.

13
CREATING OBJECTS IN A SATURATED CULTURE after the endgame

> Use your head, can't you, use your head. You're on earth, there's no cure for that!... But what in God's name do you imagine? That the earth will awake in the spring? That the rivers and seas will run with fish again?
>
> (*Endgame*, Samuel Beckett[1])

We live in a time of inundation – of images, options, information and products. Endless choices stream before our eyes, vying for our attention and our money, see Figure 13.1. Such over-stimulation can engender numbness, passivity and perhaps disillusionment or cynicism; it certainly raises questions about purpose and values. In a culture where anything and everything is possible, and where each successive novelty eventually commits the same 'crime' of familiarity, then the search for the next thing becomes the raison d'être. The stimulant for this is, of course, the economic aspiration. However, the process has reached a point where the fundamental objective seems to have been lost. The creation of functional objects has become so subsumed by the market system and the urge to profit that product permutations have become transparently pointless. We can maintain this status quo and continue to play the game, but the moves are infinite – it has become a game without meaning, a perpetual endgame.

> **This debilitating dream of a status quo is the symptom of a society which has come to the end of its development.** (Alexander Solzenitsyn[2])

There are alternatives to the mass-production, mass-culture model that has dominated recent decades. Some of these, such as craft design and folk art, have been around for centuries – but they neither threaten, nor attempt to compete with, mass production. Others, such as eco-products and 'sustainable' products are more recent attempts to lessen the harmful consequences of contemporary manufacturing. However, whether produced for global distribution or as a craft product for local markets, whether conventional or 'green', whether highly pragmatic or more decorative, all contemporary products tend to conform to the same conceptual understanding of 'functional object'.

150

Figure 13.1
**Roadside advertising
signs, Canada**

To change the game we must try to conceive of functional objects differently. Some of my own initial attempts to do this have been included in previous chapters. These exploratory designs were not created to be competitive, finished products, but merely as studies that grope for an alternative way forward which embraces various aspects of sustainable thinking. It is necessary to develop such alternatives, not for the sake of originality or novelty, but in an attempt to instil new meaning to a critical area of human endeavour that, in so many ways, has become directionless and superficial. Design work conducted within academia, protected as it is from the economic pressures of the so-called 'real world', is particularly well positioned to explore such alternatives. This is both the privilege and the responsibility of the academy.

The direction I would like to suggest in this chapter is a result of reflecting on several years of this experimental or 'academic' design work. As I noted in Chapter 9, the initial design experiments were attempts to give physical expression to ideas that marry product design with sustainable principles.[3] The process of development comprised many small, individual design projects and was, itself, a design process. As with any effective design project, the outcome was not embedded in the intention and was thus not predictable. Hence, the uncertain nature of the approach, which is a key aspect of creative design, allows the possibility of new directions and new insights to be generated through engaging in the process of 'doing'.

151

The design examples presented in this chapter build on these earlier experiments as well as on the discussion about time and design in the previous chapter. They illustrate an approach which reverses conventional design hierarchies in order to stabilize form and moderate change, but which still embraces progress. Consequently, a way of defining functional objects is suggested that provides an alternative to the barrage of often trivial and unnecessary permutations that comprise much contemporary product design. The continuing focus of the work is localization and electronic products – using new or reused circuitry in combination with locally made parts and local assembly. Because the construction of conventional product enclosures for a variety of recovered electronics and for production in small quantities at the local level is problematic and uncompetitive compared with mass production, an earlier series of designs explored the nature of enclosure

Note:
Clockwise from top left: Cable Radio, Tin Radio, Net Radio, Solar Calculator, Wallphone, Hermit Radio.

Figure 13.2
Explorations of enclosure and exposure in electronic products

and exposure of the electronic parts, see Figure 13.2, with the aim of reducing both the complexity and time of local manufacture. This led to a study prototype that consisted of unadorned electronic components mounted on recycled board, see Figure 13.3. This design prompted a reconsideration of the aims of product design and its potential links with sustainability and localization, and it provides the basis for the design explorations presented here.

The experimental designs shown in Figures 13.2 and 13.3 illustrate that for an electronic circuit, such as a radio circuit, the forms of expression given to the product can be highly diverse, from the conventional enclosing case to the circuitry being revealed and providing aesthetic interest. In general, however, aesthetic variations are usually limited to what might be referred to as the non-functioning or non-essential components, while commonality lies in the circuitry, or functioning components, at least until a particular technology is superseded. And, as I suggested in the previous chapter, the purview of the industrial designer is to define the particular, but highly variable forms of expression of the non-functioning parts, while the engineer or scientist develops the essential functionality. Admittedly this is something of a generalization, but the history of industrial design shows it to be broadly true, and perhaps especially in the fields of electrical and electronic products. An oft-cited example of the work of the designer, from the time when industrial design was emerging as a distinct discipline, is the Gestetner duplicating machine. This product was restyled in the early 1930s by Raymond Loewy, the so-called father of industrial design.[4] Loewy's contribution radically changed the outer appearance of the product but the functioning parts remained the same as those in the original version. Adrian Forty has said, 'Loewy described the design as a "face-lift" job, in which he arrived at "a form which enclosed everything that could be enclosed"'.[5] Industrial design has generally continued in this vein. Although new technologies, techniques and areas such as ergonomics have expanded the discipline, the designer still creates aesthetically pleasing enclosures for components that, if revealed, might be considered unattractive, susceptible to damage or unsafe. And, as I have said previously, this outer casing has become a tool for boosting consumerism.[6] This continues to be the attitude within the product design world; for example, the following is taken from a recent report of the Industrial Designers Society of America:

> **What inspires consumers to spend money in a
> slow economy?**
> **Frequently, it's a hot, new, attention-grabbing design
> that creates an emotional 'Gotta Have It!' response.
> Design has always been one of the most compelling
> reasons why consumers buy a product, but never more
> so than today.**[7]

With this in mind, the product can be divided into two fairly distinct categories of components, the *dominant components* that are essential to the functionality of the product and the *subordinate components* that enable the dominant components to be arranged and presented in a suitable form for use. While there might be considerable overlap between the two, the dominant components are frequently based on engineering or scientific principles and, except for a technological advance, are largely defined and fixed for a given purpose. The subordinate components can be defined more subjectively; they are infinitely variable and are usually considered in terms of a product envelope, see Figure 13.4a, or as an aesthetically pleasing façade, see Figure 13.4b. The variables for defining these subordinate components include form, colour, texture, detailing and a host of potentially semi-useful variables that might be termed 'product features'. The aim of creating so many variations is often simply to stimulate consumption through the continuous production of difference and novelty.

> **the avant garde has fallen away for, as in fashion,
> there is an expectation of novelty but no longer of
> development.** (Julian Stallabrass[8])

We can Illustrate the potential for creating a large number of permutations of essentially the same product by considering just three variables related to the definition of the subordinate components: form, colour and texture. Five discrete forms allow five different product expressions. If we add five colours to these five forms there will be 25 different combinations of form and colour. And if we add five textures, there will be 125 different combinations. The more forms, colours, textures and other variables we introduce, the more product permutations can be generated. In fact, the product possibilities rise exponentially with the increase in variables, see Figure 13.5. Thus, a virtually infinite variety of expressions is possible for any given product. A perusal of current MP3 players, cell phones or a host of other

Figure 13.3
Board Radio:
Unadorned, exposed circuitry mounted on a board

contemporary products will demonstrate our propensity for producing vast quantities of slightly different versions of essentially the same thing. But for our activities to be meaningful, especially when we are all too cognizant of the harmful consequences, we have to question the purpose of generating such large quantities of virtually identical products.

If the product is functional, aesthetically pleasing and affordable, there would seem little point in constantly creating marginally different versions. The usual argument is that it increases consumer choice. This line of reasoning, however, is seriously flawed. The constant production of slightly different models of a product, combined with the use of aggressive marketing strategies, further stimulates already soaring consumerism, and hence spiralling environmental and resource degradation. The argument has little to do with ideas that are concerned with the creation of a meaningful material culture and more to do with motives related to finance and profit. The endless generation of similar products reflects a lack of creative thinking with respect to economic welfare, a lack of meaningful purpose, and a stagnation of ideas. It reveals that we have reached an endgame where the moves are infinite but they are all without purpose, like a chess game where the only pieces left on the board are the two kings – each player can keep moving but the game has become pointless. Moreover, the structural system of mass manufacturing and distribution tends to restrict the gains of the enterprise to a relatively small number of increasingly wealthy people and corporations, while vast numbers of ordinary workers are poorly compensated and often exploited.[9] As Nichols remarked over 20 years ago in his discussion of Latin America, and well before the implementation of the North American Free Trade Agreement, which has exacerbated inequities,[10] 'The world of the multinationals is indeed the world of the poor.'[11] For sustainability, a more balanced approach is needed.

> **What I ask of a painting is that is should look like paint.**
> (Maurice Denis[12])

These issues are large and complex and any solutions lie well beyond the scope and expertise of any one discipline. Even so, the designer can and should attempt to contribute to positive change. The design academic has a particular responsibility to challenge the status quo, to generate ideas, stimulate debate and suggest potential alternative avenues. The exploration of enclosure and exposure that I have discussed here is one attempt to do this *through the activity of designing itself*. It led to the following thoughts:

- The product can be considered as comprising dominant and subordinate components.
- A primary concern for the industrial designer is the definition of the subordinate components.
- The design of these components, as enclosure or façade, is infinitely variable.
- The constant redesign of the subordinate components stimulates consumerism but can also contribute to effects that are detrimental to environmental stewardship, social justice and the creation of a meaningful material culture.

156

I have attempted to address these points via the design process but, as in previous exercises, in a manner that is provisional – the aim is not to develop a viable product. Instead, the intention is simply to explore alternative possibilities for designing functional objects by acknowledging the apparent conflicts between conventional understandings of industrial design and the priorities of sustainability. It is in the appearance or façade of a product where a particular difficulty seems to exist, at least as far as industrial design is concerned, and so this is the focus of the design exploration.

For the purpose of the exercise, the conventional way of thinking about the subordinate components can be consciously reversed.

a: Circuitry and Enclosure

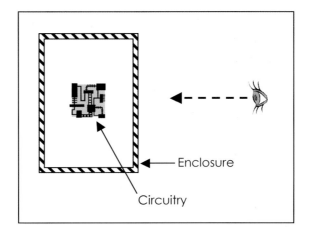

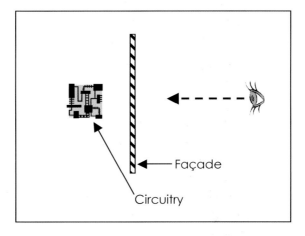

Figure 13.4a
Circuitry and enclosure

Figure 13.4b
Circuitry and façade

Figure 13.5
**Product permutations as a
function of design variables**

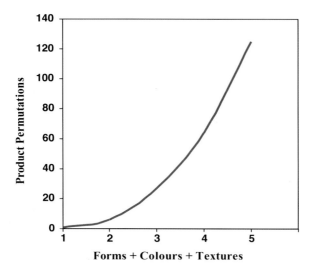

Forms + Colours + Textures

They can be standardized and stabilized in terms of form, colour and texture. Instead of considering them at the forefront, as a façade or intermediary between the user and the functional components where aesthetic acceptability, fashionable style and visual interest are important, they can be placed in the background and given a subsidiary and unadorned role as a support for the functional components, see Figure 13.6. The aim is to bring the dominant components to the fore by defining the subordinate components as an armature or chassis that provides a firm base on which to hold and reveal the functioning parts. Any aesthetic interest will then reside in the functioning parts and their juxtapositions, rather than in a consciously designed enclosure, which becomes so quickly outdated. In other words, the subordinate components must be the polar opposite of that seen in conventional product design; they must be as subdued and retiring as possible – as a necessary but unremarkable underlay. Essentially, this constitutes a reversal in component hierarchy compared with that evident in most products; this reversal is really a design device – used here to break with conventional ways of defining products. A comparison of the conventional and converse ways of thinking about the subordinate components is included in Table 13.1.

Even when the subordinate components are framed in this way, they still have to be defined in terms of materials, form, colour and texture. To provide a basis for design exploration, we can draw on examples from other contexts where a conscious intention has been to create something to be low-key, subordinate and in the background. It is here that the previous discussion about time and symbolism (Chapter 12) provides a clue. The symbolically sacred space of the white tablecloth creates a separate, inviolable area for the functional implements and the task of eating. Similarly, the white-walled gallery offers a neutral space for viewing objects of aesthetic interest and value; the absence of distracting details allows the focus to remain on the exhibited works. Similarly, the plinth within the gallery is an object used to display other objects. Again, the focus remains on the exhibited artefact, and we are so familiar with this way of displaying things that we do not read the plinth as part of the object of interest. These precedents provide a basis for considering the design of the subordinate components. The subordinate components can be standardized and consciously designed to be featureless, but even so, this does not imply a bland, unchanging object. Aesthetic interest can be created through the exposure and arrangement of the functional components themselves. Moreover, revealing these essential workings allows the user to gain a greater sense of the product's utility, not to mention its ingenuity.

159

Change can still occur over time, but it will be purposeful, based on technological development. This is often relatively slow compared to the market-led style changes prevalent today. Such technological development usually invokes a change in the form of the functioning parts, which in turn will affect the appearance of the product. Hence, aesthetic change becomes rooted in the nature of the object itself, rather than being a function of fashion or styling. Naturally, this slowing of change would also affect, and potentially reduce, the desire to replace the object – because it would no longer be susceptible to the vagaries of fashion.

This conceptual approach can contribute to rebalancing the three priorities of sustainable development – economics, environment and ethics. It is, however, antithetical to our current business and political directions and the irrational mantra of continual expansion and growth. Nevertheless, in a time where continuation of the present model seems increasingly destructive and pointless, there is an urgent need to develop different approaches. Business as usual is no longer a viable option.

Some initial examples based on these ideas are shown in Figures 13.7 – 13.10. These are fully functioning prototypes of electronic clocks and radios, but they do not conform to the way products are conventionally designed. In these examples, the functioning components are brought to the foreground, while those parts needed to hold them in place are transferred to the background and defined as a plain, white, rectangle (a white canvas) – an archetypal form based in cultural convention. Although its specific dimensions and materials may vary, the basic form can remain virtually the same even though the functional parts and technologies may change. The form can also remain the same for objects of differing functions and, depending on the use, it

can be wall-mounted or placed on a tabletop or on the floor. Hence, for the subordinate components, *form becomes largely independent of function*. The white rectangle simply serves as an armature or underlay for mounting and arranging the components so they can be acknowledged and used. The *symbolic* and the *utilitarian*, discussed in the previous chapter, come together – they are both present, but they are not integrated; the reader will recall that both Eliade and Malevich suggested that full integration is not possible. Instead, in these illustrative designs, they exist side-by-side, tenuously attached, mutually dependent, and yet separate.

This conceptual direction raises a number of issues about design for sustainability. It is an attempt to slow the unnecessary inundation of trivial change, to quieten the busy-ness and provide respite to the onslaught of visual clutter. It does not prevent change, but attempts to constrain it to that which is purposeful rather than simply a tool for stimulating consumerism. The 'white rectangle' contributes to product longevity by establishing an unembellished form that is removed from, or indifferent to, particular and ever-evolving technologies. In this sense it is symbolic, a signifier of stability and constancy, which serves as an

Figure 13.6
Reversal of convention:
From façade to chassis

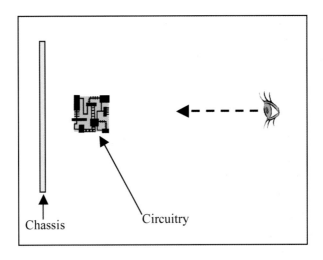

Table 13.1 Conventional and converse understandings
of the subordinate components of a product

	Conventional	Converse
Form	Variable	Stable
Colour	Variable	Stable
Texture	Variable	Stable
Details	Variable	Absent
Features	Variable	Absent
Concept	Forefront	Background
	Intermediary	Support
	Façade	Chassis
	Conspicuous	Subdued
	Obscures	Reveals
	Enticing	Plain
	Changing	Constant

impediment to the progress of relativistic but meaningless variation. It is the 'mystic white' of Malevich, the sacrosanct but featureless ground of the formal dining table or the gallery wall.

Furthermore, it provides a format for products in which the subordinate components can be created by mass-manufacturing techniques, batch production on a regional level or in small numbers in a local workshop. Hence, it enables product assembly and some component manufacture to occur across various scales, including the small scale, thus contributing to localization. This is an important aspect of moving towards more sustainable approaches, but one that can be adopted differentially and incrementally.

From the user's point of view, it provides a design approach that supports product comprehension, maintenance and repair by revealing the functioning parts and is less susceptible to change. This is intended to engender a greater sense of calm, to allow one to be 'at ease' with one's material environment; things are often less intimidating when they are more fully understood and when one has an opportunity to intervene or participate.

162

Finally, the approach raises interesting issues about the contribution of the product designer to the progress of sustainable development. Consistency in the definition of products and among different types of products might suggest that the designer has little or no contribution to make, but this is not the case. Consistency and repetition in the 'underlay' of a product by no means hamper creativity. There are precedents for this kind of stabilizing approach in other creative fields. For example, continuities and repetitions characterize the musical works of the contemporary American composer Philip Glass;[13] repeated themes and rhythms provide the foundation of the work, which are then overlaid with melodies, variations and lyrical pieces. And the Estonian composer Arvo Pärt has formalized a principle which he has termed *tintinnabuli* in which he explores the diversity of musical possibilities within a single note.[14]

The white canvas designs presented here represent a conscious attempt to move away from enclosure and façade to explore a different approach to product design and product aesthetics in order to highlight other priorities. It is obviously limited in its application, but its primary purpose is to provide a basis for reflection, for challenging some questionable aspects of current design practice and for stimulating

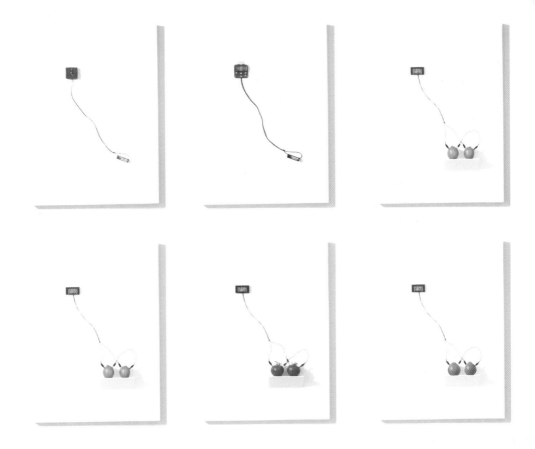

Figure 13.7
Three White Canvas Clocks:
*Analogue, digital and digital powered
by fruit 'battery'*

Figure 13.8
**Three White Canvas Clocks with
'batteries' of lime, tomato and orange**

*Dimensions of each clock
830mm × 600mm*

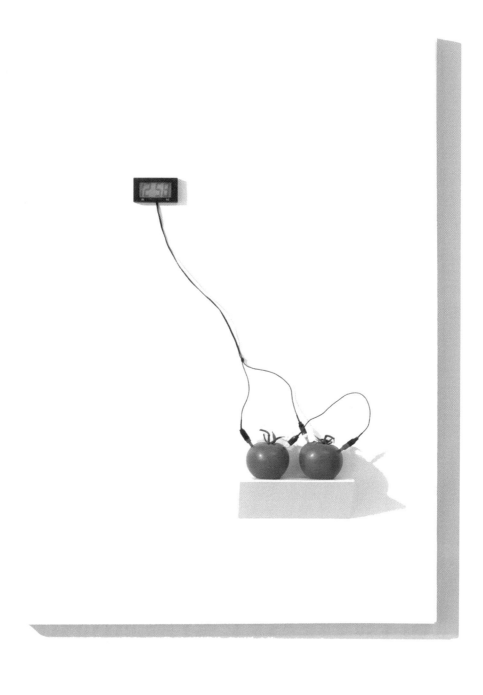

Figure 13.9
White Canvas Clock with tomato 'battery'

Figure 13.10
AM Radio,
340mm × 1620mm

further debate. So much contemporary industrial design is aimed at capturing market share by giving new styles to conventional products. While this may feed consumerism and can be seen as a valuable contribution to business, sustainability demands a different emphasis – and suggests a quite different design contribution. To be meaningful and thus to be of value, our activities have to respond to the critical issues of our time. Today we seem to have reached saturation point in terms of product variations, production and marketing, and the environmental and social consequences are now only too evident. We have reached the endgame, and after the endgame we have to start anew.

14

EPHEMERAL OBJECTS FOR SUSTAINABILITY

light touch

It is all too easy to distance ourselves from the effects of our decisions and our actions when design and manufacturing are carried out within a globalized system. When head offices are located in North American or European cities but resources are extracted, processed, formed and assembled 'somewhere else', decision makers inevitably lack a full appreciation of the consequences of their actions. Within this system, information becomes filtered down to the essential but abstracted data of production performance, unit costs and profits. A more holistic understanding of the meaning of decisions and their impacts is lacking because there is little direct connection with people and place.

This creates a world of mediated experiences (see Chapter 11) and produces a system that is increasingly divorced from the realities of people's lives and the realities of environmental devastation. It is a model of business, production and mass consumerism that exploits both people and nature.[1] These are the attitudes of convention that, according to McGrath, have been especially prevalent in western society since the time of the Enlightenment.[2] Consequently, even though many companies now espouse a commitment to sustainable development, they are often unable or unwilling to address the fundamental changes it demands. It is not uncommon to encounter complacency, indifference or even hostility, accompanied by the familiar arguments that eschew moral culpability. Rationalizations such as 'if we don't do it someone else will', or 'we have to do things this way to maintain our competitive advantage' all serve to justify an unsustainable and frequently unethical system.[3]

A significant problem in today's approaches to business is this notion of mediated experience, which leads to objectification. It creates a one-sided relationship that uses and discards at will. People become diminished and dehumanized, seen only as functional and expendable 'labour' rather than as persons,[4] and the natural environment, including animal life, becomes a resource, described in terms of tonnage or processed product. But a philosophy of sustainable design cannot be reconciled with objectification and exploitation; it has to be based on far more respectful, responsible and reciprocal relationships with people and the natural world. It requires that people are not seen merely as a *means* – an expense on the budget sheet to be 'downsized'. Such thinking fails to recognize the intrinsic value and welfare of the people involved and, ultimately, robs us of our own humanity. The same can be said of the planet itself, which behaves, in effect, as a living system[5] upon which we are dependent. If, in our business practices, we are to cultivate a more sustainable relationship with the world, then we must develop attitudes, and thence approaches that give greater emphasis to direct engagement and that recognize the inadequacies of the mediated experience.

As I briefly discussed in Chapter 11, Buber describes the mediated experience as the product of an 'I–It' attitude, where things and people are the objects of our attention; that is, they become objectified.[6] By contrast, the 'I–You' attitude has no object. The 'I' here stands *in relation to* the other. 'I–You' refers to a relationship in which people and the world are not experienced through concepts, information, facts and figures, but are encountered directly. This notion is perhaps best illustrated through some of our relationships with other people, and especially a loving relationship where there is a mutual and reciprocal encounter. For example, parents do not love their children for any particular reason – because of their smile or the colour of their

168

hair or because they do well in school – they love them irrespective of particulars, they love them in toto. The 'I–You' relationship is not dependent on particulars; it is free of specific content.[7] Papanek describes the designs of the Inuit of Northern Canada in somewhat similar terms where, traditionally, a product of art or design is seen as a transitory act or *relationship* rather than as a possession.[8]

Progress towards sustainability demands, more than anything, a transformation of attitude, and Buber's work suggests that this change should be away from an *experience of* and towards a *relationship with*. This implies a substantial shift in the way we conceive of functional objects. Today, we tend to see our material culture as property and goods that are distinct, separate and owned. However, when the world is understood as a living system with which we have a reciprocal relationship, our material culture can be better understood as a concentration of resources that achieve a desired benefit for a relatively short time. This benefit and particular accumulation of resources will, inevitably, cease to be useful. In the majority of cases, this will occur rather quickly, at which time the constituents will need to be redistributed into new applications or dispersed back into the environment. From this perspective, to continue extracting vast quantities of virgin resources, while concurrently dumping thousands of tons of waste products into landfills is clearly profligate, if not abusive. A more considerate, reciprocal attitude would suggest that the resources we take should be minimized, and then used and reused wisely for as long as possible through a continued refashioning into new functional concentrations. To design such objects requires a responsible acknowledgement of their transience, and an approach that facilitates the eventual reapplication of their constituent parts, or their re-integration into the world. Thus, a critical aspect of sustainable design is the notion of an *acknowledged ephemerality*.

169

This raises two important issues in relation to design and sustainability. Firstly, it points to the importance of *direct encounter* in the creation of material goods, and secondly, there is the need to properly recognize the *transience* of products and to incorporate this recognition in our conceptual understandings of functional objects. Before discussing the implications of these two conclusions, I would like to explore in a little more detail the problems of permanence in our current approaches to product design.

Even though the useful life of most objects is quite short, especially those based on rapidly developing technologies, they are conceived as permanent in terms of their design and materials. Hence, there is a disjuncture between the period of anticipated usefulness and the period that the object actually exists. In the case of a disposable polystyrene cup, its usefulness is a few minutes, for an electronic gadget it may be a few years, but in both cases, the constituent parts could last for centuries in a landfill and have no further useful purpose. This inconsistency is a function of the 'I–It' attitude and the mediated experience, and it raises a number of concerns for the designer. Designing products in this paradoxical manner tends to reveal a certain prioritizing of profit over accountability, a lack of concern with long-term impacts, and a view that the natural environment will continue to yield resources and absorb waste. More specific design issues include the widely recognized fact that when a variety of components of different materials are fixed together with adhesives, solders and other permanent or semi-permanent fastenings, as they are in many current products, then repair or the reuse of parts or the recycling of materials becomes highly problematic, often making disposal the only economically feasible route. And when the product casing has a multitude of intricate attachment points to hold the internal components in position, then a simple replacement to update the appearance is precluded by design.

These problems are now generally acknowledged by those concerned about sustainable product design. However, there is another factor that is not so well recognized, but which is central to the discussion. If we embark on a design project assuming our design work is going to be long-lasting and significant, then our decisions will reflect that assumption – the product will be conceived as a permanent addition to the material environment. It is this assumption that locks product design into a conceptual framework of unsustainability. Functional benefit is manifested as a self-contained, physical object, rather than as a *temporary convergence of requisite elements*.

The temporary object is, in fact, completely consistent with current business norms. Consumer capitalism actually abhors products that possess enduring usefulness and value. On the contrary, it demands products that are short-lived so that newer models can be sold, thus driving the market. Without this kind of product replacement through consumerism, our economic system would simply collapse.

For the purposes of this present discussion, we can leave aside the more philosophical arguments against this emphasis on consumerism, which I have discussed in previous chapters. The concern here is the need to develop a design approach that acknowledges the transience of products, not just in their usefulness but also in their physical manifestation, and to achieve this in a manner that is in accord with sustainable principles.

Industrial design is typically pursued through sketches, CAD illustrations and models, technical drawings and physical models. These methods tend to distance the designer from a deeper physical encounter with the material world and a more thorough appreciation of three-dimensional space, the form of objects and their existence within the larger environment. In other words, they emphasize the mediated experience; they are the techniques of visualization rather than actualization. To overcome this, a different working method is required, one that places greater emphasis on the tangible. Designs that incorporate pre-existing objects strongly indicate this kind of approach. For example, the Mozzkito lamp by Maurer makes use of a tea infuser,[9] a seating design by Madden uses old telephone directories,[10] and a birdfeeder by Wanders is created from a dinner plate and recycled plastic.[11]

171

To reinforce the nature of a more direct working method it will be useful at this point to change the discussion from the impersonal 'it' to the personal 'I', thus allowing the designer's *encounter with* design to become more explicit. I have therefore written the following section as a personal exploration of the two main areas of interest – the notion of the ephemeral functional object and its manifestation through direct encounter. I should clarify one point. The term 'ephemeral design' is sometimes used to refer to the products of the graphic designer – posters and labels, business cards and letterhead, and the paper-based ephemera of daily life. This is not what I mean when I refer to ephemeral objects. I am using the term to indicate both the ephemeral use of the object and its ephemeral existence as an object in this particular functional concentration of elements – it can be created from lasting materials as long as these can be re-integrated back into the world with little adverse effect when their use here is over.

In an attempt to implement these ideas, I embark upon the task of designing a functional object. In this transmutation from theory to artefact, I want to draw upon the things around me as much as possible, to make use of things that already exist — rather than conceiving of, defining and creating new objects from raw materials. This may not always be possible, but with all the goods and discarded products that surround us, I feel it would be extravagant and antithetical to generate more, especially because their usefulness will be short-lived. So my intention is to design an artefact that makes as much use as possible of existing items — by configuring them in new ways and in a new context — and which, for a while, will serve a utilitarian purpose as well as being of aesthetic interest. The things we create do not last, so this design, also, will not last. To think otherwise would be a conceit. When we have no further use for this design, it must be able to melt back into the built or natural environment with little or no trace.

Furthermore, the artefact must illustrate the philosophy of sustainable design that I have been exploring. It must be achieved without mediation, drawings, plans or models, but rather through my direct engagement with the items I bring together. And it must be achievable at the local level because this, too, is a part of sustainability[12] — but this need hardly be said because the working approach ensures that this will be an inherent part of the process. I will draw upon pre-existing mass-produced elements as well as simple parts that can be readily fashioned from discarded items. The artefact does not have to be complex or make use of the latest technologies. The task will be made easier by choosing a simple product to illustrate the idea; more complex examples can be explored later, once the approach is better understood.

And so I look around me, at my immediate environment. There are products in the home — some that we use every day and others that are rarely used. There are garbage bins with things we throw away, and a garage full of tools, and leftover timber and screws and glues and saved junk. There are charity stores selling sad-looking, out-of-date products, and, of course, there are stores selling new products. This is the arena from which I can draw to design an ephemeral artefact through direct encounter.

The process begins by looking. Looking around. Thinking. Making connections. I pull things from cupboards, put them next to each other, on top of each other. I try odd combinations, silly combinations — I play — searching for an idea that begins to gel and starts to articulate through form the thoughts about sustainable design that I'm striving to illustrate. I gather, gauge, combine – there is progress and doubt – but slowly a design begins to fall into place. But even when the intention and the concept become more distinct, the process continues to be difficult up to the end, to the point of completion – the final design depends on the details. As with the general concept, these details cannot be created from scratch, they cannot be an exclusive product of my imagination or my wishes. Instead, they are dependent on what already exists in the world around me – they are determined in part by the existing conditions. This, I feel, is appropriate to the nature of the exercise – the design process begins to seem more like a reciprocal relationship with the world – of acting and reacting, doing and responding through a direct, immersed engagement with the physical world. Key to this type of creative process is 'a feel for the work', it is about awareness, receptiveness and sensitivity and it is only possible through this kind of direct engagement.

Several functional objects were created by this process, and which, with varying degrees of success, begin to articulate this notion of the ephemeral object.

Two simple examples are the Potato Candlestick, Figure 14.1, and the Apple Candlestick, Figure 14.2. Conceived as one-time-use items, they can be assembled quickly from common items found in the home, used, then disassembled. The forks can be returned to the cutlery draw and the fruit or vegetables placed in the compost. Thus, there will be no evidence that the candlesticks ever existed – they have no lasting impact.

The radio design, Figure 14.3, combines a mass-produced circuit with common household items that are typically discarded – zip-lock bags and a small sweet tin. These are composed within a frame of white canvas. This enables the use of both form and space in a figure–ground relationship while simultaneously re-contextualizing familiar items so that they can be appreciated in a new way, as part of a new whole. The use of the white canvas builds on the earlier work that explored its use in conjunction with raw components (Chapter 13). Here, however, the components are once again enclosed and protected.

173

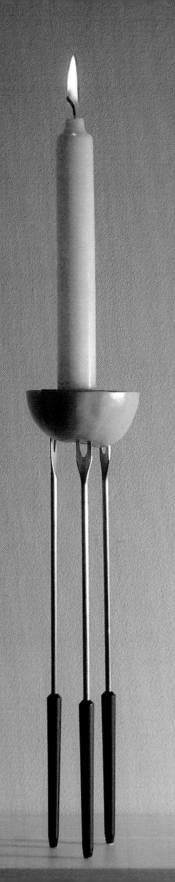

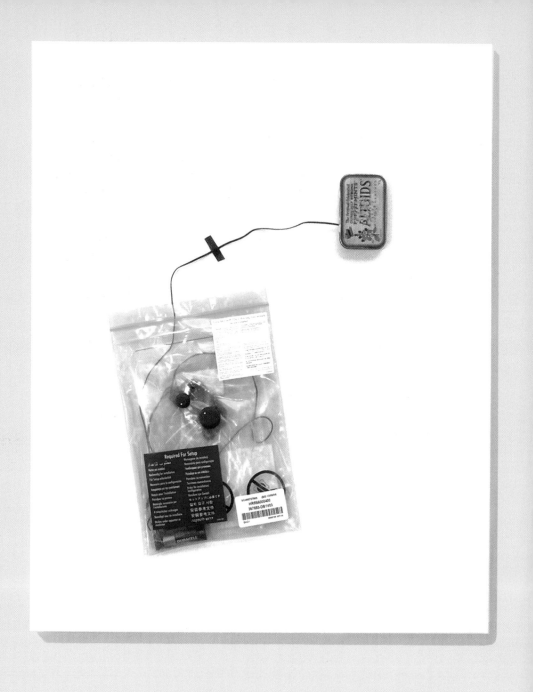

Figure 14.3
White Canvas AM/FM Radio:
*Artist's canvas, recovered circuitry, zip-
lock bags, sweet tin, adhesive tape*

The CD Player/Radio, Figure 14.4, takes recovered electronics from an outdated cassette stereo player and an outdated personal CD player and combines and re-encases them in discarded cardboard boxes, newspaper, plastic wrap and string. The main unit and two speakers are placed on three new white, mass-produced chairs. The 'product' is the whole composition, the pristine white chairs providing the means of supporting, separating and re-contextualizing the rough-hewn, locally made elements.

The Bottle Lamps, Figure 14.5, use standard electrical fittings and compact fluorescent lamps, all available from a hardware store. These stock items are combined with discarded plastic soap bottles and composed on a white shelf – which provides a means of arranging the components into a functional form while also re-contextualizing them.

The Hanging Lamps, Figure 14.6, use similar stock electrical parts and low-power lamps. In this case, they are made usable as individual lamps by wrapping them in a piece of tent fabric fastened and hung with climbing cord and stock cord spring clips. Thus, the materials added to the essential functional components are minimized and the cord and spring clips can be easily used in later applications.

177

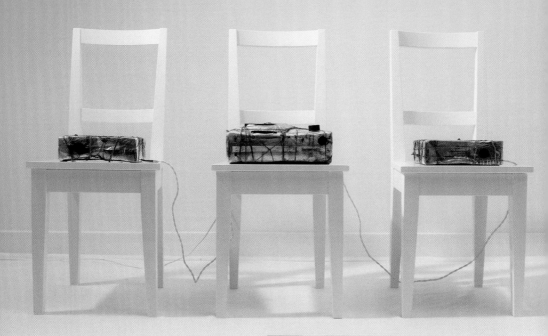

Figure 14.4a
CD Player/Radio:
Recovered circuitry, reused paper products, twine, mosquito netting, three new chairs

Figure 14.4b
CD Player detail

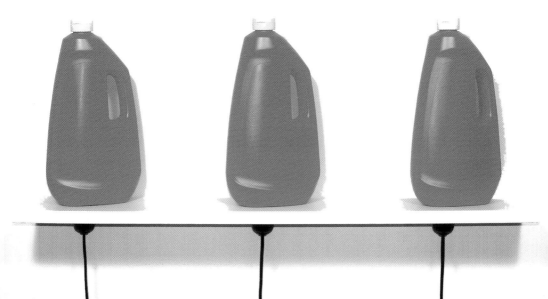

Figure 14.5a
Bottle Lamps:
*Standard electrical parts, low-energy
compact fluorescent lamps, reused
soap bottles, modified wooden shelf*

Figure 14.5b
Bottle Lamps detail:
Lamps off and on

The final design is a digital clock, Figure 14.7, which perhaps best exemplifies the ephemeral object achieved through an accumulation of elements. Here, a white shelf again provides the basis for the composition. A cup and saucer, an eggcup, a discarded envelope, a bulldog clip and a low-power LCD display are combined to form a digital clock; fruit is added to provide a natural battery. All the items can be readily dispersed and reused.

As in previous exercises, the direction explored here implies a shift in the manufacturing process from centralized mass production to a form that includes contributions at the local level. It makes use of mass-produced elements that can be included in a variety of 'functional concentrations', rather than specialized parts designed for use in just one design. It also provides an opportunity to include more redesign and re-production at the local level, enabling possibilities for local employment, culturally relevant design and promotion of a transformation from a production-based manufacturing economy to a more balanced, locally involved, production- and service-based economy. The 'ephemeral object' outlined here also begins to integrate the economic benefits of mass production with socio-economic and environmental responsibilities. Thus, this kind of approach, and the objects it makes possible, would appear to be in closer accord with the principles and objectives of sustainability.

Figure 14.6
Hanging Lamps:

*Standard electrical parts, low-energy
compact fluorescent lamps, tent fabric,
climbing cord, cord spring clips*

Figure 14.7
Off-the-Shelf Clock:
*LCD, cup and saucer, eggcup,
fork, bulldog clip, reused envelope,
crocodile clip, wire, wooden shelf*

15

INTELLECTUAL AND AESTHETIC UNDERSTANDINGS OF DESIGN

the
considered
gaze

Theory and practice, two quite different but intimately related aspects of design, will be explored in this chapter to provide a more complete basis for the design and critique of sustainable products. I will describe the relationship between theory and practice and, more particularly, the relationship between an intellectual understanding of ethics and the aesthetics of sustainable objects. To demonstrate this relationship, I consider the aesthetic qualities of one particular design, the digital clock introduced in Chapter 14 (Figure 14.7).

This chapter is intended to move the discussion from the broad overview of sustainable product design, which began the book, and the general design principles and design process of later chapters, to the specific details of one particular object and their relationship to sustainable design. This is necessary because an essential aspect of the designer's work is the aesthetic definition of an object; and aesthetics are dependent upon specifics.

Theoretical inquiry is concerned with the development of a system of ideas to explain something. It is 'based on general principles independent of the specific thing to be explained'[1] and is progressed through intellectual activity, that is, through reasoning and objective understanding. Design practice and aesthetic definition, on the other hand, require attention to specifics within the holistic development of a particular product, and not 'general principles independent of the thing to be explained'. Critique is an integral part of this designing process, and is also applied to the final object.

The intellectual and aesthetic issues of design, and their relationship, provide the basis for creating, understanding and critiquing products. In terms of sustainability, the relationship between theory and practice is such that the ethical and environmental imperatives of the sustainable rationale can inform the design process and affect the intrinsic properties of the product. In turn, this will affect one's aesthetic experience of the product and suggest a basis for sustainable aesthetics. I will discuss and illustrate these issues in terms of both the designer's *intentions* and *creative aesthetic sensibility*, and the user's *a priori knowledge* and the *aesthetic experience*.

When we set out to design a functional object, a clear understanding of intentions and a set of design criteria have to be established. The object will have to function effectively, it must be designed for a particular market and manufactured at a certain cost, and it must be safe, comprehensible and attractive to the intended user. These factors are established before the design work begins and so they represent a set of ideas about the object that are extrinsic to any particular design outcome. In this sense, the design intentions and criteria are based on general ideas and principles and, as such, they are theoretical or abstract, they do not have physical or concrete existence. They include a broad set of assumptions, knowledge and information about the context of production, the types of materials, forms and assembly techniques suited to modern mass production and knowledge about similar products already on the market. These theoretical ideas, intentions and criteria help define an object in terms of its extrinsic properties. It then becomes the responsibility of the designer, during the design process, to create concepts that bring together and attend to these factors, and this eventually results in a specific design. Hence, while intentions and design criteria are determined prior to, and independent of, the activity of designing, they find their resolution in the final design outcome. They are critical to the designer's decision making, and influence the way the final design is established, understood and judged.

Designing involves satisfying intentions and criteria in an holistic manner – and this is usually achieved by generating various design concepts. These will be developed to meet most or all the criteria and some will be judged better than others. This creative process, however, is concerned not with intellectual pursuits but with aesthetic discernment. The aesthetic sensibility requires attention to the precise properties of a particular design concept. It calls for sensational acuity, emotional spontaneity, attentiveness and contemplation, an holistic appreciation and, during the process of designing, a setting aside of the intellectual self.[2] It is in the practical process of designing the specific content and *intrinsic* properties of an object are made manifest: intrinsic properties being the base properties fixed within an object which constitute its essential nature.[3]

Thus, the design of a functional object involves theory and practice and, while each represents a different mode of thinking and a quite distinct way of engaging with the world, they are, nevertheless, intimately connected. Some of the extrinsic properties of an object will be strongly related to its intrinsic properties and, because of this, the extrinsic properties can have a bearing on one's aesthetic experience of the object. As Eaton has made clear, information about intentions is an integral part of our experience of artefacts, and intellectual information about an object can be aesthetically relevant if it draws attention to those intrinsic properties that are relevant to the aesthetic experience.[4] An example here may be useful. The musical composition The Freeman Etudes by John Cage is a difficult work to listen to – being a series of unrelated, independent, randomly generated events for violin.[5] However, knowing something of the composer's oeuvre, his intentions and the method he adopted to compose the piece, enables the listener to understand the work and appreciate the serious intent behind its form, which, in turn, can inform and enhance one's aesthetic experience. With this clarification of the theoretical and practice-based aspects of design, and the relationship between the two, we can move on to consider the link between ethics, aesthetics and sustainable design.

187

Design can be understood in terms of the added value it brings to manufacturers and consumers and the role it plays in the market system of supply and demand. However, this economic evaluation provides only a limited grasp of the meaning of functional objects. It does not account for those desires, needs and consumer preferences that cannot be expressed in economic terms.[6] Similarly, our aesthetic appreciation of an object cannot be reduced to quantitative criteria, but is based on an holistic contemplation of the intrinsic properties of the object and is informed by a host of other information, knowledge and values we bring to the experience of an artefact, which Wollheim has called our 'cognitive stock'.[7] The aesthetic experience of an object is not simply an experience of sensuous pleasure but is, in part, a reasoned response that draws upon, or refers to, values; as Scruton has suggested, the products of design must be desirable and not just desired.[8]

Product designers have extensive knowledge of the manufacturing sector and the processes, materials and practices of design and production, so their cognitive stock in this particular area will be considerable. Reference to this cognitive stock may result in one concept being selected over another, perhaps because the manufacturing stage would be easier or less expensive, or because it takes advantage of a particular technology. Significantly, such decisions can affect those intrinsic properties that are relevant to the aesthetic experience. Furthermore, there will be some, perhaps many, aspects of the design and manufacturing system that raise ethical questions. For example, the designer may be aware of practices that he or she regards as morally questionable or morally exemplary. Here again, this will be part of the background information that is brought to the design process. In other words, knowledge of the ethical aspects of product design and production, and how these affect the designer's decisions, can be linked to the aesthetic definition of the artefact.

Today, sustainability raises many issues that, in previous times, may have gone unnoticed. As I have discussed earlier, there are questions about ethical work practices, economic inequities, environmentally damaging practices and the expanding numbers of short-lived products that are unrepairable and non-recyclable. Designers who are concerned and knowledgeable about these issues will have this information as part of their cognitive stock and, as such, it can affect their design decisions. Thus, sustainable intentions can lead to designs that reflect, through their intrinsic properties and aesthetic qualities, ethical and environmental considerations. This link between the intellectual arguments surrounding sustainability and the aesthetics of a product is central to our understanding of the sustainable object and the way it is

188

created. In this regard, a barrier to the progress of sustainable product design is that conventional industrial design practice tends to constrain the intellectual understanding of what a product is or could be within extremely narrow limits, that is, those set by the assumptions, intentions and requirements of the predominant existing condition. With such a narrow intellectual basis, new and radically different conceptions of objects are often eliminated even before the design process begins. Sustainability demands a wider view of material culture and its possibilities, and a much broader intellectual base.

I mentioned above that the value of functional objects is usually considered in terms of their economic value to the manufacturer and the consumer, and the desires, preferences and needs of the consumer. However, there are other ways of thinking about and understanding objects and attributing value. It is possible to imagine a functional object that is not economically viable in normal market terms, that is not desirable in terms of the consumer's wish to possess it, and that is not needed in any practical sense, either personally or as a community ('community' here could refer to the wider community or, perhaps in the first instance, the design community). It is possible to imagine an object that performs a function, but which stands outside these conventional ways of ascribing value. While such an object may, in fact, *be* appreciated and valued by the community, this is not essential for it to be of value *to* the community. If it is true, as Eric Gill once asserted, that everyone is a special kind of artist, then the designer of products is also a special kind of artist, and as such is able to offer 'something to the community which the community does not want to accept, which the community at first finds unpalatable'.[9]

189

While this way of thinking about functional objects may seem rather paradoxical, we must recognize that significant progress in tackling sustainability requires a considerable change in assumptions, understandings of functional goods, and approaches to product manufacture. It becomes incumbent upon designers and design academics to offer to the community renditions of functional objects that are not economic, demanded, needed, desired or even appreciated and valued, but which nevertheless are of value and worth offering, at least from the designer's perspective or in terms of the thesis being explored. If the approach is based on a substantive cognitive stock, if the arguments are sound and the aesthetic sensibility is well developed, then the designer can justifiably hold the view that the work is of value, even if this is not acknowledged by the present community. Indeed, the history of art and design bears this out. The works of artists from Van Gogh to Duchamp have frequently been rejected or dismissed by the community that pays attention to art – including academics, critics, curators and commentators. Similarly, there are many examples of functional objects that have not been recognized as design by the design community. Many artefacts traditionally designed and made by women, such as quilts, needlework and knitted garments, have not been acknowledged in the histories of art and design, nor have they featured in university design courses or been exhibited in museums and galleries. Happily, in recent years this has begun to change, with dedicated books and exhibitions. For example, *Amish Art of Quilt* by Hughes and Silber (1994)[10] and, more recently, the *Knit 2 Together: Concepts and Knitting* exhibition at The Crafts Council, London (2005).[11]

There are, of course, inherent risks in taking such an approach and some caution is needed. It is all too easy for designers to become enamoured with their own creative work and to regard it favourably and uncritically. While this must always be borne in mind, it should not prevent them from attempting to challenge the established conventions of design and production, to cast the net wider and explore alternatives that address sustainable issues, and in so doing develop designs that illustrate a different direction. In fact, the very process of doing this, and publishing and exhibiting the resulting work, can be a positive step in creating change; as Orwell once wrote, 'The consequences of every act are included in the act itself.'[12] Indeed, there are many designers who have already done this.[13,14] Through this process, experimental or polemical designs start to become part of the common cognitive stock about the nature and potential of functional objects and, as such, they begin to affect one's understanding and aesthetic experience.

In the next part of this discussion I would like to illustrate the relationship between theory and practice in the context of sustainability. To do so, I will describe the intentions and outcome of a design exercise from first-hand knowledge. The primary aim of this exercise was to use a simple functional requirement as a starting point for exploring the design of sustainable objects; the actual function was not so important; in this case, it was to display time in a digital format. This is a relatively simple function and therefore useful for exploring ideas about the nature of utilitarian objects. I felt that the exercise would benefit from such simplicity because the ideas about objects that were being explored would not be overly constrained or become confused by having to deal with more complex functional requirements. An additional consideration was that a digital display of some form is used in many small electronic products and so, potentially, the exercise could have wider implications. Focusing on sustainable concerns, the main design criteria were developed as follows:

- The design should make minimal, if any, use of new resources, and cause minimal detriment to the environment.
- It should make use of readily available materials and components; these could include materials or components distinctive to a locality, locally available mass-produced components for general usage, and mass-produced elements from former applications.
- Constituent parts should be modified as little as possible so that any future reuse is not compromised by their inclusion in this design.
- It should be capable of being economically made, maintained, repaired, upgraded and 're-dispersed' or decommissioned, at the local level. This reduces the need for shipping and packaging and provides opportunities either for local employment or for users to create the object themselves, thereby offering the possibility for greater 'ownership' of their material environment.

191

The overall notion, which I described in Chapter 14, was to see this design as a temporary concentration of components that would enable a functional benefit for a finite period. As with any design exercise, aesthetic value was to be derived from decisions made during the designing process, especially the specific selection of components, with attention to their intrinsic properties and their relationships within the composition. The final design is shown in Figure 14.7.

We can now consider the relationship between intentions and the way these intentions have been manifested. This will provide a basis for judging the merits of the design. To do this we must look at the artefact in a considered manner. It is through this process of looking that we can contemplate the design in relation to the intentions, as well as the aesthetic qualities of the artefact and the potential attributes or weaknesses of its composition. We will then be in a position to recognize how the intentions and the outcome are related and, more importantly, how knowledge of this relationship affects the aesthetic experience.

The design can be viewed from a number of perspectives, all of which allow us to become aware of its aesthetic qualities and enable it to be understood or interpreted. Here, a systematic approach, a modified version of a proposition by Koren[15] will be used to look at the design from twelve different points of view, each of which allows a different aspect to be brought to the fore. This 'considered looking' enables the viewer to thoroughly see the design and reflect upon it. This will be followed by a discussion of the overall aesthetic experience and how this can be affected by the intellectual aspects of the project.

Koren's proposition for looking at object arrangements, which he has called 'a rhetoric of object placement', is derived from the application of rhetoric in other spheres. This provisional proposal for use with non-utilitarian arrangements is expanded here to include factors relevant to a functional composition.

Koren offers eight rhetorical elements under three major headings. Thus, *physicality*, the first impression of the physical arrangement, is subdivided into (1) hierarchy – the relative visual importance of the various elements, including the ground and background, (2) alignment – the relative position of the various elements, described by terms such as symmetrical, linear, parallel etc., and (3) sensoriality – the visual qualities of the components, including colour, texture and shape.[16]

The second general category, *abstraction*, relates to associations that the arrangement brings to mind. It is subdivided into (4) metaphor, which refers to symbolism beyond the arrangement itself, such as allusion and simile; (5) mystification – which includes paradoxes and ambiguities within the arrangement; and (6) narrative – the story the composition is understood to tell, or a description.[17]

The third general category is *integration*, the way in which the various elements contribute to the collective arrangement. It is subdivided into (7) coherence – the clarity or effectiveness of the composition in terms of what it is visually communicating, described by terms such as theme, rationality or logic, and homogeneity, and (8) resonance – the composition's ability to maintain visual interest and stimulate thoughts and feelings.[18]

192

Additional elements, not included in Koren's proposal, become important when considering functional arrangements. Hence, to Koren's three major subdivisions can be added a fourth, that of *utility*, under which we can include, at least provisionally, four more elements. These are: (9) purpose – the composition's intended or interpreted function and how this function is understood – it can be described as plainly identifiable, confusing, unclear or unknown; (10) connectivity – the manner in which the various primary objects are connected together to enable a given function. Connectivity can be achieved through object placement, by including additional elements in the composition, or it may be hidden. Connectivity and its relationship to purpose can be described as visually clear, implicit, puzzling, imperceptible etc.; (11) usability or the semiotics of use – the indications of how the object is to be used or operated. It might be described as intuitive, counter-intuitive, obvious, incomprehensible, ambiguous, etc.; (12) functional modality – the manner in which the function of the object occurs or is expressed. This is quite different from the function itself and how the function is understood. Functional modality can be described by terms such as pragmatic, logical, essential, fanciful, elaborate or sentimental.

This modified version of Koren's 'rhetoric', for use with a functional object arrangement, is summarized in Table 15.1. It will now be applied to the digital clock example.

193

Table 15.1 A rhetoric of functional object arrangement:
A modified version of Koren's 'Rhetoric of Object Placement'

Physicality	1. Hierarchy
	2. Alignment
	3. Sensoriality
Abstraction	4. Metaphor
	5. Mystification
	6. Narrative
Integration	7. Coherence
	8. Resonance
Utility	9. Purpose
	10. Connectivity
	11. Usability
	12. Functional modality

A rhetoric of functional object arrangement – an exercise in looking, as applied to the Off-the-Shelf Clock shown in Figure 14.7

PHYSICALITY – the first impression of the physical arrangement

1 Hierarchy

The most visually prominent elements are the two colourful fruits and the bright red wire. Next comes the liquid crystal display (LCD) followed by the spring clip, fork and arc of orange wire between the lime and orange. All other elements are in varying shades of white against a white ground. The envelope is marked with scribbles, affording it some visual weight and prominence.

2 Alignment

A cup, containing an orange pierced by a fork, is placed on a saucer. To its right is an eggcup containing a lime. Cup and saucer and eggcup are positioned asymmetrically and are not precisely aligned with, or parallel to, the front edge of the shelf. The fork pierces the orange at an angle and so is not aligned with the major horizontal or vertical elements elsewhere in the composition. The LCD is precisely mounted near the top left of an envelope which is hanging, via a spring clip and pin, on the background wall. The LCD and envelope are both positioned so that their lower edges are parallel with the horizontal surface. These principal elements are supplemented with coloured wires – a thick red wire and thinner ones in orange and white – these are attached to the various major elements but their paths are imprecise, they simply assume their natural forms.

3 Sensoriality

There is strong contrast between the plain white elements, including the ground and background, and the various coloured, black and metallic elements. The ceramic cup, saucer and eggcup are smooth, shiny rounded shapes and the coloured fruit is round with a fine-grained, smooth texture. These elements appear to be relatively heavy. By contrast, the envelope, LCD, and bulldog clip are hard-edged with angular lines and appear to be relatively light. The fork is a combination of angular and rounded and seems neither especially heavy nor light. The rounded objects are on the left of the composition and stand on the shelf, whereas the hard-edged rectilinear objects are on the right and fastened to the wall. The fork seems to belong to neither set but, in combination with the red wire, acts as an intermediary that connects them together, physically, visually and sensorially.

ABSTRACTION – associations that the arrangement brings to mind

4 Metaphor

The collection of elements suggests ideas of morning and breakfast. The stark, cool, white wall and shelf with white objects gives a lightness to the scene and this, together with the colourful citrus, brings to mind sunny climes. However, the suggestion is not explicit or direct, and the presence of the wires indicates another purpose.

5 Mystification

The arrangement creates some confusion or paradox – fruit is placed in a teacup and an eggcup; there is a fork, which is not used for eating fruit or eggs, or for stirring tea. Furthermore, the fork is electrically wired, as is the fruit. Although the overall purpose may be immediately obvious (see (9) Purpose, below) the objects selected to achieve this purpose, although functionally effective, nevertheless create some confusion. They seem to belong together, yet they do not normally go together in this way. This ambiguity creates an aesthetic tension in the composition.

195

6 Narrative

Narrative refers to interpreting the meaning of the composition as a whole, taking into consideration all the above factors. Here we are dealing with the visual aspects of the composition independent of any specific function, which will be addressed later (see (9) Purpose). From this perspective, the objects have been set out and connected together in a way that is obviously purposeful. The arrangement is not ad hoc but clearly considered – functionally and compositionally. There is an order and clarity brought about by the implied function, without which the collection would seem absurd or pointless.

INTEGRATION – the way in which the various elements contribute to the collective arrangement

7 Coherence

The predominant use of white elements gives the composition a strong coherence, and the colours of the other elements – the fruit and the wire – are of the same vibrant palette. In addition, the morning-time associations of the objects themselves – breakfast tableware, an opened envelope, and time – help to bind the different objects into a consistent whole.

8 Resonance

This initially bizarre composition soon invites the viewer to understand it. The wiring is a clue to purpose and once this becomes clear, it challenges the viewer to linger and to ask why the purpose is achieved in this manner. The flow of wires between the coloured and black elements encourages the eye to follow, in order to clarify understanding. Although asymmetrical in form, colour and weight, the composition is nevertheless balanced and stable, keeping the eye roving over it, taking in the whole, but not wandering off it.

UTILITY

9 Purpose

Although the meaning may not be instantly clear, its purpose is obviously to display time. With a little knowledge of batteries, it is evident that the clock is being powered via the wiring by the fruit.

10 Connectivity

The relationship between the various elements is reinforced by the apprehension of function, and also by the correlation between function and the physical connections, in the form of wiring. This connectivity serves as an indicator of the intentions and rationale. The connectivity between the elements is clearly stated; however, one has to assume that the wires actually connect to the fruit as these connections are, in most cases, hidden from view.

11 Usability

'Usability' refers to the way the object reveals how it is to be used. In this arrangement, while one aspect of its use is simply for the user to glance at the displayed time, others aspects are unclear. There are no visual indications of how one is supposed to set the time on the clock or how to disconnect, replace and reconnect the fruit; the clock controls are hidden, as are the connections between the wires and the fruit. The only sign that the fruit is actually connected to the wires comes from the fact that the red wire is attached to the fork which, in turn, is embedded in the orange.

12 Functional modality

The functional modality, the way in which the function of the object is expressed, seems idiosyncratic compared to the majority of designs for such products. Initially, the means by which functionality is achieved might seem rather eccentric, frivolous and impractical. However, with some idea of the intentions behind the design, it can be recognized that although unusual, the design criteria have been met, and this allows the design to be viewed in a somewhat different light; it might then be described by terms such as moderate, whimsical or sanguine.

The aesthetic experience is not simply the sum of a series of different perspectives – it is an appreciation of the whole. The rigour of this 'rhetoric of functional object arrangement' encourages a thorough viewing – it draws our attention to the visual qualities of the object, the elements within the composition and their relationships, and it asks that we ponder them. This process of looking and reflecting is crucial to the aesthetic experience of the object and prefigures any meaningful aesthetic judgement.

It becomes clear from this exercise in looking that apart from *physicality* and its subcategories, all the others elements within the 'rhetoric' are either dependent upon or can be affected by our general cognitive stock and our knowledge, or lack of it, about the artefact. Any metaphorical associations we ascribe to the object or our interpretation of functional modality are based on knowledge of other things. The coherence of the artefact, in terms of the clarity of what it is communicating, could be judged as irrational or confusing if we had no knowledge of the intentions behind it. For example, the sight of two bottles of milk standing outside someone's front door might seem, with no prior knowledge, an irrational place to have bottles of milk. We regard such a sight as normal only if we are familiar with the custom of milk delivery. It is through these external references that we begin to formulate understandings about what we are looking at. Similarly, reference to design intentions and an appreciation of their basis can contribute to the aesthetic experience. In the case of this digital clock, there is clearly a connection between the design intent and the decision to use pre-existing objects made for other purposes. In turn, this affects the intrinsic properties of the arrangement and its functional modality, which is relevant to the aesthetic experience. However, there is no *direct* or *deterministic* relationship between intentions and intrinsic properties. In the example, there is no stated requirement to use smooth-surfaced

197

white objects, an orange and a lime. The decision to use these objects was made during the designing stage and was based on satisfying the intentions while also attending to the aesthetic qualities of the composition, especially visual coherence.

'Looking' allows the viewer to become thoroughly aware of the artefact and its different features. Contemplation of the artefact requires the viewer to draw upon their cognitive stock – which can include knowledge of the intentions behind the design and their broader cultural implications. This process affords the viewer an aesthetic experience and provides the basis for aesthetic judgement. Thus, the theory of design, the practice of design and the aesthetic experience of objects are all bound together by the complex interconnections that exist between intentions, design decisions, intrinsic properties and the meaning of the object within the broader cultural context. The object is the manifestation of design thinking; it integrates a variety of issues and technical constraints within a particular expressive form, which then provides an holistic aesthetic experience.[19] Additionally, in transforming our needs, desires and moral responsibilities into tangible form we have the opportunity to create a more profound material culture, to find meaning in the mundane and to sacralize the utilitarian. At its heart, sustainability represents not so much an environmental crisis but a crisis of meaning; it prompts us to reassess many of our most fundamental assumptions, and to re-examine and change our approaches accordingly.

It follows that when the ethical and environmental aspects of sustainability are given prominence in the theoretical foundations of design, we have a robust basis for moving design forward. This should be welcomed as an exciting and important challenge to the design profession to develop a new aesthetic sensibility for sustainable design. It provides a meaningful impetus for jolting design out of its current and often trivial self-absorption and lays the basis for transformation.

Established conventions in industrial design, both in determining design intentions and in the individual design decisions made during product development, have resulted in a particular form of material culture that is ubiquitous and regarded as normal. A century of design for mass production has created a world of ever-changing, affordable consumer goods, many created by some of the most respected designers in the business. These products are generally judged to be beautiful – both by designers, as indicated through design awards, and by consumers through their purchasing habits. However, the aesthetic qualities of these goods result from a mode of creation and production that is, in many ways, ethically and environmentally insupportable. Hence, they are the aesthetics of unsustainability.

On the face of it, there is an unbridgeable chasm between the dominant existing practices of product design and the need for substantial change to address sustainability. The continuation of existing practices and our customary conceptions of products are bolstered by convention and the complacencies of familiarity; the forces to keep things as they are can often seem just too powerful to overcome. Even though business and government leaders speak powerfully and frequently of the need to address sustainable issues, the *need for change* is quite different from the specifics of *how to change*. This is where the process often becomes stalled. Change for sustainability has to occur at the ground level, in the particular decisions of individuals, but these decisions can only be made if there is some understanding of direction and some indication of possible, alternative approaches. This is precisely where the informed designer can play an important role. The products of the sustainable design process can demonstrate intentions and decisions that differ considerably from conventional approaches. Design is a potent tool because it persuades through tangible example. It has served the market system well and has been instrumental in the success of consumer culture. But today, even though the issues have changed, the conventions of design have remained essentially the same.

199

The design example presented here is a very simple artefact based on one alternative approach to design. It is not intended to suggest a definitive direction; it is but one step within a continuing process of exploration. In this small act of design and in the discussion surrounding it, however, I have attempted to highlight the critical importance of establishing sustainability within the fundamental conception of an object, and to demonstrate that when this is done, it can profoundly change decision making, the design outcome and the aesthetic experience offered by the object. It is only by providing such experimental examples, together with an explanation of their basis, that we can further the debate, advance understandings of 'how to' design for sustainability and, eventually, radically alter our conceptions of material culture and our notions of product beauty so they are in closer accord with our ethical and environmental responsibilities.

16
EPILOGUE

The design and mass production of technologically based products for use in the home began in earnest in the years spanning the 19th and 20th centuries. By the end of the first decade of the 20th century, early versions of many products that are now taken for granted were in production – the telephone, vacuum cleaner, washing machine, toaster, electric cooker and the earliest product for playing recorded music, the phonograph. Others, such as the radio and television, quickly followed. All these small domestic machines progressed from the development of larger machines that characterized the earlier years of the Industrial and Scientific Revolutions and, in turn, these revolutions went hand in hand with the philosophical revolution that spawned the Enlightenment. Over the course of the 20th century, designers struggled to define and redefine these small machines for the home and, as a consequence, have produced an endless stream of variations on a theme – variations that have both delighted and destroyed, but which, invariably, can be characterized as 'fleeting'. Despite the apparent benefits of the concepts they reify, the actual objects themselves have failed to be of any lasting value. They are here today and gone tomorrow – forever replaced with newer, more up-to-date, and more technologically advanced variations.

We can continue along this road if we choose, but to do so in the face of such overwhelming evidence of the destructive consequences would not only be foolish, we would also be relinquishing any hope of establishing a more meaningful notion of material culture and, by extension, a more meaningful notion of society itself. The almost pathological acquisition of 'newness' and the ravenous consumption of technology and style reveal a vacuous centre that is, ultimately, personally meaningless and fraught with disillusionment and unhappiness. The void at the centre of this endeavour can be traced right back to the earliest days of the Modernist project – from which stems an error that has yet to be rectified, but which is plainly evident in our contemporary products and their consequences. In the field of product design, this error lies in ascribing primary value to utility – both the functional utility of the machine and the highly questionable social utility of its style. We have assigned value to that which is useful – pragmatically useful and socially useful. This is the fallacy that lies at the heart of our present, damaging model of material culture. The value of utility can only ever be temporary because lasting value lies not in that which is useful but in that which is useless. All those things with which we associate lasting value and profundity are utterly useless – art, poetry, music, religion – they endure because they reach beyond the here and now, the transient pragmatics of the day to day. They are of lasting value precisely because they are useless.

So where does this leave us? In this book I have endeavoured, through various means, to offer an understanding of functional objects and their design in the context of sustainability. There are no simple answers to this quest to marry function with enduring value – perhaps it is flawed by an inherent contradiction. However, I hope I have offered some thoughts and ideas that will further the debate. The foregoing is not a manual for sustainable product design but a series of discussions and reflections that approach the subject from different perspectives. This, I believe, is appropriate because when it comes to sustainability we are all setting out from a place that is already permeated by conventions and precedents that are, cumulatively, destructive.

If there are conclusions to be reached from this present offering, they centre on this notion of product transience. In my view, we must reject the idea that functional objects, and especially those based in technology, will be of lasting value as objects if their primary role is their utility. We must assume that they will be merely temporary and ultimately rather trivial additions to society which enable a task to be done effectively for a short while. It is only by making this assumption that we can start seeing functional objects in a new way, in their fullness – as temporary, efficacious concentrations of resources that someday soon will have to find a place on this planet where their utility is no longer valued. Any lasting value such an object may have will not be in its utility but in meanings that surpass utility and resonate with our aesthetic and spiritual sensibilities.

203

NOTES

1 INTRODUCTION

[1] Ciambrone, D. F. (1997) *Environmental Life Cycle Analysis*, Lewis Publishers Inc., CRC Press, Boca Raton, Florida, US.

[2] The Natural Step website is at: www.naturalstep.org/, accessed: 14 December 2005. Also refer to the following publication by the founder of the Natural Step programme: Robert, K. H. (2002) *The Natural Step Story: Seeding a Quiet Revolution*, New Society Publishers, Gabriola Island, BC, Canada.

[3] Factor 10 website at: www.factor10-institute.org/, accessed: 3 December 2004.

[4] Dresner, S. (2002) *The Principles of Sustainability*, Earthscan, London, pp64–65.

2 RETHINKING MATERIAL CULTURE – The cage of aesthetic convention

An earlier version of this chapter first appeared in *The Design Journal*, vol 5, no 2, pp3–7, 2002, Ashgate, Publishing, Aldershot, UK (copyright 2002).With kind permission of Ashgate Publishing Limited, UK.

[1] Overy, P. (1991) *De Stijl*, Thames and Hudson, London.

[2] Whitford, F. (1984) *Bauhaus*, Thames and Hudson, London.

[3] Dormer, P. (1993) *Design Since 1945*, Thames and Hudson, London, p138.

[4] Bakker, G. and Ramakers, R. (1998) *Droog Design: Spirit of the Nineties*, 010 Publishers, Rotterdam; Ramakers, R. (2002) *Less + More: Droog Design in Context*, 010 Publishers, Rotterdam; Droog Design website at: www.droogdesign.nl, accessed: 23 November 2004.

[5] Bayley, S. (1980) *Little Boxes*, Horizon TV Series, British Broadcasting Association.

[6] *Marcel Duchamp (Fountain) 1917/1964* at San Francisco Museum of Modern Art, Collections: www.sfmoma.org/, accessed: 18 November 2004; *Marcel Duchamp, Fountain 1917* at: www.artlex.com/ArtLex/d/dada.html, accessed: 18 November 2004; Ades, D., Cox, N. and Hopkins, D. (1999) *Marcel Duchamp*, Thames and Hudson, London, Chapter 7.

[7] In 2004 Duchamp's *Fountain* was voted the most influential modern art work of all time in a poll of 500 art experts. Refer: *Duchamp's urinal tops art survey* (2004) BBC News, available at: http://news.bbc.co.uk/go/pr/fr/-/1/hi/entertainment/arts/4059997.stm, published 1 December 2004, accessed: 1 November 2005.

[8] Quinn, P. (2001) liner notes for *John Cage (1912–1992) Music for Prepared Piano Vol 2*, played by Boris Berman, piano, Naxos Compact Disc 8.559070.

[9] Cork, R., Long, R., Fulton, H. and Seymour, A. (2000) *Richard Long: Walking in Circles*, George Braziller Inc., New York.

[10] Dal Co, F. and Forster, K. (1999) *Frank O. Gehry: The Complete Works*, Monacelli Press, New York.

[11] Hobsbawm, E. J. (1968) *Industry and Empire*, The Penguin Economic History of Britain, Volume 3, Penguin Books, London (1990), Chapter 3, The Industrial Revolution 1780–1840, pp56–78.

[12] *Capitalism* (2001) Encyclopaedia Britannica, CD-ROM, copyright 1994–2001.

3 SUSTAINABLE DEVELOPMENT IN CONTEXT – The evolution of a contemporary myth

An earlier version of this chapter was presented at the 5th European Academy of Design Conference in Barcelona in April 2003.

[1] As I said in the Introduction, some authors maintain that 'sustainable development' emphasizes development and that 'sustainability' emphasizes the environment. Here, I use the former for a concept that refers to the triple bottom line of ethics, environment and economics, and the latter for ways of living where these issues are responsibly embraced.

[2] WCED (1987) *Our Common Future*, World Commission on Environment and Development, Oxford University Press, Oxford, p43.

[3] A wide variety of principles, frameworks and guidelines for sustainable development can be found at the website of the Canadian-based Sustainable

Development Communications Network (SDCN) located at: www.sdgateway.net, accessed: 3 December 2004.

4 For example the conservative Catholic views of proposed European Affairs Minister Rocco Buttiglione eventually led to the withdrawal of his candidacy in 2004. See Hooper, J. 'Buttiglione Deadlock Broken' (2004), The Guardian, London, Saturday 30 October 2004.

5 For example, see Bunting, M. (2003) *Secularism Gone Mad*, The Guardian, London, Thursday 18 December 2003, online edition, at: www.guardian.co.uk/print/0,3858,4821838-103677,00.html, accessed: 5 January 2004; *Bavaria Bans Teacher Headscarves*, BBC News Online, Friday 12 November 2004, at: http://news.bbc.co.uk/2/hi/europe/4005931.stm, accessed: 19 November 2004; Peterson, T. (2004) *Vatican Weighs into German Row over Religious Symbols*, The Independent Digital (UK) Ltd., 6 January 2004, at: http://news.independent.co.uk/low_res/story.jsp?story=478467&host=3&dir=73, accessed: 6 January 2004.

6 Steiner, G. (1974) *Nostalgia for the Absolute*, 1974 Massey Lectures, House of Anansi Press Ltd., Concord, Ontario, Canada, 1997, p2.

7 Jenkins, P. (2002) *The Next Christendom*, New York, Oxford University Press, p11; Jenkins quotes from Bull, H. (1977) *The Anarchical Society*, Columbia University Press, New York.

8 see Bierlein, J. F. (1994) *Parallel Myths*, Ballantine Books, New York, in which the author describes myths of 'the Fall' from the Talmudic and Biblical traditions and myths of 'apocalypse' from India, Persia, the Norse myths, North American myths and the Old and New Testaments of the Bible.

207

9 Gordon, A. and Suzuki, D. (1990) *It's a Matter of Survival*, Stoddart Publishing Co. Ltd, Toronto, p3.

10 For example: Sachs, W., Loske, R. and Linz, M. et al (1998) *Greening the North – A Post-Industrial Blueprint for Ecology and Equity*, Zed Books, London; Hawken, P. (1993) *The Ecology of Commerce*, Harper Business, New York; Hawken, P., Lovins, A. and Lovins, L. H. (1999) *Natural Capitalism – Creating the Next Industrial Revolution*, Little, Brown & Co., Boston.

11 For example: Meadows, D. H., Meadows, D. L. and Randers, J. (1992) *Beyond the Limits – Confronting Global Collapse, Envisioning a Sustainable Future*, McClelland & Stewart Inc., Toronto; Hunter, R. (2002) *2030: Confronting Thermageddon in Our Lifetime*, McClelland & Stewart Inc., Toronto.

12 Holloway, R. (2002) *Doubts and Loves*, Canongate Books Ltd, Edinburgh, p88.

13 Bulfinch, T. (1855) *The Golden Age of Myth and Legend*, Wordsworth Editions, Ware, Hertfordshire, UK, 1993, p16.

14 *The Holy Bible*, Genesis 3:22–24.

15 For example, references to riches, wealth and possessions in the New Testament include: Matthew 19:24; Mark 10:21–22; Luke 8:13–15; Luke 16:19–25.

[16] Chadwick, O. (1964) *The Reformation*, London, Penguin Books edition (1990), pp12–19.

[17] Examples include: the Mennonites and Amish (1500s); the Quakers and Baptists (1600s); the Shakers and Methodists (1700s); Christian Scientists (late 1800s).

[18] Küng, H. (2001) *The Catholic Church*, Weidenfeld & Nicolson, London. Page numbers refer to paperback edition, Phoenix Press, Orion Books Ltd., London (2002), p157.

[19] *Ibid*, pp148, 156.

[20] For example: 'The Soul of Britain' by Gordon Heald, published in the *The Tablet*, UK, 3 June 2000, describes a survey conducted by The Tablet and the BBC that reveals a drastic decline in traditional religious beliefs in Britain over recent years. However, while traditional religion may be in decline there is an increase in the number of people who describe themselves as 'spiritual' rather than religious. In Canada, while only 21 per cent of people regularly attend a religious service, 85 per cent identify with a religious denomination (*Globe and Mail*, Canada, 28 December 2002, pF3). The research of Canadian academic Reginald Bibby also shows that while Church attendance has drastically declined, there is still a strong identification with the traditional religions (see Bibby, R. W. (2002) *Restless Gods: The Renaissance of Religion in Canada*, Stoddart Publishing Co., Toronto). Thus, while there has been significant secularization of the public realm, this does not necessarily mean that people are no longer religious or concerned with the 'spiritual'. Indeed, the Tablet/BBC survey indicates that relatively few people describe themselves as atheists (8 per cent).

[21] Hill, C. (1992) *Reformation to Industrial Revolution*, The Penguin Economic History of Britain, Volume 2: 1530–1780, Penguin Books, London, pp41, 116.

[22] Thoreau, H. D. (1854) *Walden*, Penguin Books edition entitled *Walden and Civil Disobedience*, London (1983).

[23] Yellowstone National Park, US, was established in 1872 and was the first National Park in the world – see: www.nps.gov/yell/, accessed: 3 December 2004.

[24] The Sierra Club, founded 1892 by John Muir and associates – see: www.sierraclub.org/history/timeline.asp, accessed: 21 November 2004.

[25] In 1883, Germany established the first compulsory national insurance programme, starting with a health insurance programme. Britain introduced unemployment insurance in 1908. The Scientific-Humanitarian Committee, established in Germany in 1897, campaigned for the rights of homosexuals. In 1893 New Zealand became the first country to grant women the right to vote. Source: *Encyclopaedia Britannica*, 2001 Deluxe Edition CD-ROM – Timelines.

[26] Shute, N. (1957) *On the Beach*, paperback edition, Ballantine Books, New York (2001).

27 For example, James Rosenquist's 'Campaign' 1965, and Larry Rivers' 'Cigar Box', 1967; see Weitman, W. (1999) *Pop Impressions Europe/USA – Prints and Multiples from the Museum of Modern Art*, Museum of Modern Art, New York, pp58, 75.

28 Carson, R. (1962) *Silent Spring*, Buccaneer Books, New York (reprint edition 1994).

29 A brief history of the Club of Rome is available at: www3.sympatico.ca/drrennie/CACORhis.html#ClubofRome, accessed: 21 November 2004.

30 Homepage of the Environmental Protection Agency in the US is: www.epa.gov/, accessed: 21 November 2004.

31 A history of Friends of the Earth is available at: www.foei.org/about/history.html, accessed: 21 November 2004.

32 A history of Greenpeace is available at: www.greenpeace.org/history/, accessed: 21 November 2004.

33 UN Environment Programme homepage: www.unep.org/, accessed: 21 November 2004.

34 Sustainable Development Timeline: www.sdgateway.net/introsd/timeline.htm, accessed: 3 December 2004.

35 *Encyclopaedia Britannica*, 2001 Deluxe Edition CD-ROM – Timeline 1960

36 Greer, G. (1970) *The Female Eunuch*, HCP/Flamingo paperback edition, London (1985).

37 *Britannica* (35), Timeline 1973.

209

38 *1969 Stonewall gay rights uprising remembered*, CNN News Report, 22 June 22 1999, at: www.cnn.com/US/9906/22/stonewall/, commemorates the riot at the Stonewall Inn, New York, in June 1969 where gays protested against police discrimination and harassment; accessed: 21 November 2004.

39 The photo of Earth from Apollo 17, taken on 7 December 1972, can be viewed at: http://nssdc.gsfc.nasa.gov/photo_gallery/photogallery-earth.html, accessed: 21 November 2004.

40 Papanek, V. (1971) *Design for the Real World – Human Ecology and Social Change*, Thames and Hudson, London (2nd edition 1984).

41 Schumacher, E. F. (1973) *Small is Beautiful – Economics as if People Mattered*, Abacus, London.

42 Intermediate Technology Development Group homepage at: www.itdg.org/, accessed: 21 November 2004.

43 Buckminster Fuller Institute website at: www.bfi.org/introduction_to_bmf.htm, accessed: 21 November 2004.

44 Rybczynski, W. (1980) *Paper Heroes – Appropriate Technology: Panacea or Pipe Dream*, Penguin Books, New York, 1991, p100.

45 *Britannica* (35), Timeline 1983.

46 Montreal Protocol (1987) – see Sustainable Development Timeline, International Meetings and Agreements 1987, SD Gateway at:

www.sdgateway.net/introsd/timeline.htm, accessed: 21 November 2004.

[47] *Britannica* (35), Timeline 1989.

[48] Earth Summit homepage at: www.un.org/geninfo/bp/enviro.html, accessed: 22 November 2004.

[49] For example: *Britannica* (35), Timeline 1985 – seasonal reductions in the ozone layer were detected; 1986 – an international moratorium on whaling was introduced; 1988 – high rates of deforestation in the Amazon caused international concern.

[50] Grimwood, J. (1986) *Photohistory of the 20th Century*, Blandford Press, New York, p186.

[51] *Ibid*, p190.

[52] For example: Marlow, J. (1995) *Sweatshop Workers*, August 25, Commentary, *Channel 4 News*, UK, at: www.knbc4la.com/4news/comment/9508/0825_sweatshop.html, webpage no longer available; Sylvester, R. (1996) 'Sweatshop tarnishes the image of Disney', Monday 26 February, World News, *The Telegraph*, London; Lloyd-Roberts, S. (1996) 'Thai factory girls tell a different story about the cost of Christmas toys', December 20, *The Times*, London.

[53] Hawken, P. (1993) *The Ecology of Commerce: A Declaration of Sustainability*, HarperBusiness, HarperCollins, New York.

[54] Sachs, W., Loske, R., Linz, M. et al (1998) *Greening the North: A Post-Industrial Blueprint for Ecology and Equity*, Zed Books, London.

[55] Klein, N. (2000), *No Logo: Taking Aim at the Brand Bullies*, Vintage Canada, Random House, Toronto.

[56] *Eyewitness: The Battle of Seattle*, by Paul Reynolds, Thursday 2 December 1999 at: http://news.bbc.co.uk/1/hi/world/americas/547581.stm; *Protester's death mars Genoa summit*, Saturday 21 July 2001 at: http://news.bbc.co.uk/1/hi/world/europe/1448751.stm; *Protesters gather for Canada summit*, Monday 24 June 2002 at: http://news.bbc.co.uk/1/hi/world/americas/2062341.stm; *Protesters maintain Cancun pressure* by Tristana Moore, Sunday 14 September 2003, at: http://news.bbc.co.uk/1/hi/business/3107026.stm; *Many detained in Chile protests*, Wednesday 17 November 2004 at: http://news.bbc.co.uk/1/hi/world/americas/4020801.stm, all at BBC News Online, UK, all sites accessed: 22 November 2004.

[57] G8 summit police made 350 arrests, BBC News Online arrests, 9 July 2005, at: http://news.bbc.co.uk/1/hi/scotland/4666985.stm, accessed: 14 December 2005.

[58] www.live8live.com, accessed: 14 December 2005.

[59] For example, we have seen much positive change in recent years in terms of anti-discrimination measures and in areas such as women's rights and gay rights. However, in European, secular, liberal democracies such as the UK, there now appears to be far less tolerance of Christianity and Christian beliefs, at least in the public realm; see editorial by Grant, K., 'Christian

210

belief has become something to hide in "free" Britain', in *The Scotsman*, UK, 22 November 2004 at: http://thescotsman.scotsman.com/comment. cfm?id=1341342004, accessed: 22 November 2004, and 'Secular forces "pushing God to margin"' by Bruce Johnston and Jonathan Petre, *The Telegraph*, UK, 20 November 2004 at: www.telegraph.co.uk/news/main. jhtml?xml=/news/2004/11/20/wchurch20.xml, accessed: 22 November 2004.

[60] ISO 14000 website at: www.iso14000.com, accessed: 22 November 2004.

[61] *The Natural Step* website is at: www.naturalstep.org, accessed: 23 November 2004.

[62] For example, information about life cycle assessment (LCA) software is available at: www.pre.nl/, accessed: 23 November 2004; links to other sites are available at: www.life-cycle.org/, accessed: 23 November 2004.

[63] 'Auto show shines amid the gloom', pB1; 'Japanese car firms focus on the US', pB1; 'SUV's nab spotlight at auto show', pB9, *Globe & Mail,* Toronto, 6 January 2003, Section B.

[64] *State of the World Population Report 2005* by the United Nations Population Fund, available at: www.unfpa.org/swp/2005/english/ch1/index.htm, accessed: 14 December 2005.

[65] Steiner (6), pp2–4.

[66] Holloway, R. (2002) *Doubts and Loves*, Canongate Books Ltd., Edinburgh, p197.

4 DESIGN PROCESS AND SUSTAINABLE DEVELOPMENT – A journey in design

An earlier version of this chapter appeared in *The Journal of Sustainable Product Design*, vol 2, no 1–2, pp3–10, 2002 (copyright 2004), Springer/Elsevier Academic Publishers, Netherlands. With kind permission of Springer Science and Business Media.

[1] Heskett, J. (1980) *Industrial Design*, World of Art Series, Thames and Hudson Ltd., London, especially Chapter 6: The Emergence of Professional Industrial Design, pp105–119; Dormer, P. (1990) *The Meanings of Modern Design*, Thames and Hudson Ltd., London, pp46–47.

[2] Berton, P. (1976) *My Country*, McClelland and Stewart, Toronto, Chapter 9, The Franklin Mystery, pp155–176; Wilson, J. (2001) *John Franklin – Traveller on Undiscovered Seas*, XYZ Publishing, Montreal, p121.

[3] Beattie, O. and Geiger, J. (2000) *Frozen In Time: The Fate of the Franklin Expedition*, Greystone Publishing, Vancouver; also see an account of Sir John Franklin and photos of artefacts at the National Maritime Museum, UK website at: www.nmm.ac.uk/, accessed: 23 November 2004.

[4] Berton (2), Chapter 4, Samuel Hearne's Epic Trek, pp65–82.

[5] Berton (4) also see *The Adventurers – Samuel Hearne*, Historic HBC, Hudson's

Bay Company website at: www.hbc.com/hbc/e_hi/historic_hbc/hearne.htm, accessed: 23 November 2004.

[6] Bronowski, J. and Mazlish, B. (1960) *The Western Intellectual Tradition – From Leonardo to Hegel*, Harper Torchbooks, New York, Chapter 7, The Scientific Revolution, pp107–108.

[7] Martin, R. M. (1994) *The Philosopher's Dictionary*, Broadview Press, Peterborough, Ontario, p197.

[8] Tarnas, R. (1991) *The Passion of the Western Mind – Understanding the Ideas that Have Shaped Our Worldview*, Harmony Books, New York, p314.

[9] Hobsbawm, E. J. (1990) *Industry and Empire*, Penguin Books, London (originally published by Weidenfeld & Nicolson, 1968), especially Chapter 2, Origin of the Industrial Revolution, p54.

[10] Woodham, J. M. (1997) *Twentieth-Century Design*, Oxford University Press, Oxford, Chapter 3, Commerce, Consumerism and Design, pp65–85.

[11] Berliner, M. S. (1991) *Environmentalists: The New Life Haters*, The Ayn Rand Institute, California; a similar article by the same author entitled *Against Environmentalism* is available from the 'Essay and Articles' section of the Ayn Rand Institute website at: www.aynrand.org, accessed: 24 November 2004.

[12] Suzuki, D. (2002) *Quirks and Quarks*, CBC Radio 1, Saturday 6 April 2002, Interview with David Suzuki in which he referred to the Nike footwear company.

[13] Meadows, D. H., Meadows, D. L. and Randers, J. (1992) *Beyond the Limits: Confronting Global Collapse, Envisioning a Sustainable Future*, McClelland and Stewart Inc, Toronto, especially Chapter 5, Back From Beyond the Limits: The Ozone Story, pp141–160.

[14] IDSA (2004) *ID Defined*, Industrial Designers Society of America, in the 'About ID' section at: http://new.idsa.org, accessed: 24 November 2004.

[15] Campbell, J. (2001) *That Art Thou : Transforming Religious Metaphor*, edited by Eugene C. Kennedy, New World Library, Novato, California, p13.

[16] Éditions Hazan (1997) *Postcard of Marcel Duchamp* with the quote: '*Il n'y a pas de solution parce qu'il n'y a pas de problème*', Paris D.R. CN504, printed in France.

5 ENDURING ARTEFACTS AND SUSTAINABLE SOLUTIONS – Object lessons

An earlier version of this chapter was presented as a keynote address for The Third International Conference: Design and Manufacturing for Sustainable Development, Loughborough University, UK, September 2004, and appeared in the proceedings. It was subsequently published in *Design Issues*, vol 22, no 1, Spring 2006 (copyright 2006), Massachusetts Institute of Technology. With kind permission of MIT Press, Cambridge, MA, US.

[1] A number of national museums have online collections – such as the British Museum at: www.thebritishmuseum.ac.uk/, accessed: 26 November 2004, and the National Archaeological Museum of Athens at: www.culture.gr/, accessed: 26 November 2004.

[2] Amos, J. (2004) *Cave Yields 'Earliest Jewellery'*, BBC News Online, http://news.bbc.co.uk/2/hi/science/nature/3629559.stm, accessed: 15 April 2004.

[3] Betts, K. (2004) *Positional Goods and Economics. Lecture Notes*, Swinburne University of Technology, Australia, at: http://home.vicnet.net.au/~aespop/positionalgoods.htm, accessed: 14 April 2004; Lansley, S. (1994) *After the Gold Rush – The Trouble with Affluence: 'Consumer Capitalism' and the Way Forward*, Century Business Books, London, pp98, 103.

[4] Postrel, V. (2004) 'The marginal appeal of aesthetics – Why buy what you don't need?' *Innovation – The Journal of the Industrial Designers Society of America*, Dulles, Virginia, Spring edition, pp30–36.

[5] Hick, J. (1989) *An Interpretation of Religion – Human Responses to the Transcendent*, Yale University Press, New Haven, pp129–171; this interpretation of meaning, and its relationship to objects, is explored further in later chapters.

[6] Postrel (4), p36.

[7] Objects that have functional and spiritual/inspirational characteristics, without possessing some social/positional qualities are probably impossible to find. This conclusion would correspond to Maslow's suggestion that human needs are hierarchical, in which case objects that have both functional and inspirational/spiritual characteristics, would also possess some social/positional qualities.

[8] Howard, K. L. and Pardue, D. F. (1996) *Inventing the Southwest: The Fred Harvey Company and Native American Art*, Northland Publishing, Flagstaff, Arizona, p7; Papanek, V. (1995) *The Green Imperative – Natural Design for the Real World*, Thames and Hudson, New York, p234.

[9] For completeness it should be added here that ornaments and souvenirs derived from functional objects such as decorative pots can also combine functionality with social value, but in these cases the primary purpose is decorative, their functionality being largely irrelevant.

[10] *The Holy Bible*, Numbers 15:39.

[11] MacKinnon, M. (2003) 'Would-be warriors return from abroad – Iraqi call to arms', *Globe and Mail*, Toronto, A3, Wednesday 2 April 2003.

[12] Apostolic Letter *Rosarium Virginis Mariae of the Supreme Pontiff John Paul II to the Bishops, Clergy and Faithful on the Most Holy Rosary*, Section heading: October 2002 – October 2003, dated: 16 October 2002, at: www.vatican.va/holy_father/john_paul_ii/apost_letters/documents/hf_jp-ii_apl_20021016_rosarium-virginis-mariae_en.html#top, accessed: 19 October 2002.

[13] Kennedy, M. (2003) *Artist trims Tate tree*, The Guardian, Manchester, 13 December, online edition at: www.guardian.co.uk/print/0,3858,4818609-110427,00.html, accessed: 17 March 2004.

213

[14] Gribble, R. (1992) *The History and Devotion of the Rosary,* Our Sunday Visitor Publ. Div., Huntingdon, Indiana, pp130, 169.

[15] *Ibid*, p169.

[16] Wilkins, E. (1969) *The Rose-Garden Game – The Symbolic Background to the European Prayer-Beads,* Victor Gollancz Ltd., London, pp32, 56.

[17] Gribble (14), p166; Chidester, D. (2000) *Christianity: A Global History*, HarperCollins, New York, p275.

[18] Bauman, L. C. (2001) *The Anglican Rosary*, Praxis, Telephone, Texas, p4.

[19] Gribble (14), p167; Ward, M. (1945) *The Splendor of the Rosary*, Sheed and Ward, New York, pp7–9.

[20] Ward (19), p8; Pascal, B. (~1660) *Pensées*, Penguin Books, London, revised edition, 1995, Series II (The Wager), section 418,125, including footnote.

[21] Wilkins (16), p14.

[22] See reference to raking in a Zen garden in Russell, K. (1999) 'Sophia and the technologist: ways of human designing', in *The New Humanities: 2000 and Beyond* conference proceedings, School of Humanities, Central Queensland University, February, 1998. This paper is available at: www.newcastle.edu. au/school/design-comm info/staff/russell/scandal/eight.htm, accessed: 26 November 2004.

[23] Herrigel, E. (1953) *Zen in the Art of Archery*, Vintage Books, New York, p43; Needleman, J. (1980) *Lost Christianity*, Bantam Books, New York, p212.

[24] Wilkins (16), p29.

[25] Gribble (14), pp131–132; Wilkins (16), p29.

[26] For example. Harris, R. (1999) *Lourdes – Body and Spirit in the Secular Age*, Viking, Penguin Group, New York, pp144–145; Cornwell, J. (1991), *Powers of Darkness, Powers of Light*, Viking, Penguin Group, London, p68.

[27] Vail, A. (1995) *The Story of the Rosary*, HarperCollins, London, pp104–105; Chidester (17), p275; also see the website of *Our Lady of Fatima* at: www. fatima.org/essentials/facts/story1.asp, accessed: 30 November 2004.

[28] Perkins, B. (2004) 'Bottom line conjures up realty's fear of 13', at: http:// realtytimes.com/rtcpages/20020913_13thfloor.htm, accessed: 26 November 2004. Example: see Lufthansa Seating maps at: http://cms.lufthansa.com/fly/ de/en/inf/0,4976,0-0-780757,00.html, accessed: 30 May 2004.

[29] Wilkins (16), pp50, 179.

[30] *Ibid*, p49.

[31] *Ibid*, pp26, 29–30, 48.

[32] Apostolic Letter (12), especially sections 36–39.

[33] Huxley, A. (1945) *The Perennial Philosophy,* Triad Grafton Books, London, p9.

[34] Lewis, C. S. (1946) *The Pilgrim's Regress*, Fount Paperbacks, Collins, p171.

[35] Postrel (4), p36.

[36] Hick (5), pp153–171.

[37] Huitt, W. G. (2003) *Maslow's Hierarchy of Needs*, Valdosta State University,

Educational Psychology Interactive, at: http://chiron.valdosta.edu/whuitt/col/
regsys/maslow.html, accessed: 30 November 2004.

[38] Wilkins (16), p50.

[39] Dresner, S. (2002) *The Principles of Sustainability*, Earthscan, London, pp161–
164; Van der Ryn, S. and Cowan, S. (1996) *Ecological Design*, Island Press,
Washington, DC, pp57, 65.

6 REASSESSING 'GOOD' DESIGN – Objects as symbols of beauty

An earlier version of this chapter was a *Best Paper* selection at the
Industrial Designers Society Educators' Conference in San Jose,
California in July 2002 and appeared in the IDSA journal *Innovation* in
Winter 2002, pp42–45. With kind permission of the IDSA, Dulles,
VA, US.

[1] Dormer, P. (1990) *The Meanings of Modern Design*, Thames and Hudson,
London, p34; de Graaf, J., Wann, D. and Naylor, T. H. (2001) *Affluenza – The
All-Consuming Epidemic*, Berrett-Koehler Publishers, Inc., San Francisco, pp39,
143, 145.

[2] For example: Van Der Ryn, S. and Cowan, S. (1996) *Ecological Design,* Island
Press, Washington, DC, pp63–68, 79; Sachs, W., Loske, R. and Linz, M. et al
(1998) *Greening the North*, Zed Books, London, pp86, 146–152; Hawken,
P., Lovins, A. and Lovins, L. H. (1999) *Natural Capitalism – Creating the Next
Industrial Revolution,* Little, Brown and Co., Boston, pp46–47, 106–110.

[3] Rybczynski, W. (1989) *The Most Beautiful House in the World*, Viking Penguin,
New York, p186.

[4] Visser, M. (1991) *The Rituals of Dinner*, HarperCollins, Toronto, pp17–27.

[5] Jamieson, J. (2002) *Landfills Hide Computer Hazards*, Vancouver Province,
Vancouver, British Columbia, published in the Calgary Herald, Monday 4
February 2002, pC5. The European Waste Electronic and Electrical Equipment
Directive becomes law in 2005, at: www.weeeman.org/, accessed: 29 April
2005.

[6] Pathé Gazette (1931) *Gandhi Goes to England,* original newsreel footage
included on the DVD edition (2001) of Richard Attenborough's *Gandhi,*
Columbia Pictures Industries Inc., 1982.

[7] Rühe, P. (2001) *Gandhi*, Phaidon Press Ltd., London, p68.

[8] Scruton, R. (1979) *The Aesthetics of Architecture*, Princeton University Press,
Princeton, New Jersey, p72.

[9] *Bhagavad Gita* (1986) Barbara Stoler Miller (translator), Bantam Books, New
York, The Fifth Teaching, V. 22, 60.

7 DESIGN, SUSTAINABILITY AND THE HUMAN SPIRIT – How the other half lives

An earlier version of this chapter was published in *Design Issues*, vol 16, no 1, Spring 2000, pp52–58 (copyright 2006), Massachusetts Institute of Technology. With kind permission of MIT Press, Cambridge, MA, US.

[1] Riis, J. A. (1957 edition) *How the Other Half Lives*, Hill and Wang, New York, p1.

[2] Schumacher, E. F. (1977) *A Guide for the Perplexed*, Abacus, Penguin, London, pp47, 75, 154.

[3] Wing-tsit Chan (trans.) (1986) *Neo-Confucian Terms Explained by Ch'en Ch'un, 1159–1223*, Columbia University Press, New York, p146.

[4] Barilli, R. (1993) *A Course on Aesthetics* (trans. by K. E. Pinkus), University of Minnesota Press, Minneapolis, p19.

[5] Sperry in Edwards, B. (1979) *Drawing on the Right Side of the Brain*, J. P. Tarcher Inc., Los Angeles, p29.

[6] Taylor, C. (1991) *The Malaise of Modernity*, Anansi, Concord, Ontario, Chapter 1.

[7] Noddings, N. (1992) *The Challenge to Care in Schools – An Alternative Approach to Education*, Advances in Contemporary Educational Thought, vol 8, Teachers College Press, Columbia University, New York, pp49, 83.

[8] Hutchison, D. (1998) *Growing Up Green – Education for Economic Renewal*, Teachers College Press, Columbia University, New York, p49.

[9] Murdoch, I. (1992) *Metaphysics as a Guide to Morals*, Penguin Books, London, p7.

[10] Schumacher (2), p26.

[11] Taylor (6), p16.

[12] Murdoch (9), p8.

[13] *Ibid*, p21.

[14] Moore, B. (1995) *The Statement*, Vintage, Toronto, p9.

[15] *The Bhagavad Gita* 6.10, Edition consulted: Mascaró, J. (trans.) (1962) *The Bhagavad Gita*, Penguin, London.

[16] *Dhammapada* 89 and 355. Edition consulted: Mascaró, J. (trans.) (1973) *The Dhammapada*, Penguin, London.

[17] *The Holy Bible* – Old Testament: Proverbs 30:8; New Testament: Acts 4:32, Matthew 19:21. Edition consulted: New International Version (1978) Hodder and Stoughton, London.

[18] Al-Suhrawardy, A. S. (1990) *The Sayings of Muhammad*, Carol Publishing Group, New York, p110.

[19] *Tao Te Ching* 53, Edition consulted: Gia-Fu Feng and English, J. (trans.) (1989) *Tao Te Ching*, attributed to Lao Tzu, Vintage Books, Random House, New York.

[20] *The Rule of St. Benedict*, Chapters 33 and 55. Edition consulted: Meisel, A. C. and del Mastro, M. L. (trans.) (1975) *The Rule of St. Benedict,* Bantam Doubleday Dell Publishing Group Inc., New York.

[21] Sprigg, J. and Martin, D. (1987) *Shaker – Life, Work and Art*, Houghton Mifflin Company, Boston, pp22, 44.

[22] Kephart, W. M. (1976) *Extraordinary Groups – The Sociology of Unconventional Lifestyles*, St. Martin's Press, New York, pp15–16.

[23] *Ibid*, pp253–256.

[24] Sprigg, J. and Martin, D. (21), pp33, 72; Kephart (22), pp10, 15; Shea, J. G. (1971) *The American Shakers and their Furniture*, Van Nostrand Reinhold Company, New York, p33.

[25] Wittgenstein, L. (1980) *Culture and Value* (trans. by P. Winch), The University of Chicago Press, Chicago, pp31e–32e.

[26] Hick, J. (1989) *An Interpretation of Religion*, Yale University Press, New Haven, p10.

[27] Schumacher (2), p153.

8 FASHION AND SUSTAINABILITY – The attraction of opposites

An earlier version of this chapter appeared in the IDSA journal *Innovation* in Summer 2000, pp46–51. With kind permission of the IDSA, Dulles, VA, US.

[1] Wackernagel, M. and Rees, W. (1996) *Our Ecological Footprint: Reducing Human Impact on the Earth*, New Society Publishers, Gabriola Island, British Columbia.

[2] Thoreau, H. D. (1854) *Walden*, Penguin Books Ltd. (1983 edition), London, p68.

[3] van Hinte, E. (ed) (1997) *Eternally Yours: Visions on Product Endurance*, 010 Publishers, Rotterdam; Sachs, W., Loske, R. and Linz, M. et al (1998) *Greening the North: A Post-Industrial Blueprint for Ecology and Equity*, Zed Books Ltd., London, p113.

[4] Van der Ryn, S. and Cowan, S. (1996) *Ecological Design*, Island Press, Washington, DC, p57.

9 THE APPLICATION OF THEORY – Experiments in sustainable product design

An earlier version of this chapter was published in *The Journal of Sustainable Product Design*, UK, issue 7, pp41–50, October 1998 (copyright 1998). With kind permission of The Centre for Sustainable Design, Surrey, UK.

¹ Van Der Ryn, S. and Cowan, S. (1996) *Ecological Design*, Island Press, Washington, DC, pp57–81, 147–159; Hawken, P. (1993) *The Ecology of Commerce: A Declaration of Sustainability*, HarperBusiness, HarperCollins, New York, p144.

² Roseland, M. (1992) *Towards Sustainable Communities: A Resource Book for Municipal and Local Governments*, National Round Table on the Environment and the Economy, Ottawa, 1992, esp. pp7–9.

³ Perks, W. T., Kirby, R. and Wilton-Clark, A. (1996) *Edgemont II – A Study in Sustainable Community Form*, The University of Calgary, Centre for Livable Communities and Faculty of Environmental Design, Calgary.

⁴ For example: Professor Nigel Cross expresses similar views in his paper 'The refereed journal', in *Proceedings of Designing Design Research 2* (26 February 1998), available at: www.dmu.ac.uk/ln/4dd/drs2.html, accessed: 6 December 2004.

⁵ Nozick, M. (1992) *No Place Like Home: Building Sustainable Communities*, Canadian Council on Social Development, Ottawa, pp14–15.

⁶ Margetts, M. (1991) *International Crafts*, Thames & Hudson, London, p13.

⁷ Personal Digital Assistant – a type of handheld computer such as the 'Blackberry'.

10 TACIT KNOWLEDGE IN DESIGN – Visual myths

An earlier version of this chapter first appeared in *The Design Journal,* vol 6, issue 3, 2003, pp46–55, Ashgate Publishing, Aldershot, UK (copyright 2003). With kind permission of Ashgate Publishing Limited, UK.

¹ Polanyi, M. (1966) *The Tacit Dimension*, Anchor Books, Doubleday & Co., New York, p4.

² De Bono, E. (1973), *Lateral Thinking: Creativity Step-By-Step*, HarperCollins (1990), New York.

³ De Bono, E. (1985), *Six Thinking Hats*, Penguin Books (1990), London.

⁴ Perkins, D. (2000) *Archimedes' Bathtub*, W. W. Norton & Co, New York.

⁵ For example: Hannah, G. G. (2002) *Elements of Design*, Princeton Architectural Press, New York; Wallschlaeger, C. and Busic-Snyder, C. (1992) *Basic Visual Concepts and Principles for Artists, Architects and Designers*, Wm. C. Brown, Dubuque, IA.

⁶ Hawken, P., Lovins, A. and Lovins, L. H. (1999) *Natural Capitalism – Creating the Next Industrial Revolution*, Little, Brown and Company, Boston, pp2–6; Mander, J. and Goldsmith, E. (1996) *The Case Against the Global Economy – And for a Turn Toward the Local*, Sierra Club Books, San Francisco, especially Ch. 6, *Homogenization of Global Culture*, Barnet, R. and Cavanagh, J., pp71–77, Ch. 9, *New Technology and the End of Jobs*, Rifkin, J., pp108–121, and

Ch. 23, *Seeds of Exploitation*, Goldsmith, A., pp267–272.

[7] Scruton, R. (1979) *The Aesthetics of Architecture*, Princeton University Press, Princeton, New Jersey, p72.

[8] For example, Polanyi (1), pp3–25; Needleman, J. (1998) *Time and the Soul*, Currency Doubleday, New York, pp33–34.

[9] Buchanan, R. (1995) 'Rhetoric, humanism, and design', in Buchanan, R. and Margolin, V. (eds) *Discovering Design* (1995), Chicago University Press, Chicago, 1995, p27.

[10] Maugham, W. S. (1919) *The Moon and Sixpence*, Vintage International, Random House, New York, p4.

[11] Duchamp, M. (1957) 'The creative act', a paper presented to the Convention of the American Federation of Arts, Houston Texas, April 1957. Sound recording included on the CD: *The Creative Act*, Marcel Duchamp, edited by Marc Dachy, Sub Rosa, Brussels, 1994.

[12] Polanyi (1), px.

[13] Hick, J. (1989) *An Interpretation of Religion*, Yale University Press, New Haven, p131.

[14] *Ibid.*

[15] Buchanan (9), p26.

[16] Polanyi (1), p4.

[17] Holloway, R. (2001) *Doubts and Loves*, Canongate Books Ltd, Edinburgh, p93.

[18] Leeming, D. (2002) *Myth: A Biography of Belief*, Oxford University Press, Oxford, p10.

[19] Larson, S. (1990) *The Mythic Imagination – The Quest for Meaning Through Personal Mythology*, Inner Traditions International, Rochester, Vermont, pp3–5.

[20] *Ibid*, p48.

[21] Dillenberger, J. D. (1998) *The Religious Art of Andy Warhol*, Continuum Publ. Co., New York, p15.

[22] Frankl, V. E. (1984) *Man's Search for Meaning*, Simon & Schuster, New York, pp75–76.

[23] Campbell, J. (1988) *The Power of Myth*, with Bill Moyers, edited by Betty Sue Flowers, Anchor Books, Random House Inc., New York, 1991, pp6, 48.

[24] Murdoch, I. (1993) *Metaphysics as a Guide to Morals*, Penguin Books, London, pp80–83.

[25] Campbell, J. (2001) *That Art Thou*, edited by Eugene Kennedy, New World Library, Novato, CA, pp8–9.

[26] Nicoll, M. (1950) *The New Man*, reprinted edition published by Shambhala Publications Inc., Random Century House, London, 1986, pp1–16.

[27] Leeming (18), p17.

[28] *Apology 38a*, available at: www.perseus.tufts.edu/cgi-bin/ptext?doc=Perseus%3Aabo%3Atlg%2C0059%2C002&query=38a, accessed: 9 December 2004.

11 REFRAMING DESIGN FOR SUSTAINABILITY – Unmasking the object

An earlier version of this chapter was presented at the 6th European Academy of Design Conference in Bremen, Germany in Spring 2005. It was subsequently translated into Portuguese and appeared as 'Desmascarando o objeto: reestruturando o design para sustentabilidade' in *Revista Design em Foco*, vol II, no 2, Jul/Dec 2005, pp47–62, University of The State of Bahia, Brazil. With kind permission of University of The State of Bahia, Brazil.

[1] Britannica (2001) *Typology*, CD Edition, Encyclopædia Britannica, Inc, Britannica.co.uk, London.

[2] McGrath, A. (2002) *The Reenchantment of Nature*, Doubleday/Galilee, New York, pp124–125.

[3] *Ibid*.

[4] Alexander, C. (2004) *Renegade Architect*, Ideas Program, Canadian Broadcasting Corporation (CBC), broadcast 22 October 2004, 9:00pm (refer to www.cbc.ca/ideas for further details).

[5] Day, C. (1990) *Places of the Soul*, The Aquarian Press, Thorsons Publishing Group, Wellingborough, UK.

[6] Evans, W. (1959) 'Improvisation in jazz', in liner notes from *Kind of Blue* by Miles Davis, CD CK 64935, Columbia Records, New York, 1997.

[7] See De Gusmão Pereira, G. (2002) *Rua dos Inventos: Ensaio Sobre Desenho Vernacular*, Francsco Alves, Rio de Janeiro; De Bozzi, P. and Oroza, E. (2002) *Objets Réinventés: La Création Populaire à Cuba*, Editions Alternatives, Paris.

[8] Lewis, C. S. (1946) *The Great Divorce*, HarperCollins, New York, p13.

[9] East Midland Learning Resource at: www.emsource.org.uk/archive/item027/index.asp, accessed: 10 December 2004.

[10] Castiglioni (1962) Toio Lamp can be viewed at: www.evanizer.com/castiglioni/castigobjectpages/toio.html, accessed: 19 October 2004.

[11] Droog (2004) website at: www.droogdesign.nl/, accessed: 19 October 2004.

[12] I once participated in a documentary for BBC2 in the UK that explored the design process for Levi's jeans, which included discussions with locally employed scouts. Documentary: *Coolhunters*, Middlemarch Films, UK, broadcast in the UK in October 2001.

[13] Gale, M. (1998) *Alfred Wallis*, Tate Gallery Publishing, London.

[14] Matisse, H. (1996) *Chapelle Du Rosaire of the Dominican Nuns of Vence*, published by the Chapelle du Rosaire, Vence.

[15] Ades, D., Cox, N. and Hopkins, D. (1999) *Marcel Duchamp*, World of Art Series, Thames and Hudson, London, pp146–164.

[16] Dormer, P. (1993) *Design Since 1945*, Thames and Hudson, London, p85.

[17] de Bozzi and Oroza (7); de Gusmão Pereira (7).

[18] Langford, J. and McDonagh, D. (eds) (2003) *Focus Groups: Supporting Effective Product Development*, Taylor and Francis, London.

[19] Buber, M. (1970) *I and Thou*, translated by W. Kaufman, Touchstone Books, Simon and Schuster, New York, 1996, p60.

[20] Spayde, J. (2002) 'The unreal thing', *ID Magazine*, F & W Publications, Cincinnati, April edition, vol 49, no 2, pp62–67.

[21] Kawakami, K. (1997) *99 More Unuseless Japanese Inventions: The Art of Chindogu*, trans. by D. Papia, HarperCollins, London.

[22] Van der Ryn, S. and Cowan, S. (1996) *Ecological Design*, Island Press, Washington, DC, pp57–81.

[23] Steger, M. B. (2003) *Globalization: A Very Short Introduction*, Oxford University Press, Oxford, pp7–13.

[24] *Ibid*, p13.

[25] Hobsbawm, E. (2004) 'History is no longer necessary', interview with Eric Hobsbawm by Prem Shankar Jha, reported in *Outlook India*, available at: www.outlookindia.com/full.asp?fodname=20041227&fname=Hobsbawm+%28F%29&sid=1, accessed: 22 December 2004.

[26] Gray, J. (2004) *Heresies: Against Progress and Other Illusions*, Granta Books, London, pp159–166.

[27] For example, the communication possibilities offered by the Internet have allowed indigenous peoples from many different countries to link up to discuss common issues associated with changes to their lives caused by colonization and settlement.

[28] As indicated in Chapter 3, environmental degradation and increased awareness of the gross inequities between the rich and the poor countries have, over recent years, spurred protests and riots around the world. For example, protests, sometimes violent, were seen at the World Trade Organization (WTO) talks in Seattle in 1999, at the G8 Summit in Genoa, Italy in 2001, at the G8 Summit in Kananaskis, Canada in 2002, and at the WTO meeting in Cancun, Mexico in 2003; see: www.guardian.co.uk/wto/article/0,2763,1039709,00.html.

[29] Gray (26).

[30] Norman, E. (2002) *Secularization: Sacred Values in a Godless World*, Continuum, London, p171.

221

12 TIME AND DESIGN – Crushed before the moth

An earlier version of this chapter was presented at the Eternally Yours conference in Eindhoven, The Netherlands in 2003 and subsequently appeared in *Time In Design – Eternally Yours*, 010 Publishers, Rotterdam, published December 2004, pp302–332. With kind permission of 010 Publishers.

[1] The sub-title of this chapter, 'Crushed before the moth' can be found in the Bible in the book of Job, 4:19; the biblical symbolism of the moth is explained by Needleman, J. (1998) *Time and the Soul*, Bantam Doubleday Dell Publishing Group, Inc, p137.

[2] Packard, V. (1960) *The Waste Makers*, Pocket Books Inc., New York, pp45–58; Meadows, D. H., Meadows, D. L. and Randers, J. (1992) *Beyond the Limits*, McClelland and Stewart Inc., Toronto, p5; Frank, T. and Weiland, M. (eds) (1997) *Commodify Your Dissent – Salvos from the Baffler*, W. W. Norton, New York, p270; De Graaf, J., Wann, D. and Naylor, T. H. (2001) *Affluenza – The All-Consuming Epidemic*, Berret-Koehler Publishers, Inc., San Francisco, p143.

[3] Taylor, C. (1991) *The Malaise of Modernity*, Anansi Press Ltd, Concord, Ontario, pp15, 18; Tarnas, R. (1991) *The Passion of the Western Mind*, Harmony Books, New York, p396.

[4] Tarnas (3), pp419, 442.

[5] Taylor (3), p59.

[6] Frank, T. and Weiland, M. (eds) (2), pp266–274.

[7] Gelderman, C. W. (2001) *Henry Ford – Later Years*, in Britannica 2001 CD-ROM, Britannica.com Inc.

[8] Heskett, J. (1980) *Industrial Design*, World of Art series, Thames and Hudson, London, p105.

[9] Sparke, P. (1986) *An Introduction to Design and Culture in the Twentieth Century*, Icon Editions, Harper and Row, New York, pp96–97.

[10] Dormer, P. (1993), *Design Since 1945*, World of Art series, Thames and Hudson, London, p69.

[11] Stendl-Rast, D. and Lebell, S. (2002) *Music of Silence*, Seastone, Ulysses Press, Berkeley, California, p7.

[12] Needleman, J. (1), p43.

[13] Eliade, M. (1957) *The Sacred and the Profane – The Significance of Religious Myth, Symbolism, and Ritual Within Life and Culture*, translated from the French by Willard R. Trask, Harcourt Brace Jovanovich Publishers, San Diego, copyright renewed 1987, p81.

[14] *Ibid*, p88.

[15] Needleman (1), p42.

[16] Eliade (13), p16.

[17] Visser, M. (2000) *The Geometry of Love – Space, Time, Mystery and Meaning in an Ordinary Church*, Harper Perennial, Toronto, p32.

[18] Harvey, P. D. A. (1996) *Mappa Mundi: The Hereford World Map*, The British Library, London, p1.

[19] Edson, E. (1997) *Mapping Time and Space: How Medieval Mapmakers Viewed Their World*, The British Library, London, pviii.

[20] Meir, P. (2001) *Mappa Mundi: A medieval Look at Time and Space*, at: http://news.nationalgeographic.com/news/2001/08/0829_wiremappamundi.html,

222

accessed: 12 January 2005; Alington, G. (1996) *The Hereford Mappa Mundi – A Medieval View of the World*, Gracewing, Fowler Wright Books, Leominster, UK, p7; Jancey, M. (1987) *Mappa Mundi: The Map of the World in Hereford Cathedral*, Friends of Hereford Cathedral, p2.

[21] Mascaró, J. (trans.) (1962) *The Bhagavad Gita*, Introduction by J. Mascaró, Penguin Books, London, p22–24.

[22] *The Holy Bible*, Job 4:19(1).

[23] Eliade (13), pp23–24.

[24] Visser, M. (1991) *The Rituals of Dinner – The Origins, Evolution, Eccentricities and Meaning of Table Manners*, Harper Perennial, Toronto, p176; Visser (17), p33.

[25] Simmen, J. and Kohlhoff, K. (1999) *Kasemir Malevich – Life and Work*, Könneman Verlagsgesellschaft mbH, Cologne, translated from German by Paul Aston, Art in Hand Series, pp46–48.

[26] *Ibid*, p51; Stangos, N. (1981) *Concepts of Modern Art*, revised edition, Thames and Hudson, London, pp139–140.

[27] Lewison, J. (1991) *Ben Nicholson*, Rizzoli International Publications, Inc., New York, p16.

[28] Stangos (26), p194; Hughes, R. (1990) *Nothing If Not Critical*, Alfred A. Knopf, New York, pp241–242, in the essay: *Mark Rothko in Babylon*, originally published in The New York Review of Books, 1978, pp241–242.

[29] Hopkins, D. (2000) *After Modern Art 1945–2000*, Oxford University Press, Oxford, pp198–200; Stallabrass, J. (1999) *High Art Lite – British Art in the 1990s*, Verso, London, pp225–280.

[30] Stallabrass (29), pp109–111, 202.

[31] Shani, A. (2003) 'Between fact and wonder – Damien Hirst's new religious works', an essay in the exhibition catalogue for Romance in the Age of Uncertainty by Damien Hirst, 10 September to 19 October 2003, White Cube Gallery, London, Catalogues published by Jay Jopling/White Cube, 2003, pp7–11; Searle, A. (2003) *So What's New*, The Guardian, UK, online edition, 9 September 2003, Arts Features, www.guardian.co.uk/arts/features/story/0,11710,1038223,00.html, accessed: 12 January 2005.

223

13 CREATING OBJECTS IN A SATURATED CULTURE – After the endgame

An earlier version of this chapter first appeared in *The Design Journal*, vol 8, issue 1, 2005, pp3–13, Ashgate Publishing, Aldershot, UK (copyright 2005). With kind permission of Ashgate Publishing Limited, UK.

[1] Beckett, S. (1957) *Endgame – A Play in One Act*. Published by Grove/Atlantic, New York, 1994. Also available at: http://samuel-beckett.net/endgame.html, accessed: 30 December 2004.

[2] Solzenitsyn, A. (1978) 'A world split apart', Harvard Class Address, 8 June. Available at: www.columbia.edu/cu/augustine/arch/solzhenitsyn/harvard1978. html, accessed: 1 July 2003.

[3] Sustainable Principles: various sources are available, for example, The US Department of Energy at: www.sustainable.doe.gov/overview/principles.shtml and the US National Park Service at: www.nps.gov/dsc/dsgncnstr/gpsd/, both accessed: 5 January 2005.

[4] Forty, A. (1986) *Objects of Desire*, Thames and Hudson, London, p135; also see Safer, M. (1979) *Raymond Loewy: Father of Industrial Design*, 15 min. 16mm movie, CBS NEWS, distributed by Marlin Motion Pictures in which Morley Safer interviews Raymond Loewy.

[5] Forty (4), p135.

[6] Dormer, P. (1990) *The Meanings of Modern Design*, Thames and Hudson, London, pp34–43.

[7] IDSA (2003) *IDSA 2003 Design Trends Report*, available at: http://new.idsa. org/webmodules/articles/articlefiles/designtrends.pdf, accessed: 5 January 2005.

[8] Stallabrass, J. (1999) *High Art Lite – British Art in the 1990s*, Verso, London, p266.

[9] Chomsky, N. (1993) *The Prosperous Few and the Restless Many*, Odonian Press, Berkeley, California, p21; Chomsky, N. (1999), *Profit Over People*, Seven Stories Press, New York, p8.

[10] Chomsky (1999) (9).

[11] Nichols, P. (1981) *The Pope's Divisions*, Holt, Rinehart and Winston, New York, p303.

[12] French painter Maurice Denis quoted in Gill, E. (1934) *Art*, John Lane, The Bodley Head, London, p122.

[13] Glass, P. (1989) *Solo Piano*, compact disc recording MK 45576, CBS Records Inc., New York.

[14] Pitts, A. (2003) *Passio*, by Arvo Pärt, performed by Tonus Peregrinus, CD published by Naxos, UK, 8.555860, endnotes by Antony Pitts.

14 EPHEMERAL OBJECTS FOR SUSTAINABILITY – Light touch

An earlier version of this chapter was published in *The Journal of Sustainable Product Design*, UK, vol 3/3-4, January 2006, pp1-12 (copyright 2006), Springer/Elsevier Academic Publishers, Netherlands. With kind permission of Springer Science and Business Media.

[1] For example: Klein, N. (2000) *No Logo: Taking Aim at the Brand Bullies*, Vintage Canada, Random House, Toronto, pp195–229; Chomsky, N. (1993) *The Prosperous Few and the Restless Many*, Odonian Press, Berkeley, pp21–25; Meadows, D. H., Meadows, D. L. and Randers, J. (1992) *Beyond the Limits*,

McClelland and Stewart Inc. Toronto; World Commission on Environment and Development (1987) *Our Common Future*, Oxford University Press, Oxford.

[2] McGrath, A. (2002) *The Reenchantment of Nature: The Denial of Religion and the Ecological Crisis*, Doubleday/Galilee, Random House, New York, p124.

[3] See evasion of moral obligation in Hick, J. (1989) *An Interpretation of Religion*, Yale University Press, New Haven, pp150–151.

[4] Hick (3), p150.

[5] Lovelock, J. (1991) *Healing Gaia*, Harmony Books, New York, p57.

[6] Buber, M. (1927) *I and Thou*, trans. Walter Kaufmann 1970, published by Touchstone, Simon and Schuster, New York, 1996, pp53–73.

[7] McGrath (2), p125.

[8] Papanek, V. (1995) *The Green Imperative – Natural Design for the Real World*, Thames and Hudson, New York, p234.

[9] Maurer, I. (1996), Mozzkito Lamp, at: www.ingo-maurer.com, accessed: 11 February 2005.

[10] Madden, P. (2005) Phone Directory Seating at: www.core77.com/ corehome/2005/02/recycled-phone-book-seating.html, accessed: 11 February 2005.

[11] Wanders, M. (2000) '*Birdfeeder*', at: www.droogdesign.nl/, accessed: 11 February 2005.

[12] Van Der Ryn, S. and Cowan, S. (1996) *Ecological Design*, Island Press, Washington, DC, pp57–81.

225

15 INTELLECTUAL AND AESTHETIC UNDERSTANDINGS OF DESIGN – The considered gaze

An earlier version of this chapter was presented at the 'Sustainability – Creating the Culture' conference in Aberdeen, November 2005.

[1] *The Concise Oxford Dictionary* (1990) 8th Edition, edited by R. E. Allen, Clarendon Press, Oxford.

[2] Read, H. (1963) *To Hell with Culture*, Routledge Classics, London, p101.

[3] Eaton, M. M. (2001) *Merit, Aesthetic and Ethical*, Oxford University Press, Oxford, p42.

[4] *Ibid*, pp23–24; see also Berger, J. (1972) *Ways of Seeing*, BBC and Penguin Books, London, p8.

[5] Cage, J. (1977–1980) *The Freeman Etudes, Books 1 & 2*, Compact Disc, Mode Records, New York, 1993.

[6] Palmer, J. (1996) 'Need and function: The terms of the debate', in Palmer, J. and Dodson, M. (eds) *Design and Aesthetics – A Reader*, Routledge, London, pp110–122.

[7] Eaton (3), p22.

[8] Scruton, R. (1996) 'Judging Architecture', in Palmer, J. and Dodson, M. (eds) *Design and Aesthetics – A Reader*, Routledge, London, pp13–32.

[9] Read (2), p3.

[10] Hughes, R. and Silber, J. (1994) *Amish Art of Quilt*, Phaidon Press, London.

[11] Crafts Council (2005), *Knit 2 Together: Concepts and Knitting*, exhibition, London, 24 February – 8 May 2005, www.craftscouncil.org.uk/Exhib/k2together/index.htm, accessed: 23 February 2005.

[12] Orwell, G. (1949) *Nineteen Eighty-Four*, Penguin Books, London, p26.

[13] Papanek, V. (1984) *Design for the Real World*, Thames & Hudson, London; Papanek, V. (1995) *The Green Imperative*, Thames & Hudson, New York.

[14] Bakker, G. and Ramakers, R. (1998) *Droog Design – Spirit of the Nineties*, 010 Publishers, Rotterdam.

[15] Koren, L. (2003) *Arranging Things – A Rhetoric of Object Placement*, Stonebridge Press, Berkeley, CA.

[16] *Ibid*, pp41–44.

[17] *Ibid*, pp44–46.

[18] *Ibid*, pp46–47.

[19] Buchanan, R. (1995) 'Rhetoric, humanism and design', in Buchanan, R. and Margolin V. (eds) *Discovering Design*, The University of Chicago Press, Chicago, p46.

BIBLIOGRAPHY

Ades, D., Cox, N. and Hopkins, D. (1999) *Marcel Duchamp*, Thames and
    Hudson, London
Alington, G. (1996) *The Hereford Mappa Mundi – A Medieval View of the
    World*, Gracewing, Fowler Wright Books, Leominster, UK
Al-Suhrawardy, A. S. (1990) *The Sayings of Muhammad*, Carol Publishing
    Group, New York
Bakker, G. and Ramakers, R. (1998) *Droog Design: Spirit of the Nineties*, 010
    Publishers, Rotterdam
Barilli, R. (1993) *A Course on Aesthetics* (trans. by K. E. Pinkus), University of
    Minnesota Press, Minneapolis
Bauman, L. C. (2001) *The Anglican Rosary*, Praxis, Telephone, Texas
Beattie, O. and Geiger, J. (2000) *Frozen in Time: The Fate of the Franklin
    Expedition*, Greystone Publishing, Vancouver
Beckett, S. (1957) *Endgame – A Play in One Act*, Grove/Atlantic, New York,
    1994
Berger, J. (1972) *Ways of Seeing*, BBC and Penguin Books, London
Berton, P. (1976) *My Country*, McClelland and Stewart, Toronto
Bierlein, J. F. (1994) *Parallel Myths*, Ballantine Books, New York
Bronowski, J. and Mazlish, B. (1960) *The Western Intellectual Tradition – From*

Leonardo to Hegel, Harper Torchbooks, New York

Buber, M. (1927) *I and Thou* (trans. by W. Kaufman, 1970), Touchstone Books, Simon and Schuster, New York, 1996

Buchanan, R. and Margolin, V. (1995) *Discovering Design,* Chicago University Press, Chicago

Bulfinch, T. (1855) *The Golden Age of Myth and Legend*, Wordsworth Editions, Ware, Hertfordshire, UK, 1993

Campbell, J. (1988) *The Power of Myth*, with Bill Moyers, edited by Betty Sue Flowers, Anchor Books, Random House Inc, New York

Campbell, J. (2001) *That Art Thou : Transforming Religious Metaphor*, edited by Eugene C. Kennedy, New World Library, Novato, California

Carson, R. (1962) *Silent Spring*, Buccaneer Books, New York, reprint edition 1994

Chadwick, O. (1964) *The Reformation*, Penguin Books, London, 1990

Chidester, D. (2000) *Christianity: A Global History*, HarperCollins, New York

Chomsky, N. (1993) *The Prosperous Few and the Restless Many*, Odonian Press, Berkeley, California

Chomsky, N. (1999) *Profit Over People*, Seven Stories Press, New York

Ciambrone, D. F. (1997) *Environmental Life Cycle Analysis,* Lewis Publishers Inc, CRC Press, Boca Raton, Florida

Cork, R., Long, R., Fulton, H. and Seymour, A. (2000) *Richard Long: Walking in Circles*, George Braziller Inc, New York

Cornwell, J. (1991) *Powers of Darkness, Powers of Light*, Viking, Penguin Group, London

Dal Co, F. and Forster, K. (1999) *Frank O. Gehry: The Complete Works*, Monacelli Press, New York

Day, C. (1990) *Places of the Soul*, The Aquarian Press, Thorsons Publishing Group, Wellingborough, UK

De Bono, E. (1973) *Lateral Thinking: Creativity Step-By-Step*, HarperCollins, New York

De Bono, E. (1985) *Six Thinking Hats*, Penguin Books (1990), London

De Bozzi, P. and Oroza, E. (2002) *Objets Réinventés: La Création Populaire à Cuba*, Editions Alternatives, Paris

de Graaf, J., Wann, D. and Naylor, T. H. (2001) *Affluenza – The All-Consuming Epidemic*, Berrett-Koehler Publishers, Inc, San Francisco

De Gusmão Pereira, G. (2002) *Rua dos Inventos: Ensaio Sobre Desenho Vernacular*, Francsco Alves, Rio de Janeiro

Dillenberger, J. D. (1998) *The Religious Art of Andy Warhol*, Continuum Publ. Co., New York

Dormer, P. (1990) *The Meanings of Modern Design*, Thames and Hudson, London

Dormer, P. (1993) *Design Since 1945*, Thames and Hudson, London

Dresner, S. (2002) *The Principles of Sustainability*, Earthscan, London

Eaton, M. M. (2001) *Merit, Aesthetic and Ethical*, Oxford University
      Press, Oxford

Edson, E. (1997) *Mapping Time and Space: How Medieval Mapmakers Viewed
      Their World*, The British Library, London

Edwards, B. (1979) *Drawing on the Right Side of the Brain,* J. P. Tarcher Inc,
      Los Angeles

Eliade, M. (1957) *The Sacred and the Profane – The Significance of Religious
      Myth, Symbolism, and Ritual Within Life and Culture* (trans. from the
      French by W. R. Trask), Harcourt Brace Jovanovich Publishers,
      San Diego

Forty, A. (1986) *Objects of Desire*, Thames and Hudson, London

Frank, T. and Weiland, M. (eds) (1997) *Commodify Your Dissent – Salvos from
      the Baffler*, W. W. Norton, New York

Frankl, V. E. (1984) *Man's Search for Meaning*, Simon & Schuster, New York

Gale, M. (1998) *Alfred Wallis*, Tate Gallery Publishing, London

Gia-Fu Feng and English, J. (trans.) (1989) *Tao Te Ching*, attributed to Lao Tzu,
      Vintage Books, Random House, New York

Gill, E. (1934) *Art*, John Lane, The Bodley Head, London

Gordon, A. and Suzuki, D. (1990) *It's a Matter of Survival*, Stoddart Publishing
      Co Ltd, Toronto

Gray, J. (2004) *Heresies: Against Progress and Other Illusions*, Granta
      Books, London

Gribble, R. (1992) *The History and Devotion of the Rosary,* Our Sunday Visitor
      Publ. Div, Huntingdon, Indiana

Grimwood, J. (1986) *Photohistory of the 20th Century*, Blandford Press,
      New York

Hannah, G. G. (2002) *Elements of Design*, Princeton Architectural Press,
      New York

Harris, R. (1999) *Lourdes – Body and Spirit in the Secular Age*, Viking, Penguin
      Group, New York

Harvey, P. D. A. (1996) *Mappa Mundi: The Hereford World Map*, The British
      Library, London

Hawken, P. (1993) *The Ecology of Commerce*, Harper Business, HarperCollins,
      New York

Hawken, P., Lovins, A. and Lovins, L. H. (1999) *Natural Capitalism – Creating
      the Next Industrial Revolution*, Little, Brown and Company, Boston

Herrigel, E. (1953) *Zen in the Art of Archery,* Vintage Books, New York

Heskett, J. (1980) *Industrial Design*, World of Art Series, Thames and Hudson
      Ltd, London

Hick, J. (1989) *An Interpretation of Religion – Human Responses to the*

Transcendent, Yale University Press, New Haven

Hill, C. (1992) *Reformation to Industrial Revolution,* The Penguin Economic History of Britain, Volume 2: 1530–1780, Penguin Books, London

Hobsbawm, E. J. (1990) *Industry and Empire,* The Penguin Economic History of Britain, Volume 3, Penguin Books, London

Holloway, R. (2002) *Doubts and Loves*, Canongate Books Ltd, Edinburgh

Hopkins, D. (2000) *After Modern Art 1945–2000*, Oxford University Press, Oxford

Howard, K. L. and Pardue, D. F. (1996) *Inventing the Southwest: The Fred Harvey Company and Native American Art*, Northland Publishing, Flagstaff, Arizona

Hughes, R. (1990) *Nothing If Not Critical*, Alfred A. Knopf, New York

Hughes, R. and Silber, J. (1994) *Amish Art of Quilt*, Phaidon Press, London

Hunter, R. (2002) *2030: Confronting Thermageddon in Our Lifetime*, McClelland & Stewart Inc., Toronto

Hutchison, D. (1998) *Growing Up Green – Education for Economic Renewal,* Teachers College Press, Columbia University, New York

Huxley, A. (1945) *The Perennial Philosophy*, Triad Grafton Books, London

Jancey, M. (1987) *Mappa Mundi: The Map of the World in Hereford Cathedral,* Friends of Hereford Cathedral, Hereford, UK

Jenkins, P. (2002) *The Next Christendom*, Oxford University Press, New York

Kawakami, K. (1997) *99 More Unuseless Japanese Inventions: The Art of Chindogu* (trans. by D. Papia), HarperCollins, London

Kephart, W. M. (1976) *Extraordinary Groups – The Sociology of Unconventional Lifestyles*, St. Martin's Press, New York

Klein, N. (2000) *No Logo: Taking Aim at the Brand Bullies*, Vintage Canada, Random House, Toronto

Koren, L. (2003) *Arranging Things – A Rhetoric of Object Placement*, Stonebridge Press, Berkeley, California

Küng, H. (2001) *The Catholic Church*, Weidenfeld & Nicolson, London

Langford, J. and McDonagh, D. (eds) (2003) *Focus Groups: Supporting Effective Product Development*, Taylor and Francis, London

Larson, S. (1990) *The Mythic Imagination – The Quest for Meaning Through Personal Mythology,* Inner Traditions International, Rochester, Vermont

Leeming, D. (2002) *Myth: A Biography of Belief*, Oxford University Press, Oxford

Lewis, C. S. (1946) *The Great Divorce*, HarperCollins, New York

Lewis, C. S. (1946) *The Pilgrim's Regress*, Fount Paperbacks, Collins, London

Lewison, J. (1991) *Ben Nicholson*, Rizzoli International Publications, Inc, New York

Lovelock, J. (1991) *Healing Gaia*, Harmony Books, New York

Mander, J. and Goldsmith, E. (1996) *The Case Against the Global Economy*

– And for a Turn Toward the Local, Sierra Club Books, San Francisco

Margetts, M. (1991) *International Crafts*, Thames & Hudson, London

Martin, R. M. (1994) *The Philosopher's Dictionary*, Broadview Press, Peterborough, Ontario

Mascaró, J. (trans.) (1962) *The Bhagavad Gita*, Penguin Books, London

Mascaró, J. (trans.) (1973) *The Dhammapada*, Penguin Books, London

Matisse, H. (1996) *Chapelle Du Rosaire of the Dominican Nuns of Vence*, The Chapelle du Rosaire, Vence, France

Maugham, W. S. (1919) *The Moon and Sixpence*, Vintage International, Random House, New York

McGrath, A. (2002) *The Reenchantment of Nature*, Doubleday/Galilee, New York

Meadows, D. H., Meadows, D. L. and Randers, J. (1992) *Beyond the Limits – Confronting Global Collapse, Envisioning a Sustainable Future*, McClelland & Stewart Inc, Toronto

Meisel, A. C. and del Mastro, M. L. (trans.) (1975) *The Rule of St. Benedict*, Bantam Doubleday Dell Publishing Group Inc, New York

Moore, B. (1995) *The Statement*, Vintage, Toronto

Murdoch, I. (1992) *Metaphysics as a Guide to Morals*, Penguin Books, London

Needleman, J. (1980) *Lost Christianity*, Bantam Books, New York

Nichols, P. (1981) *The Pope's Divisions*, Holt, Rinehart and Winston, New York

Nicoll, M. (1950) *The New Man*, Shambhala Publications Inc, Random Century House, London, reprinted edition 1986

Noddings, N. (1992) *The Challenge to Care in Schools – An Alternative Approach to Education*, Advances in Contemporary Educational Thought, Volume 8, Teachers College Press, Columbia University, New York

Norman, E. (2002) *Secularization: Sacred Values in a Godless World*, Continuum, London

Nozick, M. (1992) *No Place Like Home: Building Sustainable Communities*, Canadian Council on Social Development, Ottawa

Orwell, G. (1949) *Nineteen Eighty-Four*, Penguin Books, London

Overy, P. (1991) *De Stijl*, Thames and Hudson, London

Packard, V. (1960) *The Waste Makers*, Pocket Books Inc, New York

Palmer, J. and Dodson, M. (eds) (1996) *Design and Aesthetics – A Reader*, Routledge, London

Papanek, V. (1971) *Design for the Real World – Human Ecology and Social Change*, Thames and Hudson, London, 2nd edition 1984

Papanek, V. (1995) *The Green Imperative – Natural Design for the Real World*, Thames and Hudson, New York

Pascal, B. (~1660) *Pensées*, Penguin Books, London, revised edition 1995

Perkins, D. (2000) *Archimedes' Bathtub*, W. W. Norton & Co, New York

Perks, W. T., Kirby, R. and Wilton-Clark, A. (1996) *Edgemont II – A Study in Sustainable Community Form*, The University of Calgary, Centre for Livable Communities and Faculty of Environmental Design, Calgary

Polanyi, M. (1966) *The Tacit Dimension*, Anchor Books, Doubleday & Co., New York

Ramakers, R. (2002) *Less + More: Droog Design in Context*, 010 Publishers, Rotterdam

Read, H. (1963) *To Hell with Culture,* Routledge Classics, London

Riis, J. A. (1957 edition) *How the Other Half Lives*, Hill and Wang, New York

Roseland, M. (1992) *Towards Sustainable Communities: A Resource Book for Municipal and Local Governments*, National Round Table on the Environment and the Economy, Ottawa

Rühe, P. (2001) *Gandhi*, Phaidon Press Ltd, London

Rybczynski, W. (1980) *Paper Heroes – Appropriate Technology: Panacea or Pipe Dream*, Penguin Books, New York

Rybczynski, W. (1989) *The Most Beautiful House in the World*, Viking Penguin, New York

Sachs, W., Loske, R. and Linz, M. et al (1998) *Greening the North – A Post-Industrial Blueprint for Ecology and Equity*, Zed Books, London

Schumacher, E. F. (1973) *Small is Beautiful – Economics as if People Mattered*, Abacus, London

Schumacher, E. F. (1977) *A Guide for the Perplexed*, Abacus, London

Scruton, R. (1979) *The Aesthetics of Architecture*, Princeton University Press, Princeton, New Jersey

Shani, A. (2003) 'Between fact and wonder – Damien Hirst's new religious works', an essay in the exhibition catalogue for 'Romance in the Age of Uncertainty' by Damien Hirst, 10 September to 19 October 2003, White Cube Gallery, London, published by Jay Jopling/White Cube

Shea, J. G. (1971) *The American Shakers and Their Furniture*, Van Nostrand Reinhold Company, New York

Shute, N. (1957) *On the Beach*, Ballantine Books, New York, 2001

Simmen, J. and Kohlhoff, K. (1999) *Kasemir Malevich – Life and Work* (trans. from German by P. Aston), Art in Hand Series, Könneman Verlagsgesellschaft mbH, Cologne

Sparke, P. (1986) *In Introduction to Design and Culture in the Twentieth Century*, Icon Editions, Harper and Row, New York

Sprigg, J. and Martin, D. (1987) *Shaker – Life, Work and Art*, Houghton Mifflin Company, Boston

Stallabrass, J. (1999) *High Art Lite – British Art in the 1990s*, Verso, London

Stangos, N. (1981) *Concepts of Modern Art*, revised edition, Thames and

232

Hudson, London

Steger, M. B. (2003) *Globalization: A Very Short Introduction*, Oxford University Press, Oxford, 1977

Steiner, G. (1974) *Nostalgia for the Absolute,* 1974 Massey Lectures, House of Anansi Press Ltd, Concord, Ontario

Stendl-Rast, D. and Lebell, S. (2002) *Music of Silence*, Seastone, Ulysses Press, Berkeley, California

Stoler Miller, B. (trans.) (1986) *Bhagavad Gita*, Bantam Books, New York

Tarnas, R. (1991) *The Passion of the Western Mind – Understanding the Ideas that Have Shaped Our Worldview*, Harmony Books, New York

Taylor, C. (1991) *The Malaise of Modernity*, Anansi, Concord, Ontario

The Holy Bible, New International Version (1978) Hodder and Stoughton, London

Thoreau, H. D. (1854) *Walden*, Penguin Books edition entitled *Walden and Civil Disobedience*, London, 1983

Vail, A. (1995) *The Story of the Rosary*, HarperCollins, London

Van der Ryn, S. and Cowan, S. (1996) *Ecological Design,* Island Press, Washington

van Hinte, E. (ed) (1997) *Eternally Yours: Visions on Product Endurance*, 010 Publishers, Rotterdam

Visser, M. (1991) *The Rituals of Dinner – The Origins, Evolution, Eccentricities and Meaning of Table Manners*, HarperCollins, Toronto

Visser, M. (2000) *The Geometry of Love – Space, Time, Mystery and Meaning in an Ordinary Church*, HarperCollins, Toronto

Wackernagel, M. and Rees, W. (1996) *Our Ecological Footprint: Reducing Human Impact on the Earth*, New Society Publishers, Gabriola Island, British Columbia

Wallschlaeger, C. and Busic-Snyder, C. (1992) *Basic Visual Concepts and Principles for Artists, Architects and Designers*, Wm. C. Brown, Dubuque, Iowa

Ward, M. (1945) *The Splendor of the Rosary*, Sheed and Ward, New York

WCED (1987) *Our Common Future*, World Commission on Environment and Development, Oxford University Press, Oxford

Weitman, W. (1999) *Pop Impressions Europe/USA – Prints and Multiples from the Museum of Modern Art*, Museum of Modern Art, New York

Whitford, F. (1984) *Bauhaus*, Thames and Hudson, London

Wilkins, E. (1969) *The Rose-Garden Game – The Symbolic Background to the European Prayer-Beads*, Victor Gollancz Ltd, London

Wilson, J. (2001) *John Franklin – Traveller on Undiscovered Seas*, XYZ Publishing, Montreal

Wing-tsit Chan (trans.) (1986) *Neo-Confucian Terms Explained by Ch'en Ch'un, 1159–1223*, Columbia University Press, New York

Wittgenstein, L. (1980) *Culture and Value* (trans. by P. Winch), The University of Chicago Press, Chicago

Woodham, J. M. (1997) *Twentieth-Century Design*, Oxford University Press, Oxford

INDEX

T